W9-BIV-053

LOVE HER TO DEATH

John Glatt

St. Martin's Paperbacks

NOTE: If you purchased this book without a cover you should be aware that this book is stolen property. It was reported as "unsold and destroyed" to the publisher, and neither the author nor the publisher has received any payment for this "stripped book."

LOVE HER TO DEATH

Copyright © 2012 by John Glatt.

All rights reserved.

For information address St. Martin's Press, 175 Fifth Avenue, New York, NY 10010.

ISBN 978-1-250-09110-9

St. Martin's Paperbacks edition / May 2012

St. Martin's Paperbacks are published by St. Martin's Press, 175 Fifth Avenue, New York, NY 10010.

P1

Dedicated to Keith Clarke,

who taught me to love English.

ACKNOWLEDGMENTS

Just after 9:00 a.m on Monday, June 12, 2006, Darren Mack exploded, changing the town of Reno forever. After months of not getting his own way during his divorce from his second wife Charla, the frustrated multi-millionaire took the law into his own hands.

First he murdered Charla, while their seven-year-old daughter Erica sat upstairs watching television. The avid hunting enthusiast then headed downtown, snipering Washoe County Family Court Judge Chuck Weller and critically wounding him, before fleeing to Mexico.

After eleven days on the run and the target of an international manhunt, Mack surrendered to the FBI and was brought back to Reno to face the music.

For the next several years the wealthy pawnbroker's dream team of criminal attorneys fought a valiant battle on his behalf. But in the middle of his murder trial Mack took a plea on his lawyers' advice, after the State presented an impenetrable case against him. But within days he had changed his mind, firing his two attorneys and hiring a new one, seeking a new trial.

This labyrinthine murder case would go on for many more months, until the Nevada Supreme Court finally ruled that Mack would have to face his just punishment.

This is my seventeenth True Crime book and by far the

most challenging. I spent almost four years researching and writing it, securing the cooperation of most of the main players, some of whom wished to remain anonymous.

I would like to particularly thank Detectives Ron Chalmers and John Ferguson, who both lead the Reno Police Department investigation. Much gratitude is also due to Charla's mother Soorya Townley, who prepared a chronology of her daughter's life, helped me throughout and kindly gave me her blessing to include Charla's moving song lyrics in the book. Sadly, she preferred not to be interviewed. I am also indebted to Landon Mack, who met me at Palace Jewelry and Loan to tell his family's side of the tragedy, and the terrible toll it had taken.

While in Reno I also met with Judge Chuck Weller and his assistant Annie Allison, who bravely told me their stories of the attack. I also spent many hours interviewing Charla's close circle of friends, including Ann and Tony Mudd as well as several others, who did not want their names in the book.

Thanks is also due to journalist Amanda Robb, who wrote the original story in *Marie Claire*, which first led me to this book. She was very generous with her time, pointing me in the direction of many who would help. Another huge asset for the book was Dean Tong, who was personally hired by Darren Mack, during his divorce. Dean was very helpful, giving me access to his expertise and some of the hundreds of e-mails Darren and Charla wrote each other in the year leading up to the murder.

I would also like to thank Alecia Biddison, Garret Idle, Corey Schmidt, Phil Pape and Rick Ross.

As always, I would also like to thank my editors at St. Martin's Paperbacks, Charles Spicer and Yaniv Soha, for everything that they do and my new agent Jane Dystel of Dystel & Goderich Literary Management, for her advice and guidance.

Gratitude also to my wife Gail, Jerome and Emily Freund, Debbie, Douglas and Taylor Baldwin, Trudy Gerstner, Gurch, Danny and Allie Tractenberg, Cari Pokrassa, Virginia Randall, Roger Hitts, Ena Bissell, Chris Vlasak and Annette Witheridge.

PROLOGUE

Monday, June 12, 2006

It was moving day for Dan Osborne, who was all packed and ready to go. For the last few weeks, he had been relying on the generosity of his old friend Darren Mack for a roof over his head and some casual work. Now, to his relief, he had found a place of his own.

The friendship dated back thirty years to Reno High School, although they had lost touch soon after graduating. But recently they had reconnected over a business idea that had never quite got off the ground.

A hugely successful multimillionaire pawnbroker and real estate magnate, Mack, forty-five, was now in the midst of a bitter divorce battle with his beautiful thirty-nine-year-old wife, Charla, a former actress who had once dated Arnold Schwarzenegger. During their tumultuous ten-year marriage, the Macks had lived a glamorous but sexually adventurous life.

When their daughter, Erika, entered preschool, Charla informed her husband that she wanted to stop swinging to become a stay-at-home mom. Darren was furious, giving her an ultimatum to either continue or their marriage was over.

Charla had then filed for divorce, and now, eighteen months later, they only communicated through high-priced lawyers.

After Washoe County Family Court judge Charles "Chuck" Weller ordered Darren to give Charla $10,000 a month in interim spousal support, based on his stated income of $44,000 a month, Darren's assets began to mysteriously disappear. The successful businessman, who had once claimed to be worth $9.4 million, finally declared bankruptcy, saying there was no money left for Charla.

The increasingly acrimonious divorce had left Darren Mack consumed with anger, likening Judge Weller's courtroom to a Nazi concentration camp. He became a radical fathers' rights activist, publicly declaring that he was not going to take it anymore. Charla began telling close friends she feared for her life

Since moving into the Mack's condominium in the luxurious Fleur de Lis gated community, Dan Osborne had often witnessed his friend's angry tirades.

"It was heavy on his mind," Osborne recalled. "He had said at one point, 'I'd just like to get rid of them all.' "

That Monday morning, Charla Mack was bringing Erika over to Darren's condo, as he was assuming custody for the first three weeks of the summer vacation. Up to now, the family court-ordered weekly handovers had always taken place at school, so Darren and Charla could avoid each other. One parent would drop Erika off at school in the morning, with the other collecting her in the afternoon.

At their last family court hearing, Judge Weller had issued a mutual restraining order for the vacation. The exchanges would now be at their respective homes, with one parent remaining in the car, while the other stayed inside the house.

But two days earlier, Darren called Charla, saying he needed to talk to her urgently when she brought Erika over on Monday.

"He never wanted to talk to her," said her friend Jacqueline Ross (not her real name), "but now he wanted to talk about the settlement. And she told me, 'I don't know why but I'm so afraid to talk to him.' "

On Monday, the morning of his move, Dan Osborne got up at around 7:00 a.m. and saw Darren Mack in the hallway.

"He told me he was going to be back shortly [and] was going to run some errands," Osborne recalled. "I said, 'Okay, I'm taking my dog for a walk.' "

A few minutes later, Osborne walked out into the bright sunshine where his 1985 Honda Civic was parked. His bull mastiff-Labrador mix, Rusty, was fast asleep in the back.

He then drove a few blocks north on Wilbur May Parkway to South Meadows Parkway, to a dog run by a pond. For the next forty minutes he let Rusty run around before returning to the Fleur de Lis condo.

Just after 8:00 a.m., Osborne pulled up outside Darren Mack's town house, seeing Darren's gleaming gold Jeep Cherokee parked across the street. Then, leaving Rusty in the back of his car, he walked into the double garage through the open right-side door.

Parked inside was the rented Ford Explorer SUV that he had helped Darren collect at Reno Airport a few days earlier. Osborne had thought that strange, as Mack already had several other luxury vehicles, including a top-of-the-line Hummer H2.

He had also been surprised when Mack had telephoned the previous afternoon, asking for a favor—something he had never done before.

"He asked me if I could take his daughter to [his mother's] house in the morning," recalled Osborne. "I said not a problem."

A little after 9:00, Charla Mack pulled up outside the condo in her silver Lexus SUV to drop Erika off. Darren immediately strode over, opening the passenger door and lifting his daughter out. Then Charla had a brief conversation with

Darren before casually walking over to Osborne and introducing herself, as they had never met before.

"Hi, I'm Charla," she said cheerfully, shaking his hand.

"Nice to meet you." he replied. "I'm Dan."

Then Darren took Erika into the condo, gesturing for Osborne to follow. As they walked through the garage, with Erika trailing behind, Charla began gathering up Erika's things outside.

Once upstairs in the living room, Mack asked Osborne to stay with his daughter, saying he and Charla needed to talk.

"I'm going to talk to your mom," he told Erika, who was turning on the television. "I'll be right back."

Then, picking up a brown paper bag from the top of the stairs. he walked down.

About fifteen minutes later, Dan Osborne and Erika were watching a dog rescue show on the Animal Planet channel, when the little girl said she could hear Rusty barking. Osborne said that was impossible, as the Labrador was locked in the back of his car. But then he, too, heard a "yelping sound" coming from downstairs.

Suddenly, Rusty rushed upstairs from the garage, looking terrified.

"He was kind of slumped down," Osborne said, "like when they get disciplined. His tail was down. He was kind of low."

Then the door leading up from the garage slammed shut and Darren Mack appeared as if in a trance, a bath towel wrapped around his hand. He walked past them without a word, turning right into his bedroom and closing the double doors behind him.

"He had a weird, scared look on his face." Osborne later testified. "He kind of had his head down."

Then Erika cried out that Rusty's fur was covered in blood.

"So I looked down and grabbed his head," said Osborne. "His muzzle had blood on it, also the chest area and the feet. And at that point I thought something has gone wrong here."

Then, remembering Darren's angry comments about getting rid of Charla and Judge Weller, he decided to get Erika out of the house immediately.

"I freaked out," said Osborne. "Then I grabbed Erika and said, 'We're going to your grandmother. Let's go!'"

A few minutes later, Darren Mack left his condo and headed downtown. Heavily armed with a rifle and other high-powered weapons, he went in search of Judge Chuck Weller. And the havoc he would wreak that morning would change Reno forever.

PART ONE

CHAPTER ONE

The Prince of Reno

Darren Roy Mack was born in January 1961, the eldest son of Dennis and Joan Mack. As the scion of one of Reno's oldest and most successful businesses, Darren was proud of his family and its role in the city's colorful history.

Present-day Reno's origins date back to the 1850s, when gold and silver were discovered around Virginia City, Nevada, with the legendary Comstock Load fueling an unparalleled mining bonanza.

In 1859, an enterprising local resident named Charles Fuller constructed a log bridge over the Truckee River, linking Virginia City to the California Trail. He soon made a fortune, charging prospectors a toll as well as providing accommodation for overnight stays.

Two years later, Fuller sold his toll bridge to Myron C. Lake, who expanded the hotel, adding a restaurant and livery stable. He renamed it "Lake's Crossing" and, using his toll profits, bought up the nearby land until it became the largest town in the newly consolidated Washoe County.

In 1868, Lake hit the jackpot when the Central Pacific Railroad reached Lake's Crossing, five years after it had started laying tracks in Sacramento. Then, in a brilliant business stroke, Lake deeded some land to railroad construction superintendent Charles Crocker in exchange for a promise to build a depot at Lake's Crossing. And from now on all trains to and from California passed through his crossing.

On May 13, 1868, Crocker proudly named the new town Reno, after Major General Jesse Reno, a Union officer who was killed in the Civil War.

For the next fifty years, Reno flourished as a business center. But at the dawn of the twentieth century, when the gold and silver mines finally dried up, the always resourceful Renoites turned their sights to new ways of making a buck.

In 1906, Reno's financial future was assured when William Corey, the president of the United States Steel Corporation, arrived in town to pursue a scandalous divorce. For under the lax Nevada State divorce laws a person only had to prove state residency for six months, to be eligible for seven grounds for divorce. Most other states only allowed adultery as the single ground for divorce, and the required residence period was far longer.

In the wake of the highly publicized Corey divorce, Reno gained notoriety as "the divorce capital of the world."

In 1926, the famous "Reno Arch" was erected on Virginia Street, right across from where Darren Mack's Palace Jewelry and Loan pawnbrokers would stand half a century later. The stunning downtown neon gateway astride Virginia Street had been built for the 1927 Transcontinental Highways Exposition. But it proved so popular that the decision was made to keep it permanently, with the then Reno mayor E. E. Roberts offering a prize of $100 for the best promotional slogan for the arch.

The winner was "Reno, the Biggest Little City in the World," which became world famous and is still in use today.

In 1931, the State of Nevada made it even easier to get a divorce, shortening the residency requirement to a mere six weeks. And after the state legislature legalized casino gambling, Reno became the original sin city, more than a quarter of a century before Las Vegas was on the radar.

The new laws instantly created a thriving industry, with hundreds of hotels, boardinghouses and other amusements catering for the thousands of people coming to get divorced every year. There were also dozens of divorce ranches, where handsome cowboy gigolos flocked to try and ensnare rich, older soon-to-be divorcées who decamped to Reno for the six weeks it took to dissolve a marriage.

Movie stars like Mary Pickford and rich heiresses like Barbara Hutton started coming to Reno for the "quickie divorce." And in 1939, writer Clare Boothe Luce immortalized her own experiences in Reno in her hit movie *The Women,* starring Joan Crawford, Rosalind Russell, and Norma Shearer.

By the late 1950s, Reno's divorce industry was waning as other states loosened divorce laws. But the casinos soon took up the slack, and gambling then became the town's life blood.

Dennis and Joan Mack first arrived in Reno on their honeymoon in 1957, falling in love with the place. And they could not have picked a better time to start a pawn business, as all the casinos springing up all over town meant more and more desperate people needing their services.

Dennis Alan Makovsky was born in Alameda County, California, on July 29, 1935, but the family soon Americanized its name to Mack. Dennis grew up in Oakland, California, and after leaving school he became a salesman for Rogers Jewelers.

Soon after he turned twenty, Dennis met a pretty young Mormon girl named Joan Rae Goodsell, who was a couple of years younger. Joan's father, Royal, was one of eight children, growing up in a tiny Mormon town in Idaho.

"My mom's side of the family was Catholic," said Joan. "They came over from Portugal to Hawaii and then to the United States."

The Goodsells were a close-knit, hardworking family. Royal was a highly skilled gunsmith and his brother Clarence was a sign painter, hand painting all the Reno casino signs in the fifties, when the town first took off as a gambling mecca.

"They were always very industrious people," said Joan, "Never asked for anything from anybody else."

In 1957, Dennis Mack married Joan at her father's house overlooking the Truckee River. They honeymooned in Reno and decided to settle down there and start a pawnbroking business. They rented a store, using their wedding presents as merchandise to sell.

In January 1958, the Macks opened Palace Jewelry and Loan on Commercial Row, Reno, backed by Joan's father, Royal Goodsell. Located in the thriving downtown casino area, between Harolds Club and the Palace, the new store was in the same three-story building as a wedding chapel, offering half-hour package deals.

And from the beginning Dennis Mack's skills as a salesman and knowledge of fine jewelry would prove a winning combination.

"He was a great salesperson," said his nephew Corey Schmidt, who would later run Palace Jewelry and Loan. "He knew his jewelry. He knew how to deal with people."

When they started, Dennis did all the pricing, while Joan kept the books. They lived in a trailer on the edge of Reno, saving every penny to plough back into the business.

And on January 31, 1961, Joan Mack gave birth to a boy, who they named Darren Roy.

"He was a very sickly child," remembered his mother. "I spent a lot of time with him during the years he was growing up."

With his father being Jewish and his mother half-Catholic and half-Mormon, Darren was baptized as well as circumcised and later at thirteen would be bar mitzvahed.

"We were a mixed marriage," said Joan, "[but] we never forced religion on the children."

Eighteen months after Darren was born, a second son named Landon arrived to complete the family.

"We grew up very meager," Landon remembered. "[We] lived in a trailer with the family until they bought their first home. I remember we used to eat whatever we caught or shot."

Both Mack boys went to The Holy Child, a local Catholic parochial school, before going to the Roy Gomm Elementary and St. Thomas schools. And little Darren seemed to have a photographic memory and craved knowledge.

"He had some qualities that were extremely interesting," said his mother. "He wanted to learn. He wanted to read before even going to school."

As toddlers, Darren and Landon spent a lot time at Palace Jewelry and Loan, where they were fussed over by the employees. During vacations they would help out in the store, where they were always given the latest toys to play with.

Their parents' hard work soon paid off, and they moved into a nice house in a good area of Reno. Dennis Mack was an excellent businessman and knew how to connect with people.

"Everybody loved him," said Joan Mack. "Dennis would sit there and talk to the people as they came into the store, listened to their problems. He had a way about him."

Dennis also expanded into real estate and other successful ventures all over Nevada and California, making him a millionaire by the end of the decade. Many of his best business deals were done on a handshake, with bankers, who considered him a personal friend.

"The family has always done that," said Landon Mack. "People would go out and loan money on a handshake, because no matter what . . . they knew they would get paid."

In 1968, seven-year-old Darren Mack joined the thriving family business.

"It was in my blood," he later told the *Reno Gazette-Journal*. "I worked here every summer. I would walk from St. Thomas School to work here every day after school."

Over the next few years, Darren learned the pawnbroking business, knowing that one day it would all be his. He started from the bottom, cleaning toilets, sweeping the floors, and learning to polish jewelry. And he soon showed a natural flair for the business.

Tall and handsome, Darren was very popular at school,

but often had a difficult relationship with his younger brother, who was always in his shadow.

"We tormented each other," recalled Landon. "It was just like brothers."

In 1969, Palace Jewelry and Loan expanded, moving into its present location on North Virginia Street's Casino Row. Occupying an entire block and standing in the shadows of the Reno Arch, the spacious new store was an immediate success.

"We went from ten to thirty employees in two weeks," recalled Joan Mack. "It was pretty wonderful."

That same year, eight-year-old Darren started a lifelong friendship with a young girl named Stephanie Finch. They would go to Reno High School, later becoming romantically involved one summer.

"Our families were members of the same synagogue," said Stephanie, "and we grew up in religious school from the time we were eight."

At the age of twelve, Darren had his first sexual experience with another girl. Years later he would tell psychologist Dr. Joseph Plaud that he had felt "scared and excited" when he first discovered masturbation.

In 1974, Darren was bar mizvahed and a year later he went to the Daniel C. Swope Middle School, where he started to get in shape, adding pounds to his once scrawny frame.

Every Thanksgiving and Christmas the extended Mack family would get together at a cabin they had built at Donner Lake on the Truckee River in North Lake Tahoe. They went hunting, sailing, and snow skiing, and during these family trips Darren and his third cousin Corey Schmidt became inseparable.

"I was closer to Darren than my own two brothers," explained Corey, who was four years younger. "All of us children were always together as much as possible. We were blessed to have so many family gatherings."

It was at the cabin that Darren first learned to hunt with a rifle, later becoming a first-rate marksman.

"We were both hunters," said his brother, Landon. "The whole family was."

In 1977, Darren began attending Reno High School, throwing himself into all sporting activities. But he especially loved baseball, dreaming of one day turning professional.

"Darren was a great athlete," said Stephanie Finch, "and excelled in any sport he put his mind to."

In his junior year, he was selected to play baseball for Reno High, serving as backup third baseman. He helped his school team win the Nevada State Championship playoffs, and was named co-MVP of the match.

"Darren was a jock," said journalist Amanda Robb, who attended Reno High in the early 1980s, "and the culture of the school gave him a lot of status. He definitely had the coin of the realm."

Soon after starting at Reno High School, Darren lost his virginity to a fourteen-year-old girl.

"I was happy, excited, and euphoric," he later told Dr. Plaud.

Corey Schmidt said his handsome cousin had his pick of girls at Reno High School.

"He was a stud," said Schmidt. "Darren always had a girlfriend. He was out dating and doing things."

The rich teenager also had his own set of friends, who cruised around Reno in expensive sports cars.

"Darren was the leader of a posse of boys who would get into trouble and do bad-boy things," said Robb.

But Joan Mack says her son could always talk his way out of trouble.

"Darren got in a few fights in high school," said his mother. "He was a very good negotiator, and he usually [walked] away and the other person became his good buddy."

Shortly before his graduation, Darren Mack attended his first Erhard Seminars Training (est) meeting and was smitten with the controversial self-motivational group. Founded in 1971 by Werner Erhard, a onetime *Encyclopedia Britannica* sales training manager, est was a radical program that offered people self-enlightenment over two weekends in an intense sixty-hour communications course.

The first est course was held in a San Francisco hotel in 1971, and over the next couple of years training programs spread like wildfire all over the United States and later Europe.

After taking his first course, Mack became a firm convert of this group, viewed by many as a dangerous cult. Over the next few years he would work his way up through the organization.

CHAPTER TWO

Stepping Up to the Plate

In 1979, eighteen-year-old Darren Mack graduated Reno High School, moving to Barstow Community College in California on a baseball scholarship. But within a year he was back in Reno, after being personally recruited by a University of Nevada baseball coach.

Darren dreamed of one day turning professional and playing in the major leagues. And during his two years at the University of Nevada, his baseball exploits at third base made headlines on the sports pages of the *Reno Gazette-Journal*.

The handsome young sportsman cultivated a worldly man-about-town image, although he still lived at home. Dennis and Joan Mack indulged his every whim, giving him expensive clothes and flashy sports cars. His mother was his biggest cheerleader, treasuring a photograph of Darren on one knee after hitting a game-winning home run.

During his second year at the University of Nevada, Stephanie Finch, now twenty-one, moved back to Reno after being away for several years. She became romantically involved again with Darren, who she had known since they were children.

"[I] dated Darren for that complete summer," Finch said. "We spent a lot of our time waterskiing, boating at [the Macks'] home in Donner Lake."

In 1982, Darren was forced to quit baseball permanently, after a sports injury led him to develop carpal tunnel syndrome.

"He got hurt," said Joan Mack. "He played until . . . he couldn't hit the ball anymore."

Darren was devastated that the painful wrist injury had ended his hopes of ever becoming a professional baseball player. So he dropped out of university to work full-time at Palace Jewelry and Loan.

At the age of twenty-one, Darren Mack was officially appointed the new Palace store manager. He immediately persuaded his parents to retire to Palm Springs and play golf while he ran the store.

He also invited his cousin Corey Schmidt to come and work at Palace as his right-hand man. The teenager, whose parents were in the midst of a divorce, dropped out of high school and moved to Reno.

On his first day at the Palace helm, Darren called his employees into his office one by one for a chat.

"I just want you all you know," Darren told them, "that my father is no longer in charge. I am now the CEO and the manager and I run this store. And you are fired."

Then, as they sadly walked out of his office, he offered to rehire them, asking if they wanted to come and work for him.

"It was a great move," explained Schmidt. "So that way they understood that it's no longer his father running things."

After Darren Mack took over Palace Jewelry and Loan, his parents divided their time between Reno and Palm Springs. Most of the week they golfed, mixing with the glamorous Palm Springs social set. But Dennis Mack was also keeping a close eye on his son's progress, buying himself a small private plane so he didn't have to drive the 507 miles back and forth to Reno.

On January 27, 1986, Dennis was flying himself back to

Reno, as Joan and her parents had decided to take the car instead. He had just been cleared for landing at Reno Airport when his tiny plane got caught in the jet wash of a Frontier Airlines 727 and crashed. Dennis was killed instantly.

"[The jet] just flew over my dad," said his son Landon, "and blew him to the ground."

Corey Schmidt was working at Palace when he got a call from an attorney friend.

"He said, 'There's been a plane wreck,'" Schmidt recalled. "'It's a private plane.'"

Darren was devastated by his father's untimely death, delivering a moving eulogy at the funeral. Joan Mack was also in deep shock, and from now on her eldest son would, in many ways, replace him in her life.

"Darren was the pillar of the family," recalled his brother, Landon. "He held it all together."

Within days of his father's death, Darren, now twenty-four, was named president of Palace Jewelry and Loan. He and his mother would now each have a 50 percent stake in the company. But from the beginning they had problems in their business relationship.

"Darren had to step up," explained Schmidt, "and fill some very big shoes that were almost unobtainable through his mother's eyes. She had very high expectations that were very hard to reach."

So Darren started distancing his mother from the family business, wanting a free hand to run it.

"When I lost my husband," said Joan Mack, "he took over the store and said, 'Mom, go out and live a little bit. Try to enjoy yourself.'"

Darren now embraced various behavioral motivational techniques, making his employers attend training seminars to maximize their efficiency and company profits.

He became deeply involved with the Landmark Education Corporation, which had recently evolved from est, whose communication seminars he had attended for years.

He started using his Landmark Education Corporation

motivational methods and communication skills to run Palace, making all his employees also undergo the Landmark course.

Over the next couple of years, Darren Mack assiduously worked his way up through the Landmark Education Corporation, eventually becoming a leader.

A few weeks after his father's death, Darren Mack struck up a conversation with a beautiful young girl in an elevator. Eighteen-year-old Debbie Ashlock had just graduated from Reno High School when she first set eyes on the rich, handsome young owner of Reno's biggest pawnshop. And he immediately swept her off her feet.

"She was an innocent and had been protected," recalled her friend Amanda Robb. "Darren seemed very worldly to her. He had a lot of money and was very slick."

They began dating and over the next few months he lavished her with attention. When he proposed marriage, she readily accepted.

"Debbie was a nice girl," said Corey Schmidt, "but I think she was a bit conniving."

On June 1, 1986, Darren Mack married Debbie in a lavish ceremony in Glenbrook, Nevada, on the banks of Lake Tahoe. Then the newlyweds settled down in an expensive home in Lakeridge, an exclusive Reno surburb.

Over the next few years, Darren Mack took Palace Jewelry and Loan to new levels, making his mark on Reno. In the often shady pawn business, appearances count for everything, so he cultivated relationships with influential state and local politicians, donating money to their campaigns and causes. He became a high-profile community activist, founding the Nevada Pawnbroker's Association.

He also courted the all-powerful Reno casino owners, who were so closely intertwined with the pawn business.

"I first met Darren Mack in the mid-1980s," said John Metzker, one of the owners of the Fitzgeralds Casino, directly opposite Palace Jewelry and Loan. "Darren emerged as a young community leader during this time."

His mother, Joan, was also very active in the Nevada political arena, donating to her favorite political campaign funds. And over the years she and her son would become highly respected among Reno philanthropists and socialites.

"Pawnbrokers prey on the most desperate people," said journalist Amanda Robb. "Palace is huge and a lot of money filters through, as it's a cash business. You've got gambling addicts, and people come in with stacks of jewels.

"So the Macks made their money that way but they also had to be upstanding members of the community, so they sponsored Little League teams. The economy's entirely based on gaming and divorce and vice of all kinds, so it's a culture and a community that is really divorced from the way it makes its money."

On August 9, 1988, Debra Mack gave birth to their first child, a baby boy they named Jory. Darren was delighted to be a father and have a son to follow in his footsteps. Two years later, on February 17, 1990, their second child was born, a baby girl named Jacqueline Elise.

But although from the outside the Macks seemed pillars of Reno respectability, their marriage was on the rocks, with allegations of infidelity flying back and forth. To this day, Landon Mack refuses to discuss why his brother filed for divorce.

"That's private," Landon said, "and what I do know I would never say."

Around that time the two brothers had a bitter argument, with Landon moving to Southern California.

Corey Schmidt—who had now left Palace and moved to Florida to start an exotic-bird cabaret act—says the divorce left Darren permanently scarred.

"When they split up," he said, "I think Darren kind of lost trust in women in general."

* * *

On August 16, 1991, Darren Mack filed for divorce in Reno Family Court. In court records he claimed that Debbie was having an affair with her psychology professor at Truckee Meadows Community College. He also alleged she had refused to end the relationship and work on their marriage.

Their bitter divorce battle would last years, with Debbie spending an estimated quarter of a million dollars on attorney fees just responding to him. Although they shared interim custody of the children, Darren made things as difficult as he could for her.

Amanda Robb, who was Debbie's friend, said Debbie did not go after his money, although she could have.

"Debbie did not make him pay," said Robb. "She settled just to get out and that's probably what saved her life."

Under their divorce settlement, the couple agreed to share custody of Jory and Elise, with Darren paying $500 a month for each child as well as monthly alimony of $2,300 for the next five years or until Debra remarried.

Now thirty-three and single again, Darren Mack became aware of his own mortality. He began keeping a life clock ticking away in reverse as a graphic reminder of his diminishing time on earth left to realize his goals.

He was now traveling all over America, leading daylong Landmark Education Corporation seminars. In May 1994 he flew to Los Angeles to lead one. And one night at dinner he found himself sitting next to a beautiful young Landmark leader named Charla Sampsel. Sparks flew instantly.

CHAPTER THREE

Charla

Charla Marie Sampsel was born on August 15, 1966, at St. Mary's Hospital in Fullerton, California, to Jan and Soorya Sampsel. Jan was working for the local police department and the couple were renting Soorya's parents' house.

"When I gave birth to Charla," said her mother, "I was twenty years old. I had to say good-bye to much of my youth to raise her."

Growing up, Soorya and her daughter were constantly on the move, with little family stability. When Charla was a toddler, her father moved the family to Santa Monica after getting a degree and going to work at the Los Angeles Police Department. The little girl loved the beach, and her mother would take her to play in the water every day.

Then, when Charla was just three years old, her father left the family to move to Costa Rica.

"Jan had a serious drinking problem." claimed Soorya, "and in 1969 we divorced."

Soorya soon met a man named Robert Broughton, marrying him a year later when Charla was five. The marriage lasted eight years, during which they had a son, Christopher.

Charla was thirteen when her mother divorced again, moving her two children to Los Angeles. Charla was already strikingly beautiful, looking far older than her years. She was naturally artistic and loved acting, setting her sights on becoming a movie star.

A few months later, Soorya moved the family to Reno, enrolling Charla at Reno High School. Once again the teenager had to start afresh, making a new set of friends in a new school.

"Her parents were divorced," said Laura Cunningham (not her real name), who would later become Charla's best friend. "She had a horrible time going back and forth."

Ironically, Charla would be in the same sophomore class as Darren Mack's future wife, Debbie Ashlock, although the two were not friends.

Soorya and her two children loved the scenic Lake Tahoe area and now really bonded together as a family.

"We had so much fun and playfulness . . . as a family," recalled Soorya. "The three of us would dress up in dorky, hilarious costumes and then drive around Lake Tahoe in a milk truck performing singing telegrams, doing comedy acts for other people's birthday parties."

In the 1983 Reno High School yearbook, sixteen-year-old Charla's photograph stands out from the rest of the students, with her wide smile and thick mane of red hair.

As a single mom, Soorya worked long hours as a masseur to support the family. And with so much freedom, Charla started getting into trouble.

"She had gotten into a wild crowd doing drugs," said her mother, "and I became apprehensive she might fall to the wayside."

So Soorya sent Charla to live with her father, Jan Sempsel, who had remarried and was now living in Missoula, Montana.

The teenager soon settled down in Missoula, starting her junior year at Big Sky High School. She was voted a cheerleader and starred in the school play.

After graduating Big Sky high School in 1984, Charla returned to Los Angeles, moving back in with Soorya and

Chris. Her mother encouraged her daughter to pursue her studies, but Charla had other ideas.

"I tried to get her to go to college," recalled Soorya, "but she had this dream of being an actress."

For the next few years, Charla's mother encouraged her to take dance, voice, and acting classes.

While waiting for her big break, Charla found a job as a waitress in a fashionable restaurant. One day movie star Arnold Schwarzenegger came in and sat at her table. He was smitten with the beautiful young waitress and kept coming back. Eventually he asked her out on a date, and the star-struck teenager readily accepted.

Later she would tell friends how the Austrian-born action hero, later California governor, had first seduced her.

"I'm European," he told her on their first date, "and people in Europe have a much more relaxed attitude about having mistresses."

For the next two years, Charla and Schwarzenegger intermittently dated, with Soorya occasionally joing them for dinner. But Schwarzenegger turned cold after Charla asked him to help her daughter get a part in a movie. He immediately stopped taking her calls, breaking off the relationship.

Then, in 1987, twenty-one-year-old Charla landed a cameo role in *Heaven*, Diane Keaton's directorial debut documentary movie. Keaton interviewed Charla and Soorya—among many others—about their perceptions of heaven.

"God has helped me through everything," said an emotional Charla in the movie. "God is wonderful."

Then Charla Sampsel fell in love with a young Malibu police officer named Scott Hobbs, and asked her mother's permission to live with him.

"I said yes," said Soorya, "since I adored him. He was funny, charming and fit right into our family. All we did was laugh, share food and life's joys."

Soon afterward a friend took Charla to a Landmark

Education communications course, and her life changed forever. After her unstable childhood, Charla felt grounded with Landmark Education, going back again and again. For the first time in her life she felt empowered, ending her two-year relationship with Scott Hobbs.

"Once Charla got interested in Landmark," said her mother, "she wanted to try living on her own, so she and Scott separated and Charla found an apartment a mile away from me in Sherman Oaks, California."

In 1990, Charla, who was now doing floral arrangements in a restaurant, met Laura Cunningham at a Landmark training course. The two young women instantly became friends, finding much in common.

"We hit it off and became close right away," recalled Cunningham. "She was just bubbly and fun and we got along very well."

A year later, Charla was finally offered a small speaking role in the movie *Poison Ivy*. In the R-rated film about incest, starring Drew Barrymore and Leonardo DiCaprio, Charla played an orderly pushing a gurney through a hospital corridor.

"She was so nervous they cut her speaking part," said her mother. "Still she obtained a SAG credit and that's what we were aiming for."

Charla had also started dating a young man named Jubal Rafferty, whom she had met at Landmark. Rafferty was training to be a Landmark Forum leader, and he and Charla moved in together. The relationship lasted eighteen months before Charla broke it off.

After her disappointment with the *Poison Ivy* movie, Charla became disillusioned with Hollywood.

"Charla became frustrated with acting," explained Soorya, "because of how unstable it was and hard on the ego."

After taking a month off to regroup and decide on her next move, she started her own flower-arranging business. It took off and she soon expanded to designing wedding floral displays.

She was also becoming more deeply involved in Landmark Education.

"Once Charla began training for and leading communication courses at Landmark, she had a full and successful life," Soorya said. "She was dating and having a lot of fun."

Then, one night in May 1994, Charla attended a Landmark dinner in Los Angeles and met Darren Mack. A lifelong vegan, she was nevertheless attracted to the handsome pawnbroker who hunted deer.

"They hit it off right away," said her mother. "Soon he invited her to fly to Reno to meet his children."

CHAPTER FOUR

Falling in Love

After his divorce, Darren Mack told friends he would be married again within a year. And when he first set eyes on Charla Sampsel, he decided she was the one. The similarities between his ex-wife Debbie and Charla were uncanny. Both had been in the same sophomore class at Reno High, shared the same birthday, and were the spitting image of each other.

Darren also liked that Charla was deeply committed to Landmark Education and, like him, led training seminars.

"It was part of their lives," explained Charla's friend Jacqueline Ross. They used all those communication words."

Darren and Charla embarked on a passionate affair, discovering an amazing sexual rapport with each other.

"Charla was very sexual, as was Darren," said Ross. "He found his sexual match."

After their first meeting, Darren started spending more time in Los Angeles. Charla soon introduced him to her best friend, Laura Cunningham.

"They hit it off," Cunningham recalled. "I mean, Darren wasn't my cup of tea, but he was very charming. He was very magnetic and charismatic. You just wanted to be around him."

As for Darren's family, his mother immediately liked Charla, thoroughly approving of her elder son's new girlfriend.

"She was fun," said Joan, "and I thought that he had finally found *the* woman—the love of his life."

Charla's warm, bubbly personality also won over Darren's son, Jory, now six, and four-year-old daughter, Elise, who immediately bonded with her.

But it would be some time before Charla met Landon Mack, as the brothers were not talking.

That summer, Darren Mack introduced Charla to a lavish new lifestyle she had only dreamed about. He wined and dined her at the best restaurants, taking on her on exotic trips to the Caribbean and Hawaii on a whim.

"So they were having fun," said Laura Cunningham. "He was very charming and the best he ever was."

When Charla's family met Darren, they were much impressed with him, thinking it an excellent match.

"It was obvious that they were very much in love," said her half-brother Chris Broughton. "He was secure and stable [and] already had two children. She was also attracted to him physically."

But Charla's grandmother was not quite so sure.

"My mother always thought that Darren saw Charla as a good showpiece," recalled Soorya.

As she entered Darren Mack's world, Charla Sampsel found herself drawn into his ongoing divorce with Debra, which was becoming increasingly ugly. Three months after the divorce had been made final, Debbie moved in with Professor Kevin Dugan. In July 1994 they married and Debbie announced they wanted custody of Jory and Elise.

Darren Mack hired a Reno divorce lawyer named Gary Silverman to stop this happening, battling his ex-wife all the way up to the Nevada Supreme Court.

One of Darren Mack's biggest supporters in the relocation battle was his new girlfriend Charla, who took an active interest in the case.

"She attended many of the conferences that we had," said Silverman. "We went to dinner with them on several occasions. They were as happy as larks. They were like two little otters swimming around in the bay."

In early 1995, Darren Mack proposed marriage to Charla, and she accepted on the understanding that he gave up hunting big game. He then had an attorney draw up a pre-nuptial agreement, stating that if they divorced she would have no claim on his family business. But Charla refused to sign it.

"Well, it was a bone of contention," said Laura Cunningham. "She was very upset about that pre-nup."

Finally, in a theatrical gesture, Darren tore up the agreement, saying he couldn't take the arguing anymore.

On May 13, 1995, Darren and Charla were married at a lavish wedding in a restaurant on the banks of Lake Tahoe. It was a Reno society wedding with around a hundred guests attending, including many of Darren's business associates.

"They were just so emotional and so passionate," said Laura Cunningham. "Really in love."

In the middle of the ceremony there was a freak spring snowstorm.

"As they were being married," recalled Cunningham, "big flakes started coming down. Looking through the big bay windows out at the lake, it kind of had a magical quality."

After the wedding, the newlyweds left for an expensive European honeymoon that Cunningham had planned for them. But immediately there were problems, as the bride and groom both had totally different expectations.

"They went to Florence, the French Riviera, and Venice," remembered Cunningham, "and I think Charla really enjoyed it but Darren hated it."

Charla later joked that Darren would have been happier going to a Caribbean resort where he could ogle topless girls.

"He didn't want to see Europe," said Cunningham. "He was a big dopey party guy and not sophisticated in any way."

During the honeymoon the couple fought constantly when they weren't in bed making love.

"It was right away they were fighting," said Charla's mother, Soorya. "Very big and loud and dramatic and emotional. That was their passion."

CHAPTER FIVE

The Ultimatum

After they returned from Europe, Darren and Charla began married life in a rented house, while they looked for their own dream home. Charla briefly went to work for Palace Jewelry and Loan, before Darren decided he wanted her home to look after Jory and Elise.

Darren was generous, buying his new wife a sports car, designer clothes, and expensive jewelry from Palace. But although Charla was finally living the lavish life she had always dreamed of, she was not happy.

"It was a very rough first year," said Laura Cunningham. "They did a lot of arguing."

Although Laura lived in Los Angeles, she regularly spoke to Charla. Almost every day her best friend would call, complaining about her and Darren's latest fight.

Occasionally, the Macks' heated arguments turned into public spectacles. One time they chased each other through a department store, screaming and yelling. Another time, according to Elise Mack, Charla slapped her father in the face during a row at an airport.

One thing that brought them together, however, was Darren's increasingly bitter custody battle with his ex-wife, Debbie. They were now squabbling over which school their two children should attend, as well as vacation plans and visitation rights.

"Sometimes he was very difficult," said Debbie. "Sometimes it was confusing. Anything I said, he said no to. I mean, I definitely had issues and differences with him."

Finally, Darren Mack filed a motion for full custody of Jory and Elise.

"She wants total control," he complained in a motion to the Washoe County Family Court.

Debbie later told friends that Charla was stalking her, attempting to get ammunition to bolster Darren's ongoing custody case.

A few months after they were married, Darren took Charla to Las Vegas, saying he had to attend a business meeting but refusing to give her any more details. Later, when she returned to Reno, Charla told Laura Cunningham how they had met a mysterious man in a bar.

"It was a hit man," said Cunningham, "and [Darren] was talking about prices. She didn't know what was going on."

Finally, the man left the bar and Charla asked what he had been trying to arrange with the strange man.

"And he goes, 'Well, I'm thinking of getting rid of Debbie,'" said Laura.

After marrying Darren Mack, Charla became very close to her new mother-in-law. Together they brokered a reconciliation with Landon Mack, who had not gone to the wedding.

The reunion took place the following Easter, when Joan Mack invited her youngest son to spend a few days in the desert with her. He arrived to find his mother, Darren, and Charla waiting to surprise him.

"Charla basically put us together," said Landon. "I didn't know about it and then it was, like, 'Why don't you guys disappear for a few hours and go shopping' So we did and it was all good."

* * *

Not long afterward, Darren Mack forced his mother out of Palace Jewelry and Loan. He secured a 51 percent proxy share of the family business and ordered her to leave. The thirty-six-year-old was fed up with her constant meddling and her claims that he was not running the business as well as his father had.

"He kicked Joan out and then ran the store for five years," explained his cousin Corey Schmidt. "Darren said, 'I'll tell you what, Joan, I'll just make you money and you stay home.'"

By now Schmidt had retired his exotic-bird cabaret act, finding a new career as a Carnival Cruise Lines director. But wherever he was in the world, he kept in close touch with Darren by phone.

Schmidt believes that Darren's sometimes difficult relationship with his mother had led him to Landmark in the first place. He was looking for leadership and the group then became his support network away from her.

"And she can shoot me for saying that," said Schmidt, "but it's the truth. It's the absolute truth."

Schmidt says Joan Mack expected unrealistically high profits from the business, blaming Darren if her quotas were not met.

"Its almost like working for a corporation," Schmidt said, "like they give you a target, you make your target, and then they raise your target. Nothing is ever enough.

"Joan is a wonderful, wonderful lady, but she has very high expectations that are very hard to reach."

Darren Mack had always enjoyed strip clubs, and he started bringing Charla along too. They became regulars at Fantasy Girls, and most nights Darren's gold Hummer would pull up at the seedy strip mall where Fantasy Girls was located, in a bad part of Reno, for an evening of fun.

The shabby East Fourth Street club boasted three poles and a back room, where Darren and Charla tipped generously for private lap dances. The couple also frequented the

BuBinga Lounge, a nightclub on the same block as Palace Jewelry and Loan, where they received the royal treatment.

They were also into pornography, often photographing themselves making love.

"Charla was a very sexual person," her friend Christine Libert later told CBS's *48 Hours*. "She did not have sexual inhibitions, and that was something she shared with her husband."

In the spring of 1997, Charla decided she had made a mistake in marrying Darren Mack. Charla told friends her thirty-six-year-old husband was immature and she was fed up with his childish behavior.

Then she accidentally became pregnant, and decided to stay.

"Well, it had been unplanned," said Soorya. "And that was when she knew that she was going to make the marriage work."

Charla later rationalized her decision to Laura Cunningham, saying she knew what it was like to grow up in a broken home and did not want her child to suffer as she had.

"She used to say, 'You know I'm going to do whatever it takes to stay married. I don't care what it is,'" said Cunningham.

Over the next few months, Charla tried to make a success of her marriage, and for a time Darren became more responsible. He used his influence to have himself and Charla voted onto the board of the prestigious Cambridge Montessori School, which Jory and Elise attended whenever Darren had custody of them.

"They seemed like an average newlywed couple," recalled Cambridge Montessori teacher Sylvia Crawford. "Charla was always vivacious and had a lot of energy. She was always smiling."

In November, when Charla was eight and a half months pregnant, Darren gave her an ultimatum. He suddenly announced that after she had the baby he wanted them to become swingers and start experimenting with sex. He said he had always dreamed of having the sexual freedom to swap partners, and if she loved him she would join in.

Then he told her that if she would not agree, he wanted a divorce so he could find someone who would.

"He was pretty crafty that way," said Laura Cunningham. "He really waited until she was about to deliver . . . until she was completely locked in. Then he unveiled certain things that he was requiring. He said it was a real deal breaker."

Charla grudgingly agreed to his terms, feeling that Darren had left her no alternative.

Then, days before their baby was born, Darren surreptitiously slipped his original prenuptial agreement in with a pile of other papers she had to sign.

It would be years before she realized how he had tricked her, effectively cutting her out of any stake in his fortune.

On December 22, 1997, Charla gave birth to a baby girl, Erika Nicole. Darren was delighted, and at New Year's he proudly showed off his new daughter at a family party at his mother's house.

A few days before Erika's birth, Darren and Charla had moved into a beautiful $1.6 million mock Tudor mansion at 5350 Franktown Road in Carson City. Built in 1979, it was set in six acres in the foothills of Washoe Valley and had its own private stream. The imposing 5,700-square-foot property boasted five bedrooms, two full bathrooms, and three fireplaces.

As soon as the Macks moved in, they spent $350,000 digging a backyard swimming pool and building a well-equipped gym with floor-to-ceiling mirrors.

But thanks to the locally hired movers, word soon spread that the Macks had "boxes of porn" and were sex mad.

CHAPTER SIX

Father of the Year

In spring 1998, when their daughter Erika was just a few months old, Darren and Charla Mack flew to Montego Bay, Jamaica, for their first swinging experience. Darren had booked them into the notorious Hedonism II Resort in Negril, on the west coast of the idyllic Caribbean island.

Advertised as "The Pleasure Seeker's Ultimate Super-Inclusive Playground," Hedonism II boasts Jacuzzis and love mirrors in every room. Anything goes on the twenty-five-acre beach resort, where clothing is optional, except in restaurants during meals.

The beach bars are open around the clock, and the staff turn a blind eye to drugs. Everyone walks around naked and couples casually hook up by the pool before retiring to the bedrooms for sex.

Soon after arriving, Darren and Charla met a handsome French business executive named Olivier who had a wife and a live-in girlfriend. Darren was immediately impressed by Olivier's sybaritic lifestyle, and he and Charla spent the rest of the vacation with him and his wife.

Later, Charla told Laura Cunningham that Darren was "enamored" with Olivier and wanted to be like him.

During their week at Hedonism II, the Macks tried Ecstasy for the first time. The popular 1990s "designer" drug was embraced by swingers for the way it dissolved inhibitions. Darren loved Ecstasy and would take it hundreds of times over the next few years.

Back in Reno, Darren decided to model himself on his new friend Olivier, who he now called "my brother." And he and Charla began exploring the lively Reno swinging scene.

"He wanted to create a life where he was [Olivier]," said Cunningham. "He was obsessed."

That summer Darren spent hours discussing his and Charla's new swinging lifestyle with his cousin Corey Schmidt.

"They would go to swinger parties and share partners," said Schmidt. "And usually the parties [would be] held at a really nice house or they [would] take over hotels."

Although Schmidt was never part of the swinging scene, he heard all about it from Darren and other friends who were.

"There's a house in Reno," he said, "where the owners have swinger parties every week. They have a DJ and food and you can just go into a room, and it's pretty much no holds barred. But everybody uses a condom and it's very clean."

The Macks also joined the swinging group Utopia, using its Web site to find local swing parties and other like-minded couples to meet.

Darren and Charla embraced their swinging lifestyle with a passion, working out daily in the newly built gym in their Franktown Road house. Darren also started consuming protein powders and other health supplements to build up his muscles, announcing he wanted to become a competitive bodybuilder.

Then Darren invited his mother-in-law, Soorya, to come and live in their guesthouse. For the next eighteen months she would run her massage therapy business out of it and babysit Erika during his and Charla's frequent out-of-town trips.

Darren also hired Charla's father, Jan Sampsel, at Palace Jewelry and Loan, putting him charge of the company's new lucrative eBay operation. He seemed to enjoy having Charla's parents rely on him, and the subtle control he exerted over them.

That July, Darren and Charla flew to Cap d'Agde, in the south of France, to vacation with Olivier and his wife and girlfriend. When Charla expressed reservations about going, as she was fast becoming disillusioned with the swinging lifestyle, Darren said they could go nudist without swapping partners.

"Then I started getting phone calls from Europe," said Cunningham. "She was freaking out, saying, 'What the hell am I doing? This has turned out to be *that* kind of trip and I don't want to do it.'"

Eventually, Darren and Olivier persuaded Charla to join in the sexual escapades.

"He sort of got the saddle on her," said Cunningham. "And then she participated."

A few weeks later, back in Reno, Charla Mack rented out a huge billboard at the corner of Cheney and Virginia streets as a Father's Day present for Darren.

It read: "The Mack Family Presents: Darren Mack. 1998 Father/Husband of the Year. A unanimous decision by his wife, Charla, and his three wonderful children."

"She loved grand gestures," said her friend Jacqueline Ross. "She had this bigger-than-life personality and that was something she would do to make him feel good."

Darren reciprocated by including Charla and Erika in his new television commercial for Palace Jewelry and Loan, introducing Jan Sampsel's new eBay operation.

"My name is Darren Mack," he proudly announced in the thirty-second spot, filmed at Palace, "and I am the third-generation owner of a small business in Reno, Nevada. My family has owned and operated small businesses in Nevada for forty-five years. I am proud of the fact that I am able to carry on the legacy left to me by my parents and grandparents.

"I've been around jewelry and diamonds since my dad

brought me down to the store when I was seven years old. I have a personal commitment to excellence in any endeavor I take on.

"And, as you can see, I am married to a lovely young lady and have three beautiful children."

As he approached forty, Darren Mack made a determined effort to establish himself as a consummate family man and pillar of society. He was a sportsman and deer hunter, with two memberships at the exclusive Canvasback Gun Club, worth $70,000. He also was a leading member of the Prospectors' Club a highly influential business association in Reno.

The pawnbroker was also actively involved in Reno politics, advocating for small businesses and campaigning against planned downtown events and a new convention center.

As the founder of the Nevada Pawnbroker Association, Darren was also very active at the state level, lobbying to protect the rights of his industry.

"He was interested in issues that dealt with his business," said pawnshop lobbyist Alfredo Alonso. "[He] would work with the state to try and police the pawn business . . . to make it a better industry."

Darren and Charla Mack now spent most weekends out of town, attending swinging parties or sex conventions. And edging into middle age, Darren was having the time of his life, with a beautiful wife and a constant supply of younger women at his beck and call.

According to Corey Schmidt, Charla was a willing participant and enjoyed sex with women. Darren told his cousin that Charla would select the girls she desired, going with them first before he was allowed to join in the fun.

"Charla wanted to do it," explained Schmidt. "I mean, don't get me wrong: it was fun for Darren too."

One night Schmidt and a group of friends were at the Macks' Franktown Road house when Charla telephoned a stripper she knew, inviting her over to party.

"The next thing you know, we were all in the Jacuzzi, naked," said Schmidt. "But then I went to bed and they went into the other room to have sex."

Despite her sometime willingness, Charla later told Laura Cunningham she had begun to tire of swinging.

"I think it got untidy very quickly," explained Cunningham. "I mean, it's pretty hard to maintain a good marriage and have swinging going on; it's just whacked."

To add to the mix, Darren was regularly taking Ecstasy and the "date rape" drug GHB (gamma hydroxybutyrate) to enhance his sexual pleasure. On party nights he and Charla would get high before doing the rounds of the strip clubs of Reno.

"He was not a drinker," said Cunningham, "but he would be at a club all night. I mean, the guy was forty, and all he wanted to do was just get the kids babysitters and go out all night."

Darren was now spending less and less time at Palace Jewelry and Loan, traveling most weekends, whether to swinging events or the occasional trip to Europe.

"They lived a very, very glamorous lifestyle," said Corey Schmidt. "Darren spent a ton of money."

In fall 2000, the Macks enrolled their daughter Erika in the Cambridge Montessori School preschool program. Charla started involving herself in school activities, becoming an active fundraiser. At a parents' meeting, she met Jacqueline Ross, whose child also went to the school.

"We had a great connection," said Ross.

The two mothers started hanging out after dropping their children at school, and found much in common.

"Charla was very charismatic," said Ross. "Very positive. Very up. We laughed a lot and she really owned her stuff."

Charla also became friendly with another Montessori mother, Ann Mudd, who had first met her and Darren years earlier at a casino opening.

"I met Charla when she first started dating Darren," Ann recalled. "I was introduced to her and she was very nice. And then I didn't see her again until years later, when we both had kids at the same school."

Charla soon became very close to her two new friends, always playing down the difficulties she was having in her marriage. It would be several years before she would finally reveal her secret life to them.

CHAPTER SEVEN

A Close Call

In summer 2001, Darren and Charla Mack befriended a local bodybuilder named Phil Pape, who owned a Reno nutri-
tion store. Pape regularly competed in Mr. Nevada contests,
training local bodybuilders as a sideline.

"They both started shopping here," said Pape. "He came
in a little more often, [to] get his protein powders, meal re-
placements, weight gainers and advice on dieting. He wasn't
a real big guy but he was in decent shape, because he had his
own gym. He knew what he was doing."

Soon after they met, Darren hired Pape to train him to
compete in the upcoming Mr. Nevada competition. Over the
next few months, Mack devoted himself to building up his
body to compete in the lightweight class. He went on a high-
protein, low-carb diet for his muscles. And he placed himself on the Fit for Life program, which advocates eating only
fruit and high-water-content foods in order to lose excess
body weight.

"It was all about having 3 percent fat," said Jacqueline
Ross. "He carried his food around with him and he was very
particular about what he ate."

Mack was now regularly going to Phil Pape's gym for a
bodybuilding master class.

"He knew what he was doing already," said Pape, "so I

just kind of dialed him in. I helped him get his posing, choreographed his routine, and did his diet for him."

Outside the gym, Pape often saw the Macks at the BuBinga Lounge at the Eldorado Casino, directly opposite Palace Jewelry and Loan. And, sometimes to his embarrassment, he'd see Charla sitting on other men's laps, right in front of her husband.

"Charla was a flirt," said Pape. "She would be giving me hugs and I was kind of nervous, as Darren was right there. I was, like, 'That's kind of odd.' But then someone told me they were swingers."

By spring 2002, Darren Mack's body had undergone a remarkable transformation. His five-foot-eleven-inch frame was now bursting with muscles, and he had started taking illegal steroids for added definition.

"I don't know when the steroids started, but at some point they did." said Laura Cunningham. "With an already aggressive guy who's got impulse control things, that was a bad situation."

Darren's trainer, Phil Pape, denies any knowledge of Mack ever taking steroids.

"As far as he ever told me, he was natural," said Pape. "And if my clients tell me they're natural, they're natural. If you're juicing, you're juicing—doesn't matter to me. It's easier when you're juicing."

With all the drugs he was taking, Charla told friends that Darren was having problems achieving an erection and had started taking Viagra.

In May 2002, Darren Mack won fifth place in the Mr. Reno lightweight competition, and Charla and Erika were there to cheer him on. His runner-up trophy became one of his most prized possessions, taking pride of place on his desk in his second-floor Palace office.

To celebrate, he commissioned a life-size photo portrait of himself flexing his muscles, which he placed on the wall directly above the urinal of his master bedroom.

"It was the *Darren Mack Show*," said Laura Cunningham. "He wanted you to acknowledge him and how great his body was every day, incessantly."

That summer, Darren Mack almost died. He and Charla were checking out of the Mandalay Bay Hotel and Casino, after a swinging trip to Las Vegas, when he started talking gibberish. Realizing something was seriously wrong, Charla dialed 911 for an ambulance to take him to the nearest emergency room.

After they arrived, Darren was left in a room as his condition visibly deteriorated. Finally, unable to take it any longer, Charla stormed into the doctors' offices, screaming for someone to come and examine her dying husband.

"Charla created such a fit that they got a doctor out of bed to come and see him," said Laura Cunningham. "She saved his life."

By the time the doctor arrived, Darren had fallen into a coma and was close to death. As the emergency staff fought to save his life, a tearful Charla called the family with the terrible news.

Corey Schmidt was in San Francisco when an emotional Landon Mack called, asking him to come to Las Vegas as quickly as possible.

"Lanny was crying," he recalled. "He says . . . Darren's not going to make it."

So Schmidt and his fiancée caught the first plane to Las Vegas, going straight to the hospital.

"By the time I got there," said Schmidt, "he was already in a coma."

By now, the doctors had diagnosed spinal meningitis, a sometimes fatal bacterial infection that inflames the membrane covering the brain and spinal cord.

For the next three days, Charla and other close Mack family members kept a round-the-clock vigil in the infectious diseases ward as Darren hovered between life and death. Then he started to come back from the brink.

"I was actually feeding him ice chips," recalled Schmidt. "When he opened his eyes, I was the first person he saw. I look at him and he goes, 'That's amazing!' "

Then Darren closed his eyes and went to sleep with a smile on his face.

"I mean, normal people would die," said Schmidt. "But he was a bodybuilder and he ate right, so he was able to pull out of it."

Darren Mack spent the next two weeks in the hospital, until he was strong enough to fly back to Reno and convalesce.

"It affected about 30 percent of his hearing," said Schmidt. "I mean, he could barely move, because this bacterial disease just eats up your entire system."

For the next three months Darren remained at home, nursed twenty-four hours a day by Charla and her mother.

When he was fully recovered, Darren Mack informed Charla that his near-death exprience had given him an epiphany. He said he now needed to explore his sexuality by turning their Franktown Road mansion into his personal Plato's Retreat.

"After he had meningitis, it became more urgent to him that they swing," said Laura Cunningham. "I think it was his brush with death that made him feel that it was his life's mission."

Mack now wanted to bring other women into their home, just as his mentor Olivier was doing in Paris.

"He wanted to be the Hugh Hefner of Reno," said Cunningham. "He had this whole fantasy that all these people were going to live there. I mean, he was a real sex addict. He really ratcheted things up."

Charla said she wanted no part of that lifestyle, as it was incompatible with her being a good mother to Erika. She begged him to forget it and save their marriage.

"She was trying to get out," said Cunningham. "She was, like, 'I seriously want out. I don't want to do this. This is wrecking our marriage.' "

After that, their already troubled marriage went downhill, as Darren kept pressuring her to join in his swinging escapades. Sometimes she would give in, knowing he could turn violent if he didn't get his way.

"There was an incident where he had choked her," recalled Cunningham. "He got mad and just flew off the handle."

When Charla tearfully told her about the attack, Laura advised her to call the police if it happened again. Darren risked losing his pawnbroker's license if he was arrested and charged with a felony.

"So a lot was at stake," said Cunningham, "and she was afraid. I said, 'You've got to tell him that if he touches you, you're going to call the police and it's going to threaten his whole livelihood. You've got to say something.'"

A few weeks later, Cunningham got a furious phone call from Darren Mack after Charla had mentioned their conversation.

"He called me, livid, " said Cunningham, "and he thought that I was trying to destroy him. He was aggressive and he wanted me to back down."

Laura told him that she just wanted him to stop physically abusing Charla.

"You just need to keep your hands in your pockets," she warned him, "and no one will need to call any policeman."

When Darren Mack finally returned to work at Palace Jewelry and Loan, he used a cane for the first few months, although there was little sign of his near-fatal illness. The Macks were now leading virtually separate lives, with Charla staying at home to look after the children and Darren coming and going as he pleased.

That fall, four-year-old Erika started therapy with psychologist Dr. Joann Behrman-Lippert. The little girl was having emotional problems and falling behind at school as a result of her parents' increasingly troubled marriage.

At Christmas, Laura Cunningham flew to Reno to spend the holiday with the Macks, and found things had drastically changed. As usual, Charla had decorated the Franktown Road house with a huge Christmas tree and a Santa's foot coming through the ceiling. But there was an uncomfortable coolness between her and Darren.

During the visit, Charla finally told her friend about their swinging lifestyle and how desperately she now wanted to stop.

"She was really embarrassed about it," said Laura. "She was ashamed. She said they did it for about three years, and that for her it was about two years, three months too long . . .

"They had been having problems because he was right back into [swinging] and she was drawing the line," said Cunningham. "And he was *very* frustrated."

Acute spinal meningitis can result in brain damage, and Laura Cunningham now believes that Darren Mack could have suffered this.

"He got darker and darker," she said. "It was a subtle thing, but I thought there was a difference. Little things that once would have been like water off a duck's back frustrated him. Everything was a catastrophe."

CHAPTER EIGHT

"I Will Crush You!"

Two weeks after Christmas, at the start of 2003, Charla Mack moved out of Franktown Road, renting another house near her friend Jacqueline Ross. She told Darren that she wanted a separation, as he refused to stop swinging.

"I don't think she wanted a divorce," said Laura Cunningham. "I don't think she even wanted a separation. I remember thinking, *Why is she so hopeful?*"

For the next six months, Darren Mack lived the bachelor life. He was frequently out of town swinging, while Erika stayed with her mother in her newly rented house.

He was also neglecting the family business, delegating management of Palace to several employees while he was away, being a playboy.

"It got to the point where the store was suffering," said Corey Schmidt, "because Darren was the man when it came to running the store, so when he wasn't around, people stole from him."

On February 4, Washoe County Family Court ordered Darren Mack to pay his first wife. Debbie Ashlock-Dugan, $2,000 a month in children support for Jory and Elise as well as hundreds of dollars of arrears he owed. And their custody battle—which had now been going on for twelve years—was still far from being settled.

By June, Darren begged Charla to move back in with him and save their marriage. He gave her an expensive diamond ring, saying he loved her and could not live without her.

Charla agreed to move back to the Franktown Road house and try and make a go of it.

"And that summer he wooed her back," said Laura Cunningham, "so she let her place go and moved back in. Everything was fine. Everything was okay. He was in love with her."

In October, Darren and Charla flew to Jamaica to attend a swingers' convention at the Hedonism III resort in Montego Bay. Darren had decided to combine it with a Mack family vacation, calling his cousin Corey Schmidt, who was now working as the cruise director of the brand-new *Carnival Conquest,* the largest "fun ship" ever built.

The plan was for Darren and Charla to join the rest of the Macks on the cruise ship after it docked at Montego Bay. They would all then continue on the cruise to the Cayman Islands and Cozumel, Mexico.

Corey booked Darren and Charla an ocean-view stateroom, deciding to surprise them by getting Landon a cabin next door. Then Joan Mack, also attending, decided she wanted to go on the entire seven-day cruise with her boyfriend, Bryn, and invited other family members to come.

"It was all the Macks," said Schmidt. "Even his grandma Helen."

After the cruise ship docked at Montego Bay, Schmidt and his English girlfriend drove straight to Hedonism III.

"And there I saw Darren and Charla," said Schmidt, "and they had brought a girl with them. They were in the pool naked with all their friends, and we dropped our draws and just went in."

Afterward, everybody went white-water rafting at the breathtakingly beautiful Dunns River Falls. Then they proceeded to Jimmy Buffet's famous Margaritaville Bar and Restaurant for dinner and cocktails.

Later, Schmidt brought Darren and Charla back to the cruise ship, where Joan, Landon, and other family members were waiting to surprise them.

"It was awesome," said Schmidt. "Yeah, it was huge."

On October 22, the *Carnival Conquest* docked at Grand Cayman. Everyone went ashore to go fishing at Sting Ray City, where the fishers were given squid meat to attract the sting rays to the feeding spot.

"I'll never forget," said Corey. "I stuck a whole handful of squid down Darren's pants. It was hysterical."

According to Schmidt, Charla was in a bad mood that day, so Corey and Landon decided to go ashore, leaving Darren to sort things out with his wife.

Later that night, everyone went to the disco for a cocktail.

"Whatever started earlier," said Schmidt, "escalated to the disco that night."

During the course of the evening, Schmidt was talking to his cousin Landon when he suddenly went: "Wow!"

"I turned around and Darren was getting up," said Schmidt. "Charla had punched Darren in the stomach . . . Darren left the disco very disgruntled."

Then Schmidt went to their cabin to see if he could help.

"And that's when Charla came into the cabin," said Schmidt. "She started screaming and yelling, 'You ruin everything!'"

Schmidt claims Darren tried to calm Charla down, saying she was overreacting. Then they moved to the outside deck and Charla began screaming again.

"I'm, like, 'Charla, you've got to stop,'" said Schmidt. "'I'm the cruise director. I'm in your cabin and I don't need to have security in here.'"

The next morning, when they docked at Cozumel, Corey took his cousin to one side.

"I remember saying to Darren, 'Oh my gosh, so this isn't the perfect marriage,'" said Schmidt. "And he said, 'You just got the chance to see the other side.'"

* * *

Three weeks later, Charla Mack went to Los Angeles, leaving Erika with her father. While she was away the little girl burned her hand. Instead of applying an antibiotic ointment, Darren used another cream.

"So, by the time Charla got home," said Laura Cunningham, "Erika's hand was totally infected and she had to go to the hospital."

When Charla confronted Darren for not even noticing that Erika's hand was infected, he stormed out of the house in a fury.

"It was like Doomsday," recalled Cunningham. "He felt he was being attacked to the core. He had to survive, and the only way was to cut himself off. That was the end."

When Laura Cunningham arrived for Christmas that year, Darren and Charla were barely speaking. Charla told her that Darren had said he no longer loved her after she had accused him of neglecting Erika.

"He was so gone," said Cunningham, "and it was very strained. I mean, he was in the room but he didn't look at you. He didn't speak. It was very weird."

On Christmas Day, Darren refused to get out of bed and join in the celebrations with Charla and the children.

"I'd never seen anything like it," said Cunningham. "He was literally, like, asleep on Christmas morning . . . not wanting to be there. Being so very removed."

At the beginning of 2004, Darren Mack finally reached a custody agreement with his first wife, Debbie, thirteen years after their separation. It was agreed that Elise would live with her mother in Panama City, California, while Jory remained in Reno with his father and Charla.

In March, Darren and Charla Mack brought the children to Palm Springs to spend spring break with Laura Cunningham and her kids. Throughout the trip Darren was absorbed in a psychology textbook about borderline personality disorder.

"He was carrying it around like a Jehovah's Witness takes their Bible," recalled Laura. "He took it everywhere, making weird notes in the margins and underlinings."

One day, while the kids were playing, Charla said Darren wanted her to be psychologically evaluated. Charla had refused to have any part of it; it had really upset her.

"So that precipitated a kind of irritation between Darren and Charla," said Cunningham. "She wasn't even talking to him and was looking at the ground. I think she was scared of him."

At the end of the trip, Laura took Charla to one side for a chat.

"I said, 'That guy is getting ready to divorce you. He's been looking for a reason because you won't swing and he's found it. He's latched onto borderline personality disorder, so you get ready, because it's coming to an end.'"

In May, Charla Mack told Laura Cunningham that Darren wanted her to move out—but on his terms. He had devised a five-year plan in which they would remain married but Charla would move into an apartment with Erika while Darren remained in the Franktown Road mansion to pursue his pleasures.

"That was his fantasy about how it was going to go," said Cunningham. "Of course, she wouldn't date anybody and would be available sexually if he ever wanted to come over."

Darren said they would stay "super-friendly," with Erika staying at whichever house she wanted to. Then, after five years, she could move back in with him and continue the marriage.

Charla told him there was no way she would agree to this. After seeing a marriage counselor, an angry Darren Mack reluctantly agreed to move out.

In July 2004, Darren and Charla Mack separated. A month later, Darren moved into a luxury condominium rental in the Fleur de Lis gated community. The luxurious complex boasted its own twenty-thousand-square-foot clubhouse, acres of landscaped gardens, and a series of ponds.

Darren rented the condo from a friend called Carol Kelley, who he affectionately called his "life coach." The two-bedroom apartment on the Wilbur May Parkway in southeast Reno cost $3,295 a month, not including club fees.

Soon after their separation, Darren and Charla met in a restaurant to discuss a future financial arrangement, as Darren wanted to avoid paying expensive divorce lawyer fees.

"He made a financial offer that was written on a napkin," said Cunningham. "It wasn't unreasonable and it was a monthly thing. But he would not disclose any other assets or show her what they had in retirement. Nothing."

When Charla said she needed detailed information of his financial assets, and not just a few numbers on a napkin to show her divorce attorney, he flew into a rage.

"He leaned in," said Laura, "and he said, 'If you do not take this deal, I will crush you!' Those were his exact words."

CHAPTER NINE

"You Have Always Hidden Your Sexual World"

That September, Erika Mack began first grade at Mountain View Montessori School as her parents' marriage spiraled out of control. With the six-year-old still in therapy, Charla was concerned about how the divorce would affect her.

Darren Mack's mind was elsewhere. He was already busy arranging future swinging trips.

On October 4, he sent Charla an e-mail, demanding a meeting to discuss the offer he had scribbled on the napkin.

"I gave you a copy of the offer that I was proposing for our divorce settlement," he wrote. "Can you please let me know when we can meet to complete this matter and file for divorce?"

The following day, Darren informed her that he had hired a divorce attorney, so she made an appointment with Reno divorce attorney Shawn Meador.

"I am just trying to figure everything out," she wrote Darren.

On October 11, Charla angrily e-mailed Darren after discovering he had arranged to have all her telephone bills sent directly to him in future.

"I would like to have my cell phone bill be mailed to me," she wrote him, "since you have a history of monitoring my calls."

Then Darren accused her of cheating on him with someone named Tim, but saying he no longer cared.

"I only was reviewing the bills when we were married," he wrote, "and you said you were not calling Tim and he kept showing up on the bills. This is no longer important and will not be reviewed."

Charla e-mailed back, accusing him of just wanting her out of the way so he could go swinging.

"For the record," she wrote, "I NEVER spoke with Tim in secrecy and I was NEVER unfaithful. I do not appreciate the implication. I know you can't wait to get rid of me but I would appreciate a little sensitivity around the process. Unlike you I am devastated by this divorce and messages like that are extremely hurtful."

On Thursday, October 28, Darren Mack informed Charla that he was leaving for Newport Beach, California, to spend the weekend at a Landmark Education Leader Days course. But instead he went to a swinging weekend at a resort in Cancún, Mexico.

Late Sunday night, after arriving back from Mexico, Darren turned up at the Franktown Road house, pleading with Charla for sex. He swore he had not been with anyone since their separation. Presumably she agreed to his request, but soon regretted doing so.

"Stop initiating being with me," she wrote him, "hugging me, having sex with me. If I'm such an abuser gnarly person then leave me alone."

Earlier that Sunday, Charla had taken Erika to a Halloween party at a friend's house. During the party she met another Montessori School parent named Tony Mudd, who had just divorced her good friend Ann Mudd. Tony also knew Darren Mack, as they went to the same gym.

"We first met through the school and a Halloween Party," said Mudd. "She said she was separated and going through a divorce."

They exchanged phone numbers, and over the next week

started talking on the phone and became friends. Then Mudd invited her over to his house on a dinner date.

"She came over and we had some wine and I cooked her dinner," he said, "and because she's a vegetarian I cooked her a vegetarian dinner. I'm a hunter and it's two different worlds, but she was a neat lady and I enjoyed her company."

After their separation, Darren Mack never bothered to change his passwords to his swinger Web sites. So Charla was able to secretly log in and monitor his swinger activities. To her shock, the dates he was attending out-of-town sex parties and swinger conventions often matched the dates he was supposed to care for Erika. Charla realized that Darren was having his mother care for their daughter while he played around.

After discovering he had lied to her about the Landmark leaders' conference at Newport Beach, Charla called him out on it, accusing him of "slinking around" and "living a lie."

"What is upsetting," she wrote him in an email, "is not that you are seeing other people it is that you lie about where you are going and what you are doing. I HATE IT WHEN YOU LIE TO ME. YOU SHOULD HAVE MORE RE-SPECT FOR ME THAN THAT!!!!!"

Charla told him that she could "deal with [her] jealousy" about his new life and girlfriends, but couldn't take his lies.

"I already know where the parties are. If I wanted to I could fly down in a heartbeat and be there and wreck it for you but I don't. But you lie always."

Then, in another e-mail, she detailed all his betrayals and lies over the years.

"You always had/have secrets," she wrote, "blocked palm pilots with passwords emails I could not see. You have already hidden your sexual world. You have lied and kept secrets for years and that is part of your sexual addiction.

"There has always been lies in our marriage/separation," she told him. "I have caught you a hundred times most of them I have not pointed out. I do not confuse charm like 'If

I was living half of what you think' as the truth. I am much too clever for that."

Darren Mack then angrily fired back, saying he did not have to tell her anything.

"I don't want to discuss those matters with you," he wrote coldly. "We are in the process of divorcing and we should each have the right to our own personal life.

"The whole tone of your emails remind me how . . . I am not what you want in a man and how the glass (man) is always half empty. After reading both your emails I am clear how your view of who I am causes you much misery and discontent. I am no longer committed to be the object in your life that you make responsible for your negative emotions."

He said they should finalize the divorce as soon as possible, so they could each move on and find happiness.

"Please respond by 11/15/04," he wrote, "so we can move this matter along."

Charla responded, saying she had the right to know where he was, as she took care of the children.

"Darren," she wrote. "I did not ask what girl you were seeing. You told me . . . we could not afford to spend money but since all your trips were business it was ok. Then you proceed to go to Cancun on a vacation, Vegas with the guys . . . to party. If you can't see where your lying to me can cause riffs I will NEVER GET ALONG EVER WITH YOU!!!!!

"I guess I feel used. I open my heart to you, we have sex and you give the big I am working on what does not work about me I want to hear. What I ask for is honesty and you are just not up to that.

"Darren take a look at how you constantly con people . . . I manage myself to communicate in an email because you don't like to speak on the phone when I'm hurting and your response is to invalidate me and push for the divorce? That you want an answer by the 15th? To get rid of me."

She wrote that she would now instruct her defense attorney, Shawn Meador, to move forward with the divorce.

"It takes everything in me not to use the phone to say

what is on my mind, and I went to email," she said. "But again you can't handle the truth. Lying is very poisonous. It rocks the foundations of who you are and after a while noone [*sic*] will respect you.

"You may not care how that affects my relationship with you or if we even have one. But I hope one day you will care how it affects the rest of your family. You can't isolate lying.

"I love you Darren, a lot. You were the only man I have ever loved. I am also the only one in your life who has the courage to say it like it is. I know it will cost me a relationship with you. But I refuse to pretend. Charla."

CHAPTER TEN

"He's a Bad Guy"

On November 16, Charla met Darren and Jory, his son from his first marriage, in a dental office where she had taken Erika for an appointment. Then, in reception, Darren got in a big argument with his sixteen-year-old son in front of Erika, prompting Charla to intervene.

Later, back at home, she e-mailed Darren, urging him and Jory to see a psychologist to work on their relationship.

"It does not work for me when you fight with Jory in front of Erika," she told him. "The receptionist and I could hear everything you were saying, it was A) embarrassing and B) right in front of Erika.

"Then after I came out and asked you not to fight for the second time tonight you leaned in and I did not hear all of it but what Jory said when I asked him was, 'You're a fucking asshole, don't call me anymore.' Did you say anything close to this??? He got in the car and started crying."

Charla wrote that Erika was very upset to see her father fighting with her big brother.

"You keep saying it doesn't happen," she wrote, "but I have witnessed [it] on numerous occasions and three times tonight."

Half an hour later Darren replied, apparently welcoming her advice that he and Jory undergo counseling.

"[Jory's] attitude is totally disrespectful and obnoxious with me," he wrote, "and I don't want him with me until that changes. If he insists on being disrespectful and arguing with everything I say and do he can do it somewhere else."

And he warned that if Jory's attitude didn't change after "a reasonable amount of time" in counseling, he would send him away to boarding school to learn "responsibility, appreciation and respect."

On November 28, three days after spending Thanksgiving together, Darren and Charla got into a violent argument at the Franktown Road house. After an incident outside the garage door, Charla dialed 911, accusing him of hitting her in the eye and trying to strangle her. But when Reno police arrived to investigate, they determined it to be a domestic dispute and took no action.

Later, Darren would accuse Charla of going berserk and hitting him.

"He showed up at the house where she and Erika were," said Charla's friend Ann Mudd, "and they had some kind of confrontation. He grabbed her by the neck and she was afraid he was going to choke her to death. He was so angry with her. And his comeback is that she was violent and attacked him. I'm sorry, but he was a bodybuilder and a guy and she was very small, very petite."

After hearing about the incident, Ann decided that she no longer wanted her daughter to have sleepovers with Erika. She called her ex-husband, Tony, warning him that Darren was dangerous.

"'He's a bad guy and I don't feel comfortable,'" she said she told Tony. "'I do not want my daughter at his house or having sleepovers at Charla's house.' I said, 'It's nothing against her, I don't trust *him*.'"

As their marriage spiraled out of control, Charla and Darren were both in close touch with Laura Cunningham, frequently calling her for advice.

"Sometimes you just listen," she recalled. "And it was

funny, because they would both call me about the same incident. I would hear two sides of the story and the perspectives, but basically the nuts and bolts were the same.

"His version would be the most ridiculous. It missed entire huge chunks, like the part where he was an asshole. When Charla told me her part, she'd be, like, 'I shouldn't have said it.' It would include all the parts that make her look bad and all the parts that make her look good. But it was a complete picture."

Finally, Cunningham confronted Darren about leaving out vital information that she'd already heard from Charla.

"He was upset," she said. "That was the last time he ever called me."

After Charla Mack summoned the police to Franktown Road, Darren went into survival mode. He punished her by restricting her access to Jory and Elise, announcing that she was no longer welcome at a family Christmas get-together with the children, as previously planned.

In the two weeks leading up to Christmas, they battled over holiday arrangements.

Then, on December 10, Darren Mack suddenly suggested they dispense with divorce attorneys to save money.

"I am recommending that we hire an experienced mediator to work with us on a flat fee "that has a vested interest in creating win/win resolution for all concerned," he e-mailed her. "Attorneys have an interest in keeping the conflict alive to get their part of it."

He ordered her to start researching financial mediators and to give him a list so he could select one.

Charla said she needed to first run the idea past her attorney, to see if it was in her best interest.

"I'm open to all of it," she told him. "Right now I am just not informed enough to proceed with a mediator."

The next day, Darren informed her there was no money left in their checking account, and the credit had run out on their Visa card.

When Charla received this e-mail, she was stunned he was now using money as a weapon against her, especially with the holidays approaching, not to mention a European trip she had planned.

"I do not understand why there is suddenly no money after 10 years," she replied. "I am going to London and will need cash as well as credit card use."

Darren then warned that from then on they would have to "pull in our belts financially," as they had overspent. And the added expense of his new condo rental and auto payments meant they now had to cut spending.

Then he offered to go over their financial situation with her with a third party present.

"I recommend my mother," he wrote, "since she knows us both and understands finances as well. I can show you where all the money is going. We must speak immediately to come up with a plan for your spending in England. Please call me right away."

On Christmas Eve, Darren Mack cut off all of Charla's credit cards and closed their joint checking account.

"Do not write any checks," he told her, "or attempt to use any of the credit cards or ATM as they will not work. If you have any questions please email me and I will respond."

Two days after Christmas, Charla called their bank, trying to withdraw money for her trip. When the representative refused her request, she burst into tears.

"I just received a call," Darren e-mailed her on December 28, just hours before Charla was due to leave for Europe, "stating you were trying to withdraw funds from our joint account. He said you were crying on the phone and sounded desperate."

Mack then admonished her for not telling him she needed money for her trip.

"I assumed that your finances were in order," he wrote. "I was very surprised to get the call . . . informing me of your frantic call."

He then told her to call him immediately to arrange funds for her London trip.

The following morning, Charla Mack flew to London and then on to Paris to ring in the New Year with Olivier. But before leaving, she removed all her jewelry and computers from the Franktown Road house.

"I told her to get rid of anything important," said Laura Cunningham, "because he's going to ransack this house while she's gone. He's all about control."

As Charla Mack celebrated the New Year in Europe, Darren did indeed raid the family home. Accompanied by several Palace Jewelry and Loan employees, he backed a truck through the locked garage doors of the Franktown Road town house and broke in.

Then he systematically removed $50,000 of Charla's personal possessions, including her wedding dress. He also seized personal scrapbooks, family photos, and special albums she had been making for the children. He even broke down Charla's locked bedroom door, opening her personal mail and reading it.

Finally, his employees dismantled the home gym, loading the weights and other expensive fitness equipment into his truck.

CHAPTER ELEVEN

Hardball

On Tuesday, January 11, 2005, Charla Mack arrived home in the middle of a major blizzard to discover that the electronic gates leading up to the long driveway were wide open. There were already several feet of snow and ice on the ground, and when she got the snowblower to clear a path to the front door, she found that someone had removed the rip cord and it was unusable.

"Charla called me," said Laura Cunningham. "She said, 'I can't get into my house [because] he's ransacked it. I can't get the garage door open. Everything's frozen shut.'"

Laura flew to Reno to help her friend get back into her house.

"And I helped her shovel it all up," she recalled. "Darren was nasty. He just ransacked it and as soon as he was done he pulled out the rip cord from the snowblower so she would have no way to dig herself out."

Then Charla called the alarm company, telling them to put her name on the contract. But when they contacted Darren, he insisted that he remain on it.

"He wouldn't sign a piece of paper that allowed her to put the security system in her name, so that if she was feeling threatened, she had recourse," said Ann Mudd.

Three days after arriving home, Darren sent Charla a

stern e-mail with the subject, "Regarding our finances and selling the home."

"We need to make some decisions to help sell the 5350 Franktown house," he wrote. "I am getting feedback from the realtor that he has had some interested parties but the home has been in less than showable condition. We need to discuss a strategy we can both align on. I will get you more information once the realtor gets me a list of the problems with the cleanliness of the home."

In early January, Darren Mack fired his divorce attorney, replacing him with Richard Young, who had represented him in his earlier custody battle with Debbie. Then he canceled a long-scheduled meeting with Charla's attorney, Shawn Meador, with only two hour's notice.

That same day, Mack sent Tim Lukas, another divorce attorney he had hired, a list of Charla's bills, saying he refused to pay the $900 fee for Erika's counseling or Charla's $179.99 monthly Cingular cell phone bill.

"I am not paying unless [she] makes me," he wrote Lukas.

He also forwarded Lukas an e-mail he had just received from Charla entitled: "Protecting yourself rather than resolving anything." In it she had said she was "suspicious" that his accusations of her being violent were merely "a campaign" for divorce court.

"Regarding abuse," she had written, "I do not point out all the abuse I sustained in this relationship and I would like to remind you that I do have records of many types to verify the violence. I would appreciate it if you stop trying to turn this around and put it on me.

"The fact that you continually bring up abuse leaves me [to think] that you must have a deep sense of guilt [about] this and I want you to know that I forgive you. It is time to let it go because it is really counterproductive."

The next day Charla demanded that Darren return the items he'd taken from her house while she was in Europe.

"I am worried about some of it being damaged in the warehouses," she wrote, "as well as it is not good for the sale of the house that you dismantled the gym room, etc. Are you willing to return the items from the house? If so by when?"

Two days later Charla pleaded with Darren not to cancel her cell phone because of $900 of calls from Europe. She admitted it was "really high," saying she had not been able to use a calling card in France.

"PLEASE DO NOT PUNISH ME WITH CANCELING THE PHONE," she wrote him. "It was not done maliciously."

A few days later Darren Mack responded that his accounting office had now gone through the phone bill, noting that $500 of the calls were to Tony Mudd.

After receiving this e-mail, Charla called Tony Mudd to warn him of possible trouble.

"She called me and said, 'Darren's asking all these questions about you,'" said Mudd.

A few days later Mack quibbled over Erika's orthodontist's bill, complaining that it could destroy his "impeccable" credit.

"We are under extreme financial stress," he reminded Charla on January 25, adding that he had now sent the dentist a $1,260 deposit for braces.

"Even though this is for Erika's teeth," he wrote, "we still need to plan and not overspend."

He again urged her to meet with "a mediator or my mother" to try to resolve their issues before bringing in expensive attorneys.

"I still care for you very much," he wrote, "and do not want to lose our relationship and the possibility of being friends once this is complete. I ask you to help me stop the direction this is headed and to re-group for a fair and peaceful resolution."

Darren Mack now became obsessed with Charla's relationship with Tony Mudd, and why she had called him so often from Europe. He repeatedly asked her to explain.

Then he began calling every number on her cell phone bill, checking up on who she was in contact with.

"My friends are saying you are calling and hanging up on them," Charla complained on January 30. "So you are obviously re-calling people from my phone bill. You are now . . . violating my privacy. I do not see this working out for me. Your words and your actions are completely the opposite. If you want to work together perhaps you should demonstrate good faith."

On January 31, Charla told Darren that unless they agreed on an interim support arrangement within a week, she would file for divorce.

"Dear Darren," she began. "You say you'll give me $1,000 per month. We have never lived on $1,000 a month, as you know that does not even cover groceries. When would I receive more support? If we could simply reach a temporary agreement that you will pay certain defined bills and that you will give me $X per month for my personal expenses, then we could have the conflict and anger about temporary money behind us and could focus on final resolution."

She said she was still willing to take the mediation route, but first needed more information about her rights.

"I am not a lawyer," she said. "I am not a sophisticated business woman. I don't know what my legal rights are. It seems like you want me to agree to a deal having the information you think I should have."

She said they needed an interim support arrangement in place until they agreed to a final one.

"It isn't fair to me," she wrote, "to have to come and beg for money or ask for an allowance like a child asking her father."

Darren Mack's response was "I am truely [sic] sorry for the hate in your heart you must have that you continue to relate and act out the way you do towards me."

A few days later, Darren Mack secretly detailed his financial assets to Wells Fargo Bank to secure a new $500,000 line of credit for himself. He claimed he and Charla together were worth more than $12 million, and he alone was worth

$10.67 million. Then, on February 1, he closed their remaining bank accounts, refusing to pay her outstanding Visa bill.

Charla fired off a furious e-mail, accusing him of "actively attacking/violating" her.

"By the way you are legally responsible for me," she reminded him, "and the income you are taking is ours. I can't imagine any Judge would look at what you are doing right now and think favorably of you."

CHAPTER TWELVE

"I Am in Terror of Charla!"

On Monday, February 7, Charla Mack seized the initiative and filed for divorce. In her nine-point divorce complaint, lodged in the family division of the Second Judicial District Court of Nevada, she asked for primary custody of Erika as well as "adequate and appropriate" child support.

"The parties are incompatible in marriage," read her complaint. "Plaintiff is not presently employed . . . and has no income or ability to support herself at this time. Defendant is a fit and able bodied man who has sufficient income to provide substantial permanent alimony to allow the plaintiff to maintain the standard of living enjoyed during marriage."

In an attached motion for preliminary orders, Charla's attorney, Shawn Meador, asked the court to designate Charla and Darren as their daughter's joint legal guardians and keep the current custody schedule. He also asked the court to grant Charla exclusive use of 5350 Franktown Road until it was sold and award her "appropriate interim support," as well as sufficient money to pay her attorney to prosecute the case.

The motion outlined their troubled marriage and how Charla had "stood by Darren's side and supported him" in his lengthy divorce from his first wife Debbie.

"She then co-parented the children with him," it stated.

"And, while they are not her biological children . . . Charla loves the children as if they were her own."

Early in their marriage, read the motion, Charla had worked for Darren's family business. Then they had both agreed that it was in the children's best interests for her to become "a stay-at-home wife.

"At that time he repeatedly promised her that she need not worry about money, and that he would support her forever. Therefore, Charla has not worked outside the home since prior to Erika's birth. Charla has no career, no college degree and no ability to support herself. She is entirely dependent upon Darren and the community estate.

"Darren, on the other hand, remains employed by the family business. According to the most current documents in Charla's possession, Darren estimated his net worth as of December 31, 2003, at $9.4 million."

Charla's complaint claimed Darren earned $44,336.72 every month from Palace Jewelry and Loan and his other businesses, with an annual adjusted gross income of $532,400.66 for the years 2001, 2002, and 2003.

"He has not provided Charla with his income information for 2004," the complaint stated.

The complaint also noted that even though the Franktown Road house was now listed at $1,599,000, there would be little equity to divide up when it was sold, as the monthly mortgage alone exceeded $8,300.

"Charla appreciates that following the divorce she cannot afford to maintain such an expensive home, the costs of which exceed $13,000 a month," it read.

It also explained that although Charla knew from personal experience how "emotionally and financially devastating" custody litigation could as well as "the harm" it could inflict on children, there was no alternative.

"However, the reality at this time," Charla's complaint stated, "is that the parties cannot reach agreement on temporary support and other rules governing their conduct and financial affairs pending resolution of this divorce.

"Darren has insisted that Charla clear all her spending with him in advance, but makes no effort to clear his with her."

The complaint indicated that Charla believed her filing for divorce and requesting interim financial support would upset Darren, potentially creating "the acrimonious, contested battle" they both wanted to avoid.

"However," the complaint noted, "their inability to reach agreement on interim financial issues is creating incredible stress and hostility between them."

Regarding custody arrangements, Charla's complaint stated that she believed that Darren is a "loving father," with a great deal to offer Erika. Therefore custody should not be decided on the basis of who the better parent was but rather on the best schedule for them and Erika.

Charla asked the court to order Darren to pay her $25,042 a month in family support, out of which $13,000 would be needed to maintain the marital residence until it was sold.

"She appreciates that this is an extraordinary sum, but spending to maintain the standard of living is relative. Darren's historic income exceeds $500,000 per year or $44,000 per month."

The complaint pointed out that although Darren claimed they were in "a financial crisis," he had offered no proof to back this up.

"He continues to spend lavishly himself," it stated, "going on frequent out-of-town trips, applying for expensive credit lines at Las Vegas Casinos, etc."

The complaint also asked the court to order Darren to pay all her legal expenses for what looked like a long, drawn-out divorce.

"Based on his . . . angry statements (hopefully made out of frustration)," the motion stated, "that if litigated he will destroy her, and his history of being prepared to litigate issues that are important to him, Charla must prepare herself for the possibility, if not probability, of protracted and expensive litigation. Charla has no funds with which to pay these legal expenses."

One week later, Darren Mack's divorce attorney, Richard Young, responded by applying to Washoe County Family Court for a temporary protection order (TPO) against Charla, saying his client believed he would become a victim of domestic violence.

"Charla is a verbally and physically abusive person." Darren Mack wrote on the TPO application form. "This abuse has been an ongoing problem throughout our marriage and since we have separated."

On numerous occasions, according to Darren, Charla had threatened to kill him if he ever left her.

"I am in terror of Charla," he wrote. "Coupled with her mental state and her excessive use of alcohol, I believe her totally that she will make good on her threats."

After reading the restraining order, Charla was terrified. She called Laura Cunningham, saying she now feared for her life, as Darren had always projected his feelings on those closest to him.

"That's when she became truly scared of him," said Cunningham, "because she saw the restraining order. She's like, 'OK, this guy really means business. He's actually considering doing away with me. I think he's seriously thinking of killing me.'"

On February 25, both sides agreed to enter into a mutual restraining order, with Darren withdrawing his application for a temporary protection order. Later he claimed he had backed down after Charla had threatened to accuse him of marital abuse, making it just his word against hers.

"It doesn't matter about proof," he said. "The women are always protected in those courts."

Soon after Charla filed for divorce, Darren Mack celebrated with some friends at the renowned Moonlite Bunny Ranch.

He was no stranger to the notorious brothel, located thirty-four miles south of Reno and featured in the popular HBO documentary series *Cathouse*.

"His friends brought him out here to play," one of the Bunny Ranch girls told *48 Hours*. "He was, like, 'You know I'm getting a divorce. I'm having fun. I don't have no reason to worry about it. To hell with her! I don't need her because I've got all these girls here.' It was your average, everyday divorce party."

In late February, real estate agent David Morris visited 5350 Franktown Road to inspect the property, which remained unsold. Eleven months earlier, he had appraised the 5,749-square-foot property at $1,470,000, although Darren Mack had listed it for $1,599,000.

"The home is in need of major updating," he wrote in his subsequent report. "[It] appears to have been neglected for a number of years."

He estimated that it would require an investment of more than a quarter of a million dollars to maximize its value.

Then he warned that his showing agents had raised "concerns," including: various items of clothing strewn around the house; toys, CDs and games spread out everywhere; and, food, dirty dishes and utensils littered the kitchen.

"Sadly, in one case, dog feces was evident in two rooms," Morris's report stated, "making for an unpleasant showing. The seller appears to be overwhelmed by taking care of this home . . . and is under great pressure to keep up and maintain all that is required for a home of this size and price range. This is not unusual when a divorce is ongoing."

The real estate agent recommended reducing the price to $1,429,000 and immediately vacating the home, so it could be professionally cleaned and repainted.

"Please review this report," wrote Morris, "so that we may meet and generate the best offer possible in order that you may close this chapter of your lives."

CHAPTER THIRTEEN

"Mr. Mack Has Certain Sexual Interests"

On March 3, 2005, Judge Chuck Weller of the family division of the Second Judicial District Court of Washoe County was officially assigned the contentious Mack divorce case. The charismatic fifty-two-year-old judge, grew up in southern New Jersey and graduated St. Joseph's University, in Philadelphia, before going to Georgetown University Law School in the late 1970s.

He then moved to Reno, Nevada, where he had a solo law practice for twenty-one years. He also hosted his own weekly legal advice show on KOH Radio, called *Chuck Weller and the Law*, and wrote a column in the *Reno Gazette-Journal*.

"I was active in the community," he said. "I tried to give the law away to the people."

Like Darren Mack, who he had never met before the Macks' divorce case, Judge Weller was active in the controversial Reno downtown redevelopment scheme. He successfully led the fight against an $86 million courthouse construction bond issue. After the bond was defeated, he was elected chairman of the Justice Facilities Working Committee to make recommendations about future court redevelopment.

"We came up with a plan," explained Weller, "and it resulted in the construction of . . . the Mills B. Lane Justice Center."

On January 21, 2001, Darren Mack told the *Reno Gazette-Journal* he supported the sweeping new downtown development, but with reservations.

"I don't know how you negotiate when that gun [of condemnation] is at your head," he explained. "Are [small businesses] the ones that are going to be swept aside?"

After his successful campaign, Weller decided to run for judge, citing his years of experience as a family court lawyer. In November 2004, he was elected to Washoe County Family Court, replacing retiring judge Scott Jordan.

"You can do a lot of good work in the court," Weller told the *Reno Gazette-Journal* at the time. "There are a percentage of cases that are hopeless. But that's a small percentage."

That same week, Darren Mack began secretly investigating Charla. He contacted family members and mutual friends, seeking any dirt he could use against her in the upcoming divorce.

One of the first people he contacted was his "brother" Olivier in France, sending him an e-mail entitled, "I need your Help":

> *Can you please write down everything that was told to you from Charla about anything that might help me. As in all cheating or sexual relations . . . Anything she told you about the divorce, Erika, or anything else you think might help.*

Five days later, Olivier replied"

> *Here is what she told me.*

> 1) *Last June . . . she met a man with whom she spent the night in her hotel room. This man was a soldier going to Iraq . . .*

2) *In August she visited a swinger couple in San Francisco. She [said] [. . .] she had only 'a breve [sic] sexual intercourse' with the woman but she confessed that on the other hand it is with the man that she had more fun the most rest of the time.*

After receiving his email, Darren tried unsuccessfully to telephone Olivier in France, looking for more damning information on Charla, but he had the wrong number, so he wrote to thank him and ask for more dirt.

Darren was also compiling for his divorce attorney a log of violent threats he alleged Charla had made against him. He called this seven-page, single-spaced document "Diary of Incidents of Unacceptable Behavior by Charla."

He prefaced it by writing that these threats only happened when Charla was "in her demonic state" and "angry and raging."

"Many times throughout the marriage," he wrote, "[she] has threatened that 'I will kill you if you ever leave me' or 'I will cut your penis off and put it in the freezer.' When I would tell her it was not funny and she shouldn't make threats like that she would justify [it] by telling me that she watched Court TV all the time and she knows how to do it so she could get away with it. She also at times would say it in a very loathful [sic] and hateful deminer [sic]."

He also claimed that Charla had threatened to make "false allegations" against him to the police in order to destroy his reputation.

"Many times Charla would threaten me that she would tell everyone of her views of how horrible in her eyes I am," he wrote. "She threaten[ed] to destroy my reputation, take me for everything I have and make my life a 'living hell.' She would say things like 'If you think it has been bad with Debbie, you've seen nothing yet.'"

He also accused Charla of telling Landmark Education

leaders about his immoral behavior to have him thrown out of the organization.

"And then I would have to account to the Course Leader," he wrote, "for why my wife would say such things."

Darren's diary also alleged that Charla had threatened to make his life "a living hell" and ruin him financially; that he suffered "months of withheld sex"; and that she "tried to kick me in the balls but missed."

He also accused her of calling him "multiple times a day" at work, just to berate him.

"I always felt most of this was just her attempts to manipulate me," he wrote, "but when she called the police because we were in a minor disagreement and . . . then called the police/911 [and told] untruths to the police then told my mother and I assume her attorney that I hit her in the eye when this never happened. After that incident I now fear for all the threats she has ever made to me including death threats being realized."

On March 18, attorney Richard Young filed his client's reply to Charla's divorce petition and his counterclaim. He argued that Darren Mack, not Charla, should be granted primary custody of Erika.

"Charla M. Mack suffers from mental or emotional disorder(s)," read the counterclaim, "and as a consequence, is subject to wide mood swings, from rage to bouts of incessant crying."

Mack claimed that since Charla had filed for divorce, her behavior had "rapidly declined," to the point where she could no longer safely care for Erika.

"She has become incapable of taking care of the parties' residence on Franktown Road," it read, "and providing for a clean, sanitary and safe living environment for the parties' child Erika."

He asked the court to order Charla to undergo a "comprehensive psychological evaluation" before deciding on any parenting plan for Erika.

The counterclaim also maintained that Charla was quite capable of working and paying child support. And it asked that she be ordered to pay half of all Erika's out-of-pocket medical and dental expenses.

Citing grounds for the divorce, Mack told the court that he and Charla had "numerous irreconcilable differences" and were now "incompatible."

On March 23, Darren Mack officially responded in family court to Charla's motion for preliminary orders. His attorney, Richard Young, informed Judge Weller that the separation was due to Charla's "uncontrolled spending," "wide mood swings," and "uncontrolled anger and rage."

"Mrs. Mack appears to be engaging in a campaign to belittle and denigrate Mr. Mack in the eyes of Erika," read the motion. "Mr. Mack is observing the results of Mrs. Mack's efforts to parentally alienate Erika against him."

Young then asked Judge Weller to order psychological evaluations of both his client and Charla as well as a physical inspection of their homes.

"Mrs. Mack has allowed the marital residence in Franktown Road to deteriorate into such a terrible condition that it is unsanitary and maybe hazardous to Erika's health," the motion stated. "Mrs. Mack appears to be incapable of managing the simple task of keeping the residence clean and sanitary. She has allowed dog feces to remain on the floor of the residence. She allows animals to urinate in the house and does not clean it up."

Darren Mack asked Judge Weller to order Charla to vacate the marital home within thirty days, offering to rent her a "reasonably priced" three-bedroom residence.

That spring, Charla Mack met a handsome young weight lifter named Mark Phillips at a bodybuilding competition and they fell for each other.

Within a few weeks they were living together and Charla warned him about her estranged husband.

"She was concerned about her own safety," Phillips later told the *Reno Gazette-Journal*. "She said in passing that she feared he would hurt her someday."

Despite all the pressure she was now under, Charla was bravely trying to forge a new life for herself. She began taking singing lessons and started performing regularly at a Reno nightclub. She also began writing country-and-western-style songs about her painful divorce, some of which she recorded.

On April 5, Charla Mack's divorce attorney, Shawn Meador, asked Judge Weller to grant his client primary custody of Erika. The motion claimed that the alternate weekly visitation schedule that Darren was demanding was not in their daughter's best interests.

"Mr. Mack's conduct demonstrates that his position regarding custody is about his ego, money and, most importantly, about CONTROL," the motion maintained.

It claimed that Darren's promiscuous lifestyle kept him away from home too long to be a good father: "Mr. Mack's lifestyle simply does not support a joint physical custody arrangement. Mr. Mack is often out of town and works late hours. In 2004 alone, Mr. Mack was out of town no less than 109 days."

The motion also dismissed any allegations that the Macks' marital breakdown was caused by Charla's mood swings.

"The truth is that Mr. Mack has certain sexual interests," it stated. "While Mrs. Mack was prepared to participate and go along in an effort to save the marriage, she ultimately decided that his interests left her feeling unloved, unsupported and unfulfilled.

"His sexual interests are such that many people in the community would disapprove and would suggest that they bear on his fitness for parenting. It would be embarrassing to most people to have this information played out publicly or before the court."

It then stated how Charla had previously taken the high road and not dished the "dirt" on Darren to gain the upper hand in the custody battle. But after his unfounded allegations against her, she had no other choice.

"Unfortunately, there were incidents of domestic violence in the marriage," it said. "As late as November of 2004, Mrs. Mack was forced to call 911 due to a violent incident."

Once again it pointed out that Charla could easily have used this to her advantage in seeking custody of Erika, but decided not to "turn up the emotional heat."

"Mrs. Mack elected not to raise the violence as an issue. Rather than appreciating that Mrs. Mack did not seek to obtain an advantage from this sad set of circumstances, Mr. Mack's response was to run down to the courthouse in an attempt to try to convince the TPO [temporary protection order] master that Mrs. Mack was the violent one, that he lives in fear of her, and that he should have custody of Erika."

The motion also dismissed as "absurd" Darren's claims that Charla suffered from any mental illness, saying she was willing to undergo psychological testing by an independent expert.

"Mrs. Mack is mentally sound," read the motion. "Coincidentally, Mr. Mack also claimed that his former wife was mentally ill and attempted to use this claim as a weapon in a prior custody battle. Clearly, labeling ex-spouses as 'mentally ill' is simply Mr. Mack's way of justifying his failed relationships and his inability to get along with the mothers of his children."

A few hours after Charla Mack's motion was filed, Darren's attorney, Richard Young, hand delivered a letter to Charla's attorney, Shawn Meador, announcing that his client would no longer be paying her "unnecessary monthly expenditures."

It began by stating that between them the Macks owed the Internal Revenue Service $23,524 with their individual 2004 tax returns.

"As a result," wrote attorney Young, "I am instructing Mr. Mack to stop the following services and cease payment of the following:

- Yard care at Franktown residence - $600.00 per month
- Terminate second telephone line with Nevada Bell
- Terminate satellite television - $100.00 per month
- Terminate Tahoe Pool Service - $300.00 per month
- Terminate TTI long distance telephone service - $90.00 per month
- Terminate pest control - $36.00 per month
- Terminate Charla's singing lessons with Kim Sandusky - $400.00 per month
- Terminate Crystal Springs water delivery - $50.00 per month
- Close charge account at Village Dry Cleaning for Charla - $200.00 per month
- Terminate payment of counseling for Charla with Rebecca Jankovich, Ph.D. - $640.00 per month
- Cancel AOL internet service for Charla - $30.00 per month
- Cancel Charla's 24-Hour Fitness membership - $40.00 per month

"All of the above items are luxury items and not necessary for Charla Mack's monthly support."

On April 11, attorney Richard Young asked Judge Weller to seal the Mack divorce file, which contained the potentially explosive revelations about his client's swinging lifestyle. Darren Mack was well aware that if these scandalous details were ever made public, they would destroy his well-crafted image as a clean-living family man.

A few days later, Shawn Meador lodged another motion, demanding Judge Weller award Charla interim monthly support payments so she would "not be left to the whims of a vindictive husband."

"Mr. Mack has used his tremendous wealth in the past," read the motion, "and will use his wealth in the future to try and control and manipulate his wife."

It strongly disputed that the expenses he was now refusing to pay were unnecessary luxuries, demonstrating that his needs came before his daughter's.

"Mrs. Mack can't even make a long distance phone call from the home," it read. "This, from a man whose stated net worth exceeds $9 million."

CHAPTER FOURTEEN

"Toomuchfun"

As his divorce battle escalated, Darren Mack veered out of control. He now rarely went to Palace Jewelry and Loan, spending his days locked away in his condo getting high and watching porn.

"I know that when they were split up in that last year," said Laura Cunningham, "he watched just an amazing amount of porn. I mean, the guy was watching porn all day. I don't think he was even going to the office anymore."

He was also hitting the gym at all hours, often taking Erika, now seven years old, with him at 4:00 a.m. to watch him work out. When Charla discovered this, she accused him of child abuse.

"She said I was abusing my child because I was working at four o'clock in the morning," Mack would later explain. "My daughter loved to go work out with me. It was, like, one of the high points for her, and now I'm being told it's child abuse."

Charla's friend Tony Mudd went to the same gym and often saw Darren there.

"He was fanatic about his appearance," said Mudd, "and doing the drugs to get the appearance. He hardly ever went to work now."

He also spent hours every day on his computer, hitting

his favorite swinger Web sites to find sexually adventurous partners. Using the name "toomuchfun," he described himself as a straight "divorced dad of three, friendly, a flirt and the life of the party." He posted the same smiling photograph of himself, in a white tee shirt and leather jacket, on MySpace, Yahoo, Match.com, and Cupid.com.

"Inquire only if you want too much FUN," he posted on MySpace, saying he was there for "Networking, Dating, Serious Relationships, Friends." He also described himself as "White/Caucasian, 5' 11"/Athletic with the Zodiac sign of Aquarius." He was a "proud parent" with "some college education and a business owner."

Darren wrote that he wanted to meet "a beautiful, sensual, sexual, smart, fun woman with a respectful attitude to enjoy all life has to offer. Get ready for too much fun."

Darren's motto was to "[live] life so there are no regrets in the end."

He then listed some of the swinging groups he belonged to as "Ultra Nightlife, NapkinNights.com (Las Vegas, Arizona, San Diego, San Francisco & Sacramento), Bay Area Nightlife/NorCalNightsd.com, California Love and Hook-It-Up Part 11."

On the personal section of Yahoo.com, he posted: "I am looking for someone to connect with, enjoy great times together and to explore life outside the typical relationship structure that everyone seems to be so unhappy in."

His Match.com profile read in part: "I have done a lot of work to become very present and grounded in life. I am successful and happy with my life and very fun loving.

"I am looking for a woman who is very attractive, is very happy and complete with herself who would be a partner and companion exploring life together. Must not be controlling, jealous, mean or insecure."

The first week of May, Darren Mack fired his divorce attorney, Richard Young, replacing him with Tim Lukas. Then on May 10, six days before their first scheduled case management conference with Judge Chuck Weller, he made Charla a new offer.

Darren now proposed to pay her $849 a month in temporary child support and $4,000 a month in temporary spousal support, but only after the Franktown Road house was sold.

"Until that time," the offer stipulated, "no additional support is warranted. Wife has $30,000 in funds obtained just prior to her filing for divorce."

Lukas had also drawn up an elaborate six-page parenting agreement for Charla to sign, requesting joint custody of Erika. Darren now wanted them to share their daughter equally, with holidays split between them in odd and even years.

But the plan demeaned Charla's character, putting her at an unfair disadvantage from the beginning.

Clause 10 of Darren's new parenting plan—entitled "Other Arrangements and Additional Comments"—stated: "If assumptions are confirmed by a highly qualified psychologist/custody evaluator that the mother has an alcohol problem and or has any personality disorders, then the following are recommended for the safety of Erika."

It then recommended "Counseling for MOM," including help for substance abuse and having her medication evaluated.

"MOM may benefit from a mood stabilizer," it stated, "to address PTSD [post-traumatic stress disorder] and possibly Bipolar concerns (OR BORDERLINE PD [personality disorder])."

Friday, May 13, 2005, would have been Darren and Charla Mack's tenth wedding anniversary, and that morning they spoke on the telephone about Erika's schedule for the upcoming weekend. At 1:52 p.m. Charla sent him an e-mail.

"Hi Darren," she wrote. "Today is our 10 year wedding anniversary, sad we couldn't make it . . . I hope you have a nice day today!"

Darren's reply came a few minutes later: "Charla, Happy Anniversary, Darren."

The following Monday at 3:30 p.m., Charla and Darren

met in Judge Chuck Weller's chambers for a case management conference. At Darren's side was his new defense attorney, Tim Lukas, and at Charla's, Shawn Meador.

"The first time I met with the Macks was in my chambers," Judge Weller remembered. "It was my practice to have initial meetings with clients to try and resolve things. We try to bring them to agreement as opposed to having traditional litigation, because in traditional litigation where there are winners and losers, the children always lose."

After the meeting, Judge Weller agreed to seal the Mack divorce case. Then a week later he issued his rulings, which would remain in effect for two months, when a settlement conference would be held. By then he would have more information available, allowing him to fine-tune his order until a possible trial.

First off, he handed Darren a victory by awarding him and Charla interim joint custody of Erika.

"Nothing in the record," wrote the Judge in his May 27 order, "suggests that the child won't thrive in the care of both parents, jointly."

Judge Weller ruled that they would share Erika's physical custody on an alternate weekly schedule. But he ordered the exchanges to take place at school, so they would never have to meet face-to-face.

During the remaining school year, the parent relinquishing custody would drop Erika off at the Montessori school on Monday morning. Then the parent assuming custody would collect her after school on Monday afternoon.

During the long summer vacation, custody would be exchanged on Monday mornings at 9:00 a.m. at the home of the parent assuming custody.

"The parent relinquishing custody shall drive and shall remain in the car during drop off," Judge Weller ordered. "The parent acquiring custody shall remain in the house during drop off. Darren has represented to the court that he will arrange his schedule so that he will not be out of town during his custodial weeks."

Judge Weller then ordered Darren to pay Charla $10,000 a month in interim spousal support, backdated to May 1. He also ruled that the noncustodial parent should pay 18 percent of his or her gross monthly income in child support. Since Darren's gross monthly income was $44,000 and Charla's zero, 18 percent of his would have been almost $8,000 a month. But under a state law capping child support, he was only required to pay $849 a month, as he had already agreed to do.

Judge Weller also allowed Charla to remain at 5350 Franktown Road as long as she fully cooperated with its sale.

"She is ordered to keep the home clean and presentable for showing," Judge Weller wrote.

Darren would also have to pay all monthly expenses for the house, including the two mortgages, taxes, lawn maintenance, gas, electricity, telephone, satellite TV, and pool/Jacuzzi costs.

"Darren is to pay these bills promptly when they arrive," ordered the judge. "Darren is not to enter the marital home without obtaining Charla's prior permission."

Then, at Darren Mack's request, Judge Weller issued an ex-parte mutual restraining order, freezing both parties' properties and assets until the divorce was made final.

Darren Mack was furious with Judge Weller's interim orders. He was livid at having to pay Charla $10,000 a month as well as her living expenses.

Over the next few weeks he began investigating Judge Weller's past, discovering that he had made many enemies during the six months he had been on the bench.

"He is increasingly earning himself the reputation of being one, if not the most abusive and unfair judges [sic] anywhere to be found in America," read one posting on the Courthouse Forum Web site.

Mack joined Nevadans for Equal Parenting, a local advocacy group that campaigned for joint custody.

He started attending group meetings and making contact with other disgruntled fathers who felt that the family court system—and especially Judge Weller—had violated their rights.

The pawnbroker now threw himself into a new mission to change the family court system and champion fathers' rights.

CHAPTER FIFTEEN

"You Are Acting Like a 5-Year-Old"

On June 3, Shawn Meador filed a fifteen-page motion in family court, demanding that Darren Mack provide a complete disclosure of all his financial assets, business holdings, and Palace Jewelry and Loan's financial statements going back to 1993. When Darren Mack read the scope of what Charla's lawyer wanted—to obtain a comprehensive financial picture for an eventual divorce settlement—he was enraged.

Three days later he quietly transferred 1 percent of his Palace Jewelry and Loan interest to his mother, giving her a controlling 51 percent share of the company by proxy. This violated the mutual financial restraining order he had requested and then signed a few weeks earlier. It meant, at least on paper, that he was no longer a wealthy man.

Later, Joan Mack would claim her son had called her back to run Palace Jewelry and Loan so he could concentrate on his divorce.

"He asked me to come into the store and take over so he could spend his time taking care of other affairs," she said. "He couldn't keep his mind on business then."

One of Joan's first actions as the new boss of Palace was to cut her son's monthly salary from $44,000 to $5,000 and demote him to salesman.

"When I came in everything was pretty much in disarray," said Joan. "Our controller had walked out and I was trying to assemble where we were."

Soon afterward Corey Schmidt, who had recently retired from Carnival Cruises, was summoned back to Reno to manage Palace.

Darren immediately found his cousin a condo to rent, directly opposite his on the Fleur de Lis estate.

"He had lived a very extravagant life," said Schmidt. "playing the player, playing the swinger, playing the big deal—the house, the cars, the watches and everything else. All I know is he spent a shitload of money . . . and then he called Joan back in. He said, 'Joan, I need you to start running the store.' "

On Friday, June 17, Darren Mack collected Erika from school, flying with her to San Francisco to help him celebrate Father's Day weekend. But he neglected to tell Charla he was taking their daughter out of state.

When she discovered that Darren had left Reno with their daughter, Charla desperately tried to track him down. But Darren ignored her numerous texts and voice messages.

Finally, at 10:00 p.m. on Saturday night, Erika telephoned her mother from a restaurant in Mill Valley, California, where she was having dinner with her father and two friends of his. When Charla asked to speak to her father, she heard Darren whisper, "Tell your mom I told you to call her."

Later that night, Darren sent Charla an e-mail apologizing for not telling her he was taking Erika to San Francisco.

An hour and a half later, Charla replied with an e-mail entitled, "protecting yourself rather than solving anything," copying Shawn Meador and Tim Lukas. It accused him of violating Judge Weller's order by taking their daughter out of state without her permission.

"It's is completely inappropriate," she told him. "Stop doing this!!! You are acting like a five-year-old."

On Sunday evening, Darren Mack sent his divorce attorney, Tim Lukas, a draft of an e-mail he proposed to send to

Charla, asking him to review it and supply input, before he sent it off.

He began by apologizing to Charla that their "interaction" had broken down. "I was simply attempting to have [a] quiet, fun and memorable Father's Day weekend with Erika, Darryl and Britney. I hadn't planned on going due to my bronchitis."

He explained that on Friday he had stayed in bed before his friend Darryl called at 1:00 inviting him and Erika to San Francisco. "[He] pushed me to get out of bed, get away from Reno and all the stress that I am under and bring Erika down for a Daddy/Daughter weekend for Father's Day."

After hanging up, he bought tickets and rushed to the airport, barely catching a 1:45 flight. He had not even thought about the court order and notifying her. "For that I am guilty," he conceded. "This is new to me and I am trying to deal with the stress of being financially broken and tying to save the company and again I am sorry. It was not intentional." He said he understood that if she decided to complain to Judge Weller he would have to face the "consequences" for his "lapse in judgment." He then methodically outlined their various issues as he saw them, and how he proposed they be resolved.

"Charla," he wrote, "I am attempting to do whatever I can to get through this tough time but one thing I will not give into is to be verbally or physically abused ever again by anyone including you. Please show a little grace I am doing the best I can while my whole life is being shattered." He then added a postscript, begging Charla not to ruin him financially. "I ask you to think of everyone this effects [sic]," he wrote. "It is not just about breaking me but it includes my mother, the kids, and really you. Please trust what I say. Remember I have always taken care of you from the beginning. Remember who gave and did everything to let you live the way you got to live and have a little empathy . . ."

After reviewing the email, Lukas advised Mack not to include his postscript, and on Monday morning at 11:02 a.m. Darren sent it off to Charla without it.

Then, just after midday, Darren Mack sent his attorney a frantic e-mail, revealing his true state of mind. He had now read the court order five times, finding that he was under no obligation to notify Charla if he went out of state. "I just re-read it again," he told his attorney, "and I was attacked for something she thought was in the agreement and ISN'T."

He complained that Charla had "attacked" him in text messages that he had recorded, calling him names and making threats. "SHE MUST BE DIAGNOSED WITH HER PERSONALITY DISORDER," he thundered. "I am being held to account to getting along with someone who has a SEVERE PERSONALITY DISORDER WHICH IS IM-POSSIBLE!!! TO COME TO TERMS WITH. I DID NOT SAY DIFFICULT, I SAID IMPOSSIBLE. EVERYONE IS EXPECTING ME [TO] GET ALONG WITH HER. IT IS IMPOSSIBLE." He said it was imperative that she be properly diagnosed as suffering from a personality disorder. "Until then I am being expected to fulfill the IMPOSSIBLE. I didn't say DIFFICULT, I said IMPOSSIBLE. I was nothing but nice. Please understand the disorder and help me."

CHAPTER SIXTEEN

"Stop the Insanity"

Charla Mack's threats to introduce evidence of Darren's violent abuse into family court terrified her estranged husband: any abuse allegations could lose him custody of Erika. So he now decided to go for his daughter's full custody at any cost.

The next day, while trawling the Internet, he came across parents' right's campaigner and forensic consultant Dean Tong's Web site: www.abuse-excuse.com.

Dedicated to helping fathers counter accusations of abuse, Tong provides personal case analysis relative to many mental health issues, including borderline personality disorder. He utilizes his own personal experiences of wrongful arrest for child sexual abuse and domestic violence, together with twenty-five years of professional experience, to help his clients in family court.

Darren Mack was impressed by Tong's credentials, believing he might be useful in countering any future abuse allegations from Charla.

"Tim, I want you to review this man's website for supporting full custody," he e-mailed his attorney on Tuesday afternoon. "He is one of the foremost experts in gaining full custody from Borderlines. Please review his website and get back to me as soon as possible."

Later that day, Darren Mack called Dean Tong at his office in Riverview, Florida, and put him on a retainer.

"So I was hired to give him the best divorce settlement," explained Tong, "and ultimately he did want custody of Erika."

On Monday June 27, Tim Lukas's office mailed Tong a $5,000 retainer check along with a discovery package, including all the family court motions and hundreds of Charla and Darren's e-mails since their separation.

That afternoon, Darren e-mailed Lukas and Tong a breakdown of the harassment Charla—who he called "a monster"—had subjected him to.

"You must find something in the law to protect me from her," he wrote them. "Just because I was frauded into a marriage with a sick woman and gave everything I had to make our marriage work, should not leave me at the effect of this for the rest of my life. Please find something to stop the insanity."

Then, in an attempt to change Nevada custody law, Darren used his family's political connections to lobby influential members of the Reno establishment. He wrote letters to powerful politicians and decision makers, complaining about the way Judge Weller was handling his divorce case.

"He went to state senators," said his brother, Landon. "He went to judges, pleading that [he was] being absolutely unfairly handled in the family court system."

He also met Washoe County district attorney Richard Gammick for lunch at the plush Prospectors' Club inside Harrah's Reno casino, lamenting the bad treatment he was receiving in family court.

"He asked me if I knew some names of lawyers who could help him out," Gammick said.

In late June, Darren received a letter from Nicolas C. Anthony of the Nevada Legislative Counsel Bureau, who had been asked by state senator Maurice Washington to research new changes in the Nevada's child custody laws. The recently passed Assembly Bill 51 expanded the number of factors that judges should consider in determining child custody.

Mack was most concerned about how the new bill impacted domestic violence allegations, for which family court judges were now compelled to hold evidentiary hearings.

The new law ruled that if there was "clear and convincing evidence" that either parent had engaged in domestic violence, there would be "a rebuttable presumption" that sole or joint custody by the perpetrator would not be in the best interests of the child.

A few days later, Dean Tong held a conference call with Darren in Tim Lukas's office to discuss countering any possible accusation by Charla of domestic violence.

"We had a one-hour powwow," recalled Tong. "I said that in my professional judgment, Darren's going to have to go for psychological testing, because she's made this subtle allegation."

Tong also warned that if Judge Weller ever heard the allegation, Darren was probably going to lose custody of Erika.

"So it was very important that Darren get a clean bill of abuse health," Tong explained, "to show he had no propensity to be the monster Charla was painting him to be."

That summer Charla Mack broke off her relationship with Mark Phillips, feeling it had no future. She told her best friend, Laura Cunningham, that she was not in love with Mark.

After learning that Charla was single again and had joined the Match.com dating site, Darren hired a private investigator to date her. But Charla soon discovered what was going on and sent him packing.

"They were both on dating Web sites," said her friend Jacqueline Ross. "He hired somebody to date her and get information. She really should have been an investigator, because there was nothing she couldn't uncover. She was very intuitive and she uncovered him pretty damn fast."

According to friends, Charla was now becoming increasing fearful of Darren, realizing the extreme lengths he was prepared to go to get custody of Erika.

"You know she was scared," said Ross. "She was scared the whole time, as he had put a hit out on his first wife. Many times she said to me, 'One day he's going to kill me. When you find my body you'll know it was him and this is what I want you to do."

Convinced she was going to die, Charla gave her closest friends precise instructions for what she wanted them to do in the event of her murder.

"We all had little lists of what we were to do after he killed her," said Ross. "She wanted her mom to get Erika. Taking-care-of-business-type things. Everybody had their little jobs."

On June 30, Shawn Meador filed a motion of civil contempt against Darren Mack, asking Judge Weller to send him to jail. The motion accused Darren of violating the mutual financial restraining order on three counts: not paying the first $10,000 a month to Charla; transferring a voting interest in Palace Jewelry and Loan to his mother; and moving $280,000 in cash from his personal account to his business.

CHAPTER SEVENTEEN

"A Good Sexual Partner"

On Monday, July 11, Darren Mack drove his Hummer H2 to Las Vegas to meet Dean Tong for a breakfast meeting at the Golden Nugget Casino. On the agenda was the fathers' activist's strategy to have Mack evaluated by a psychologist to measure his propensity for domestic violence and physical child abuse.

"[Darren] was a Reno guy who looked like he belonged in Vegas," recalled Tong. "He was handsome, charismatic, but very overbearing."

For the next two hours they discussed his divorce case in depth, and the trial consultant told Darren what he would need to do to get the upper hand.

"I had already gone through the discovery from the divorce case," said Tong, "and I told him, 'Look Darren, I have three rules in custody cases. They may be a bitter pill to swallow, but if you violate any of them, I'm gone.'"

Then Tong told him that from now on he would have to put Erika's needs before his own, nurture his daughter's relationship with Charla, and never "vilify nor denigrate" her to Erika.

Tong told him that in his case there was a fourth rule: he would have to clean up his act.

"He had cavorted in these brothels and sex swinging clubs from Nevada to Mexico and wherever," said Tong. "This is not emotionally healthy for the kid."

At the end of the two-hour meeting, Tong ordered Darren to stop swinging or lose Erika.

"I pounded my fist on the breakfast table," he recalled. "And I said, 'Darren, this has got to stop now! The sex swinging has to stop. I'm not asking—I'm telling you.'"

Mack took a deep breath and promised to address the problem.

On July 19, Darren Mack flew to Whitinsville, Massachusetts, for a psychosexual evaluation by Dr. Joseph J. Plaud. The evaluation, spread over three days, focused on Mack's sexual habits and desires. It would also determine if he was at any risk of engaging in inappropriate behavior toward children.

During the fourteen hours he spent with Darren, Dr. Plaud subjected his patient to a battery of tests, later noting that Mack had been evasive at times.

"Mr. Mack tends to be guarded and defensive regarding self-disclosure," the doctor noted.

A large part of the report was devoted to Darren Mack's sexual history and whether or not he was attracted to young children.

"Mr. Mack presents himself as having normal libido and drives," Dr. Plaud reported, "and denies at any time sexual interest or arousal towards males. Mr. Mack stated that he thought he was a good sexual partner."

Mack estimated that he had had sex with approximately a hundred women, denying ever visiting prostitutes or indulging in any "obsessive or excessive" use of pornography.

"Mr. Mack did not indicate that he was now easily ashamed about sexual matters" wrote the doctor. "Mr. Mack denied any deviant sexual fantasy behaviors."

In his conclusions, Dr. Plaud found that Darren Mack did not present a danger to the community or display "sexual interest or behavioral patterns" that would place him in a risk category.

On August 11, while Darren Mack was at a swinging convention at the luxurious Grand Velas Spa and Resort on the Mexican Riviera, he filed for Chapter 7 bankruptcy. He now claimed to be worth $5.5 million less than he had reported six months earlier, with assets only totaling $4.3 million and $2 million in liabilities. And he stated that he was unable to pay his debts.

Now many of Darren Mack's assets would come under the jurisdiction of the bankruptcy court, no longer subject to Judge Weller's eventual divorce settlement.

At the beginning of November, Charla Mack filed a complaint in U.S. Bankruptcy Court, stating that her estranged husband was responsible for her child support and alimony payments ordered by the family court.

In the three months since Judge Weller's ruling, Darren had only paid Charla $9,000 of the $40,000 he owed in alimony. He also had not paid anything toward the Franktown Road mortgage or any of the essential bills, as Judge Weller had ordered.

To survive, Charla had resorted to borrowing money from her friends and family.

"She was selling stuff on eBay," said Laura Cunningham. "Junk, paintings, to live. I mean, we lent her money for food."

As the months went by, 5350 Franktown Road went to rack and ruin through neglect; there seemed little hope of it ever being sold. Eventually, the electricity was turned off after several months of bills went unpaid.

"It looked like a haunted house," said Cunningham. "It went straight to hell. Have you ever seen a yard when no one services it? I mean, the weeds came through. The pool was full of algae and he would not pay for a single thing."

On September 28, Joan Mack sued her daughter-in-law, accusing her of refusing to return a $200,000 diamond ring and an eighteen-carat-gold lady's Rolex watch worth $13,000 that belonged to Palace. Charla claimed they had been gifts from Darren.

"Within the first year of our marriage," Charla said in a court filing, "Darren sold my wedding ring off my hand. I was very upset and hurt. He replaced it . . . and promised he would never sell it or other gifts out from under me."

Even though he was now claiming poverty, Mack had visited Mexico twice that year, as well as Costa Rica, San Francisco, and Las Vegas.

"Despite his claim of bankruptcy," read the filing, "Darren has continued to maintain a lavish lifestyle after the couple's separation, and has traveled outside of Reno with various women almost every weekend to alternative lifestyle or swing parties. In fact, he was in Mexico with a young woman at such a party on the date his bankruptcy petition was filed . . . All the while his wife and daughter are left without financial resources."

At 11:00 a.m. on Tuesday, November 15, Darren Mack appeared at a family court hearing to rule on Shawn Meador's civil contempt motion. Just a few days earlier he had returned from a swinger's group vacation at the Meliá Cabo Real beach and golf resort in Mexico.

Prior to the hearing, Tim Lukas had filed an amended financial declaration on behalf of his client. Where before Darren Mack had listed his occupation as a pawnbroker and jeweler, he now described himself as a sales manager for Palace Jewelry and Loan. And he claimed to be earning just $5,000 a month, as opposed to the $44,000 salary he had previously filed.

It was a tense atmosphere in Judge Weller's courtroom as Darren and Charla Mack sat across from each other with their respective lawyers, Tim Lukas and Shawn Meador.

"I have trouble believing your client," Judge Weller told Lukas, "who had $280,000 available to him and who is receiving approximately $44,000 a month."

The judge then admonished Mack for disregarding his orders and doing exactly what he wanted.

"Sir, I'm not a judge because I know more than anyone else," said Weller, "it's just that somebody gets the job and I happened to be in the chair this year."

"I understand," replied Darren Mack.

"And courts can't function if you, or anybody else, gets to say, 'I heard what you said, Judge, but I know better than you, and I'm going to do what I think.'"

"I didn't say that, sir," Mack retorted. "Can I explain?"

"Of course," replied the judge.

"I objected at the time that you awarded her $10,000," he continued, "because there was not $10,000 to pay her."

Then Mack said he had suddenly received an additional tax bill for $23,000, as well as having to pay $20,000 owed to the IRS for the previous year.

"Taxes are critical," he told Judge Weller. "You have to pay those things. I did the best I could."

Mack then claimed to have given Charla two out of every three "spendable dollars" he had earned that year.

"I did everything I could," he said, dramatically gesticulating with his hands, "and then I'm being judged."

Shawn Meador then accused Darren Mack of playing games with the court.

"Every time we hear the numbers from Mr. Mack," he said, "they change."

Meador told the judge that Darren Mack was all about control, and he had wanted to carry on paying Charla's expenses, rather than giving her any money.

"The minute Your Honor said, 'Well, you're [going] to give her some cash,'" said Meador, "that's when we started having problems. That's when everything changed: the minute you said, 'No, you're not going to have complete control.'"

At the end of the hearing, Judge Weller said he was seriously considering sending Darren Mack to jail for contempt.

Then the judge asked Darren Mack exactly how much money he could give Charla that day.

"I can give her a thousand dollars," he replied. "That's all I have, Your Honor. I mean, I cannot pay the rest of my bills. I can pay her probably $2,000, and that would be every dime I have."

Meador reminded Judge Weller that Darren Mack's extravagant lifestyle appeared unchanged since the separation.

"Is your client still living the high life?" Judge Weller asked Lukas.

"No, Your Honor," replied the attorney, claiming that Mack had used frequent flier miles for all the foreign trips.

"That was the sky miles that paid for an all-inclusive trip," explained Mack. "Your Honor, can I say something about the three trips?"

Darren Mack then explained that a friend had paid for the Costa Rica trip after Darren told him he could not afford it.

"The two Mexican trips," he said, "the total out of pocket for me was $640. If I would have stayed in town and just paid food and gas for myself, it would have been $1,200. For the three trips, I spent less than I would have done not going out of town."

After hearing this, Judge Weller started losing patience.

"I'm changing my inclination as we go through this," he told Mack. "My inclination now is to require you, sir, to give her $10,000 by Friday at 5:00, or if you don't do that to report to 911 Parr Boulevard [the Washoe County Sheriff's Office] for incarceration. And that you will remain in that jail for twenty-four days until $10,000 is delivered to her, based upon your contempt. That's what I'm thinking now, Mr. Lukas."

"All I can ask is that the court put it in writing," said Mack's attorney. "My client doesn't have $10,000."

"Your client obviously has control of lots of other things." replied the judge.

Judge Weller then held Darren Mack in civil contempt, warning he would go to jail if he didn't get the voting interest back from his mother.

"I'm going to delay imposition of the sanction," Judge

Weller said. "Mr. Lukas, I want you to take a look at what we can do to terminate that voting right."

Addressing Mack, Judge Weller told him to pay Charla $2,000 that day and ordered another hearing when he could examine Darren Mack's financial accounts and see his true worth.

That night Charla Mack told Tony Mudd that Darren's behavior at the hearing had terrified her.

"Right after the meeting with the judge and the attorneys she sent me an e-mail that she feared for her life . . . ," said Mudd. "She was really afraid."

By the next family court hearing on Tuesday, November 22, Darren Mack had heeded Judge Weller's warning, regaining control of Palace Jewelry and Loan.

"During the week he got that voting interest back from his mother," said the judge, "so I imposed no sanction at all."

Joan Mack attended the afternoon hearing along with her attorney and a Palace accountant. The judge began by asking Tim Lukas if his client had paid Charla the $2,000 he had been ordered to. Lukas reported that Mack had gone straight back to his office after the previous week's hearing and electronically transferred the funds.

"We're not looking at criminal contempt here, Mr. Meador," said the judge. "How much money do you believe that this gentleman owes your client under existing court orders?"

Sean Meador replied that Mack owed Charla $31,000 through August. Lukas agreed it was accurate "within a couple of dollars."

Charla's attorney then complained that Darren Mack was "playing money games" by pretending that he now only earned $5,000 a month instead of the $44,000 salary as previously claimed.

"You heard Mr. Meador," the judge told Lukas. "He believes that your client's lifestyle hasn't changed—that he's living on Palace credit cards and that he has available to him as much money as he had previously."

"Your Honor," replied Lukas, "I would invite Mr. Meador to ask Joan Mack."

Then, complaining he did not have all day, Judge Weller asked Joan Mack's accountant, Randal Kuckenmeister, if her son was living beyond his reported earnings. Kuckenmeister replied that the only financial records he had of Mack's spending were his June and July credit card statements.

"[They] indicated that Mr. Mack was still spending a significant amount of funds on credit cards," said the accountant. "And we would like to see further credit cards."

"What do you need to figure out the truth here?" asked Judge Weller.

Kuckenmeister replied that he would need copies of Darren Mack's Palace Jewelry and Loan credit card statement for 2005, several other personal credit card statements, as well as ones from Mack & Mack LLC, a branch of the family business dealing with real estate.

Tim Lukas said that would not be a problem and that he could produce them within two weeks. But he pointed out that in as much as Mack & Mack LLC belonged to Joan Mack and Palace, they would have to give permission first.

Then the judge ordered those documents be produced within two weeks, telling Darren Mack to make his best efforts to get the bankruptcy court and his mother to release the other documents.

"I'm sure in the fullness of time I'll appreciate more of the relationship between you and Palace, sir. And I hope that you're acting reasonably in relation to this person, who was somebody you loved for a very long period of time and has a right to get on with her life, as you have a right to get on with yours."

In early December, Wells Fargo Bank petitioned the U.S. Bankruptcy Court in Reno to have Darren Mack pay back $500,000 he owed.

The bank claimed that eight months earlier Mack had told Wells Fargo that he was worth $10.67 million and his interest in Palace Jewelry and Loan was worth $5 million, but now he claimed to the bankruptcy court that it was only $550,000. He had also told the bank he held commercial real estate holdings worth $3 million, later telling the court they were worth just $450,000.

He had also claimed in April to hold a promissory note worth more than a million dollars from Palace, later valuing it at $470,000 in his Chapter 7 bankruptcy filing. And whereas he had told the bank he had more than $150,000 of personal property, he was now scaling it back to just $16,000.

Based on all the financial discrepancies, Wells Fargo's attorneys were asking the bankruptcy court to stop Darren from getting away with what he owed the bank.

That Christmas, there were few celebrations at 5350 Franktown Road, which was now in foreclosure. The electric company had still not turned on the power, as the bill had not been paid, and the only lighting came from candles. Nevertheless, Charla did everything she could to make it into an adventure for Erika.

"She didn't have any power and it was winter," said Jacqueline Ross, "so she and Erika lived by the fireplace and roasted marshmallows and things. And she made it a camp. You know, it was hard. It was very hard. She didn't know how she was going to feed her child."

Over the holiday season, Charla organized a lot of play dates for Erika with their friends to get out of the house.

"We'd meet for coffee," said Ross, "hung out a lot. We did a lot of kids' stuff together."

It was during this difficult period that Charla started telling her closest friends about her former swinging lifestyle with Darren.

"She did mention that was part of their issue," recalled Ann Mudd. "She said, 'You know, I did a lot of things that I'm not proud of to try to keep my marriage together. But it just wasn't for me, and he didn't want to give it up.'"

While Charla was struggling to survive, Darren Mack

celebrated the holidays by attending a nine-day Utopia group swinger's convention, at the luxurious Meliá Cabo Real beach and golf resort, where he had attended a similar event in June. He shared a $170-a-night room with a woman he had brought along, engaging in sex by the pool and other open areas of the hotel, which had been taken over by Utopia.

Resort bellboy Jesus Reyes later remembered Darren Mack, because he had a different girl on his arm every time he saw him.

CHAPTER EIGHTEEN

The Sex Photographs

At 12:52 p.m. on Monday, January 9, 2006, Darren and Charla Mack were back in family court, having tentatively reached a financial settlement. And Darren had a new divorce attorney named Leslie Shaw, his third, after firing Tim Lukas.

"He made grave, grave errors," Mack later explained, claiming to have paid Lukas around $80,000 for his work. "He was not prepared for the contempt hearings."

After the Macks were sworn in, Judge Chuck Weller addressed them.

"We are awfully close to a settlement of the financial issues in this case," he said. "And in the interests of time I'm going to recite what I believe to be the agreement. This can fall apart but we're so close I think I can state it close to right."

Under the settlement, Darren would pay Charla $480,000, within forty-eight hours of the formal agreement being drafted and signed. Charla could spend $50,000 on whatever she wanted, using the balance to buy a house and a car. Darren would also pay her $500,000 from his Palace pension fund over the next five years, so she would continue to receive $10,000 a month. Both parties would split Erika's school tuition fees and the costs of her extracurricular activities, although Darren would pay her dental treatment.

When Judge Weller noted that child support would be based on Darren's current income of $5,000 a month, Shawn Meador began shaking his head.

"It's not acceptable, Your Honor," he said. "I think we've got to deal with the bigger pictures of custody, and I was hopeful we were going to get a deal today that gave us that opportunity."

Judge Weller said Erika's custody would be settled at a later hearing. Then he ordered Mack to pay Charla an additional $15,500 of spousal arrears within forty-eight hours of the agreement being signed.

Finally, Judge Weller asked Darren Mack if there were any personal belongings that he wanted from the Franktown Road house.

"I believe the only thing that's really of any significance to me is just a feather that was given to me by an Indian chief," he replied.

"You have any problem with that, ma'am?" asked Weller.

"No," Charla replied.

"And then there's a $10,000 TV," Darren continued, "that would probably only fit in that house that I think we should probably sell and split the proceeds."

"I mean, he took, like, $50,000 worth of merchandise out of the house," interrupted Charla. "I mean—"

"I don't want to reserve jurisdiction," said Darren angrily and rising to his feet. "I want to settle the property stuff."

"So you want to sell the TV," Judge Weller, losing patience. "What else?"

"I think that's really the only thing that has any significance in the house," said Darren.

"Fine!" replied Charla in obvious frustration.

The judge then told Darren to let her just take the TV and be done with it, asking what the value of a used TV could be, anyway.

"Well, it's worth a few thousand dollars," said Mack's attorney, Shaw, "but I thought she said that was fine with her."

"No," replied Charla, "I would rather not do that, in honor

of the integrity of how this is played out. He came with four movers and a U-Haul while I was out of town and took a ton of stuff. And I just think in the spirit of this just . . . I'll give you the—"

"All I want is my feather," snapped Darren, cutting her off.

"Fine. Fine," said Charla.

Then Shawn Meador told Judge Weller that although Charla had accepted the agreement, it was going to take time to draft it and she needed cash immediately.

"Can Charla have some money right now?" Judge Weller asked Mack. "Some credit against the amount you owe her?"

"Your Honor," replied Darren Mack, "I don't have any money."

"Sir," said the judge, "you get $5,000 a month."

"What's that?" said Mack, sounding surprised.

"You get $5,000 a month."

"I get $5,000 a month," said Mack. "I've just paid her sixteen hundred dollars yesterday."

"No," Charla told the Judge, "and it'll take me a week because he's mailed it."

"No it doesn't," Mack snapped back. "It gets there in two to three days—every sixth of the month."

Then Judge Weller ordered the attorneys from both sides to prepare the agreement order to sign on Friday so Charla could have money the following week.

He also asked everyone if they had heard the agreement that was now on the record.

"I have one other thing that we'd agreed on at the beginning," said Darren Mack. "That our family photographs being held by Mr. Meador are destroyed."

"What the sex photos," laughed Charla. "OK."

"Yeah, let's get over that issue," said Shaw, "because we're going to beat this horse to death. The sex photographs . . . okay, we'll say it as many times as we need to . . ."

"All right, let me stop you," said Judge Weller. "Sir, aside from the photographs, have you heard the entire agreement that's been recited her today?"

"I have, sir," replied Mack.

"Have you had an opportunity to discuss it with your attorney to the full extent that you would like?"

"This is a change," replied Mack. "I'd like to spend just one minute."

The judge then called a short recess so both parties could discuss the photographs with their respective counsels.

"We need to destroy those photos," Meador told the judge. "I did tell Darren that when we got it resolved, we'd destroy them."

"I trust Shawn," said Charla. "That's fine."

A few minutes later the court reconvened and Leslie Shaw announced that he had now discussed this "sensitive" matter with his client.

"We just want to make sure how this additional element we talked about is handled," Shaw told Judge Weller. "Mr. Meador is in possession of some private and sensitive photographs which are going to be destroyed. Mr. Mack simply asks that he be allowed to come to Mr. Meador's office, look at them, and make sure they're all there. He would know whether they are or not. If they're not there, they need to be turned over . . . immediately and destroyed."

"I told Mr. Mack," said Meador, "that when this case was over we'd destroy the photos. When the money's paid I'm happy to do it."

"Is that acceptable?" the judge asked Darren Mack.

"Do I get to see them?" Mack asked. "And then we'll destroy them."

"If you want to see them again," said Meador, "we can make arrangements for that."

"That's fine, Your Honor," said Darren.

Then Judge Weller polled both parties, ensuring they fully understood the agreement and knew exactly what they would be signing.

"Mr. Mack," asked the judge, "do you agree to be bound by this agreement?"

"I do," replied Darren Mack.

"Ma'am, do you agree to be bound?" asked Weller.

"Yes," said Charla.

"Then this agreement is accepted by the court," Judge Weller told them, "and shall be the order of the court and shall be binding upon the parties."

In late January, Darren Mack backed out of the million-dollar divorce settlement. His attorney, Leslie Shaw, filed a motion into family court claiming his client had been "coerced" into it with a contempt of court jail threat hanging over him. It also stated that Joan Mack had refused to sign a release dropping any litigation against Charla.

Mack now maintained that his final financial settlement with Charla was contingent on her agreeing to his custody demands for their daughter.

"He wanted to start all over," Judge Weller explained later. "The deal shouldn't be enforced. He wanted to throw the agreement out and begin again."

On February 2, Shawn Meador filed a motion to enforce the settlement agreement, describing the present situation as "chaos."

"He had seller's remorse," Clark County special prosecutor Robert Daskas would later explain. "He voiced his frustration to anybody and everybody who would listen, and he found an audience for his frustration."

During the next month, until a family court hearing could be held to rule on whether the settlement was binding, Darren Mack embarked on a bitter campaign to discredit Judge Weller.

In early February, Darren Mack again lunched with District Attorney Richard Gammick at the Prospector's Club at Harrah's Reno casino. They were joined by Palace's chief operating officer, Eric Maiss. Mack dominated the conversation, bitterly complaining about how he was being victimized by Judge Weller in family court.

"This one was really getting under his skin," recalled Gammick. "[He was] really obsessed with it to the point of that's about all he could talk about."

A few weeks later, Gammick met the pawnbroker again for lunch. This time they were joined by Washoe County assistant district attorney John Helzer.

During lunch, Darren Mack produced some of his divorce documents, asking Gammick and Helzer to review them and offer their opinions of how Judge Weller was conducting proceedings.

Suddenly the judge entered the Prospector's Club, heading straight for their table. As soon as Mack saw Judge Weller he grabbed the documents, hiding them under the table, away from his view.

Darren Mack also lobbied the governor of Nevada's wife, Dawn Gibbons, asking her to have her husband, Jim, intervene in the matter. He cornered her in a car park, spending two hours telling her the injustices he had suffered in Judge Weller's courtroom.

"But she didn't know what to do," said Mack, "other than to tell me to get a good attorney. I spoke to numerous senators and tried to get them to do [something]."

But even if the politicians and other powerful players did little more than lend a sympathetic ear, there were plenty who would. Darren was now regularly attending meetings for Nevadans for Equal Parenting as well as several other fathers' rights groups. And he soon began meeting others who also disliked Judge Weller.

"He felt Judge Weller wasn't listening to him," said Michael Small, a former child actor who met Mack at a meeting. "[He was] disillusioned, frightened, and could not believe this was happening. He was about to lose a lot of money."

The two men decided to join forces to wage a campaign against Judge Weller, determined to reform the injustices of the family court system.

"We felt something big did have to happen," Small told CBS's *48 Hours*, "in order for people to know what is going on."

One night in February, Darren Mack was on the San Francisco–based Legal Reader Web site when a January 13 posting by "Alecia" with the heading "More Bad Judges" caught his attention.

"This Judge and his conduct needs to be addressed," read her posting, responding to an earlier one about Judge Weller. "We have rights and resources. I too have experience with this judge and his obvious bias against women. I just need your support."

Darren Mack sent Alecia an e-mail, railing against Judge Weller and the Washoe Valley family court system. They discovered an immediate rapport in their common hatred of the judge, and within a few days had struck up a lively on-line correspondence.

CHAPTER NINETEEN

"Darren Mack Could Not Be Rejected"

An attractive blonde in her early forties, Alecia D. Biddison is a major in the U.S. Army Reserve who has served in the Middle East. Holding a bachelor of arts degree from California Polytechnic University, Biddison is also a managing partner for the Busick Group, a government appropriations consultancy.

According to the Busick Group Web site, Biddison has ten years' experience working in both the public and private sectors, generating more than $20 million in revenue for her clients.

"Her persuasive, organized and energetic attitude," reads her site CV, "enable her to clearly communicate technical and business information to members of Congress and senior management of diverse organizations."

The site also boasts that she cofounded a Silicon Valley software company that in just two years went from a garage shop to an $8 million company. She then positioned it for acquisition at $60 million.

But Biddison is also a Reno-based political activist with a mission to reform the Nevada judiciary. And the overwhelming catalyst for Biddison's radical reform campaign was her experiences of Judge Weller in her child custody case.

"I was shocked and horrified about what was taking

place in his courtroom," Biddison would later testify, "and accusations that were being made about my military service and about my character."

After her first family court hearing in front of Judge Weller, Biddison blamed her attorney and fired him. Then she discovered that the father of her then five-month-old son had allegedly contributed to Judge Weller's election campaign.

"And so there was no way I was going to prevail," she explained.

In November 2005, Biddison successfully managed to transfer the custody case out of Judge Weller's court to the state of California.

In February, Darren Mack and Alecia Biddison began exchanging e-mails, joining forces to expose Judge Weller and the alleged corruption in his family court.

"We shared a certain level of frustration," recalled Biddison.

At 1:15 p.m. on Wednesday, March 1, Washoe County Family Court judge Chuck Weller held a three-way telephone conference with Leslie Shaw and Shawn Meador. The conference call came ten days before Charla had to move out of 5350 Franktown Road.

Judge Weller began the conference call by refuting Darren Mack's claim that the financial deal agreed in January was contingent on Erika's custody.

"I've reviewed the documents," said the Judge, "and I just don't accept it."

Judge Weller also said that although he did not believe Darren could get his mother to sign an indemnity release for her daughter-in-law, he was still obligated to use his "best efforts" to get her to cooperate.

"So I'm not going to take Shawn's recommendation that we incarcerate this fellow," said the judge. "I'm going to give some money to Mom today."

He said he wanted an interim agreement in place for Charla's welfare.

"What I have in mind," he said, "is giving her enough money so that she's not forced into the street. And that money is not used as a weapon in this case."

Shawn Meador said he had been "shocked" to hear that Joan Mack refused to sign a release settling the financial part of the divorce.

But then Darren Mack's attorney Leslie Shaw explained that Palace Jewelry and Loan was now contemplating further legal action against Charla Mack.

"Apparently the business is looking into additional things that Miss Mack may have taken that have substantial value," said Shaw. "Joan Mack feels that she has been treated in a very offensive and abrasive manner in the negotiations for this release."

Charla's lawyer said this was nothing more than a smoke screen.

"What's really happening here," said Meador, "is Darren got cold feet about the custody, and so he's holding up the money to try and work her on custody."

Then the judge asked Meador how much money his client needed.

"A hundred thousand dollars," he replied.

"Break it down for me," asked Weller.

Meador told the judge that Charla desperately needed money; she also owed him a "tremendous" amount in legal fees.

Then Judge Weller ruled he would give Charla Mack a qualified domestic relations order (QDRO) ordering Darren Mack to pay Charla $60,000 immediately.

"There's nothing to prevent the two of you from resolving the remaining issues and doing the settlement," he told the attorneys. "And you're free to treat this as an advance on the settlement. If you're not able to agree, we'll have a trial."

In the wake of the family court hearing, the following posting appeared on the "More Bad Judges" page of the Legal Reader Web site from "Nevada Parent":

"THE NEW TERRORISM! Judge Chuck Weller of Washoe County Family Court had people (both men & women) running from his courtroom in TERROR. He threatens to take your children, your freedom, your property!

"Weller uses whatever tactics to force you to submit to his imperial demands and tyrannical orders. Every story from each person that I have talked to in my investigation has similar experience. They are terrorized and don't understand why he is being so aggressive when they've done nothing wrong.

"Does Weller ever rule on the law or does he just rule on his whims?"

And directly underneath this posting was one by "Reggie", comparing Judge Weller to Adolf Hitler.

"Family court Judge Chuck Weller of Reno, NV, lied to everyone by saying he was going to defend father's rights to get elected. Once on the bench he has single handed[ly] destroyed more GOOD father's [sic] with his [shoot-from-the-hip] punishing motions. He takes all statements against fathers as true despite all evidence opposing them and then makes impossible orders which fathers can never comply with. Then punishes the fathers for not following his impossible order. Everyone should [be] outraged at his bias [sic] behavior and do everything that can legally be done to get this HITLER off the bench."

When Judge Weller read this posting, he was horrified, believing he could be in danger, as he had received death threats in the past.

"I was made aware that I was being attacked online on blogs," said the judge. "And there were just some horrible attacks on me, calling me Hitler and saying I was unfair, that I was biased and corrupt."

The judge happened to know a member of the Nevadans for Equal Parenting group, running into him by chance a few weeks later at a social affair.

"And I said, 'Why is Nevadans for Equal Parenting coming after me?' " recalled the judge. " 'I'm sympathetic to your views; why is this happening?' And he told me that Darren Mack was the source of it."

After several weeks of corresponding through e-mails and telephone calls, Darren Mack invited Alecia Biddison out for dinner. They met at one of Mack's favorite Italian restaurants in Reno, and over wine and pasta they got to know each other better.

"We talked about our families," she recalled. "We talked about the community, about my business and what I do as far as judicial reform."

They also spent a good deal of time discussing Judge Weller and their dislike of him. Alecia was much impressed with the handsome pawnbroker.

"He was very articulate," she remembered, "very intelligent. He was chivalrous, which is kind of a lost trait, and opened doors and was very respectful and courteous. He was respectful of me and . . . valued my opinion."

In mid-March, Darren Mack attended the monthly Nevadans for Equal Parenting meeting in Sparks Library. And he struck up a conversation with Garret Idle, who was also embroiled in a heated custody case in Judge Weller's courtroom.

After the meeting, the two men talked further, finding much in common. They both believed that the family court system was corrupt and needed to be torn down and rebuilt from the ground up.

A couple of days later, they met at the Brew Brothers brewery at the Eldorado Casino, directly across the street from Palace Jewelry and Loan. Darren Mack then took Idle upstairs to his second-floor office, which he had renamed the "War Room" because it was packed with boxes of files from his divorce cases.

"Darren was on a quest to expose Weller and bring him down," explained Idle. "And he was focusing all his efforts on what he needed to do to get that accomplished."

* * *

In mid-March. Charla Mack moved out of the Franktown Road house, renting a new home at Alder Bridge Court, Reno, until the divorce settlement could be finalized.

"She told me that she was having to borrow money from friends." said Ann Mudd, "so that she could come up with enough money to rent another house. She said, 'I just want to stay home and be a mom. If he's not going to give me any money, that's his ball.'"

By now Charla was so scared of Darren that she refused to give him the address of her new home, only providing a Mail Boxes Etc. number for any correspondence. She told friends that she feared that he might be following her home after she collected Erika from school.

At the beginning of April, Darren Mack and Alecia Biddison decided to take their relationship to the next level and became lovers.

"We were both seeing other people when we first met," explained Alecia. "But it was becoming more and more exclusive as things were moving on forward, rather than just out there, playing the field."

Before long Biddison introduced Darren Mack to her one-year-old son, Brandon, for the first time.

"I really enjoyed his companionship," said Alecia. "My friends really liked him and certainly both of us were interested in seeing where it would lead. I don't think either one of us were at that point saying, 'Oh this is it.' We both had a lot on our plates."

Biddison says that when Mack told her about his swinging lifestyle, she told him she wanted no part of it.

"That certainly was not going to be an element in our relationship," she said. "That was openly discussed."

In mid-May, Darren Mack reconnected with an old Reno High School friend called Dan Osborne after more than thirty years. Osborne, who worked in the computer industry, had approached Mack about buying up excess inventory of IBM computers cheaply and then making a killing on eBay.

"Darren hired me out," said Osborne. "It might have been a pretty good, lucrative deal."

Osborne was in the process of moving back to Reno, so Mack invited him to move into the Fleur de Lis until he found a place.

"I'd been looking for work and trying to get a place," explained Osborne, "and Darren said, 'Why don't you stay here? You're more than welcome.'"

So Osborne moved into Erika's room, and his pet dog, Rusty, stayed in the garage.

Over the next few weeks, Osborne tried unsuccessfully to get the IBM computer deal off the ground while helping his friend research Judge Chuck Weller.

But Osborne became increasingly uncomfortable about Darren's gnawing obsession with how Charla and Judge Weller were trying to destroy him.

"He talked about it all the time," explained Osborne. "I knew Darren was displeased with the judge. He thought the guy was running him over the coals and not giving him a fair shake. You could tell he's being tormented by it and it's on his mind."

Having been through a painful divorce himself, Osborne empathized, but warned his friend to calm down and play by the rules.

"It scared the hell out of me," Osborne recalled. "There were a lot of times we talked [and] I said, 'You really don't want to say stuff like that.'"

On Tuesday, May 16, Darren Mack told Garret Idle that he was ready to move against Judge Weller. He planned to orchestrate Judge Weller's downfall by lodging a judicial complaint against him and having a local television station expose him at the same time.

"We are getting ready to file judicial complaints against Weller," Idle posted on the Legal Reader's "More Bad Judges" page.

On May 19, Darren Mack and Idle arrived at KRNV-TV studios in downtown Reno and urged news reporter Shelby Sheehan to investigate Judge Chuck Weller for corruption. Several weeks earlier, Mack had contacted Sheehan and several other news outlets to suggest a possible investigative piece on family court corruption, but refused to give any details.

"They said they wanted to gather some evidence and come in and meet with me," Sheehan recalled, when later interviewed on cable TV. "They did come in and basically alleged that the judge bases his decisions on the attorney and if they are a contributor or not."

Sheehan remembered Darren Mack as being extremely upset, accusing Judge Weller of being corrupt.

"He was very well-spoken, very intelligent," recalled Sheehan. "He said to me, 'You know, my case is basically over. I have lost. I have lost my children. I have lost money, a home. But I don't want other people to be in the same situation.'"

Shelby refused to commit to an investigation, saying it was far more complex than Darren seemed to appreciate.

"And I told him, "'You're coming to me with these allegations [but] these types of cases take a lot of footwork and just checking into the issues,'" Sheehan said. "'And we can't necessarily turn the story around in one day.'"

Dean Tong believes Darren was devastated when his idea for a judicial corruption investigative piece was turned down.

"I think that's the thing that finally broke the camel's back," said Tong, who was no longer on the divorce team. "Darren took his 'discovery' to the Reno media and he was rejected. And Darren Mack could not be rejected."

CHAPTER TWENTY

"He Gets So Angry"

At 10:00 a.m. on Wednesday, May 24, Judge Chuck Weller convened an all-day family court hearing, determined to settle the financial aspect of the Mack divorce case. Darren Mack and his attorney, Leslie Shaw, sat across the chambers from Charla and Shawn Meador. Joan Mack was also in the courtroom with her attorney, Robert Lyle.

Judge Weller began by asking Darren Mack what progress he had made in having his mother waive litigation against her daughter-in-law.

"You tried to get your mother to go along with the deal," said Judge Weller. "What was her response?"

"She responded in a number of different ways," replied Darren, taking a sip of water. "She told me that she doesn't trust Charla . . . because of the things that Charla has done through this whole case."

Judge Weller then noted that Joan Mack's reluctance to sign a waiver release was holding everything up. Leslie Shaw replied that it was more complicated than that and all the family businesses—Mack & Mack One, Mack & Mack Two, and Palace—also had to sign releases.

"So even if Ms. Mack says, 'I'm ready to do it,'" asked the Judge, "we still don't have a deal from your perspective?"

Then Judge Weller called Joan Mack to the witness stand, to explain exactly her position toward Charla.

"I guess there's suspicions on my part, too, as president of Palace," Joan Mack told the judge, "because there's other things that are happening in the interim that I am not comfortable with. So at this time I'm not willing to sign releases."

Judge Weller then dismissed her from the stand.

"I can't forget the fact that this is your client's mother," Judge Weller told attorney Shaw. "OK, how would you propose that we resolve this case then?"

Darren Mack's attorney then informed the judge that a recent audit of Palace Jewelry and Loan had put Charla Mack under even more suspicion.

"They have discovered some inaccurate record keeping of items that are taken out of inventory, like the watch and ring," Shaw explained. "And that reflects that Charla Mack has taken far more personal things than is involved in the lawsuit. That is what I am told."

Then the judge asked Darren Mack what property Charla had allegedly taken from Palace.

"There's a whole list of them," he replied. "It's like hundreds of CDs, TVs, stereos, tape recorders, Walkmans— lots of miscellaneous items. Somewhere I believe, if I remember rightly . . . between twenty-five and thirty thousand dollar[s in] value."

Then Darren Mack angrily accused Charla of trying to ruin him by sending out his bankruptcy notices to hundreds of vendors and pawnshops.

"[Our] office has fielded over forty calls," said Mack, "that interpreted it as the Palace Jewelry and Loan was in bankruptcy. We don't have proof of who did this, but right now we're working on getting some forensics done."

Shawn Meador told the judge that all these Palace items had been gifts to Charla from Darren, and they had a sworn affidavit from a former Palace employee to prove it.

Meador told the judge that his client vehemently denied sending out any bankruptcy letters to anyone, but even if she had, it was accurate information about a public legal proceeding.

After restating his intention to rule on the financial aspects of the Mack divorce that day, Judge Weller recalled Joan Mack to the witness stand to be questioned by both sides.

Shawn Meador asked her who else had been involved in the decision to sue her daughter-in-law.

"It would be just me," Joan Mack replied, adding that after she had learned about the alleged missing jewelry, Charla had been asked to return several times.

"And did you talk with Darren about the issue before you filed the lawsuit?" asked Meador.

"I don't recall," she replied.

"Are you aware," asked Charla's attorney, "that your refusal to execute mutual releases is the holdup in the settlement between Charla and Darren?"

"I'm not sure of that," she said.

"Has Darren told you anything to the contrary?"

"Darren doesn't discuss very much with me," she said.

Then, visibly frustrated, Judge Weller personally appealed to Joan Mack to help prevent years of expensive and damaging supreme court litigation.

"Mrs. Mack, I address you," he told her. "The holdup here is whether or not you, on your own behalf and on behalf of various entities that you control, are ready to say that you're not going to sue this women for anything, or whether or not you want to keep open that option."

The judge then said he wanted everyone to think about what he had said during lunch, because when they returned he was making a decision.

After the lunch break, Joan Mack retook the stand to be questioned by her son's attorney, Leslie Shaw. She told Judge Weller that she would never have sued Charla if she had returned the watch and ring when she was asked to.

"Let me state this," she explained. "I'm wearing a hat for Palace Jewelry and Loan. And the hat was simply to request

that a ring and watch be returned that Charla was in possession of."

She said that someone had informed Palace's competitors
that her son was in bankruptcy, putting their business in jeop-
ardy. And she was also concerned that signing any releases
could affect her legal standing as Erika's grandmother.

"Would I be able to see my grandchild," she asked, "and
still remain the grandparent that I have always been? And I
think I have been a good grandparent and I care for my grandchild very much."

Judge Chuck Weller then assured her that any releases
she signed would not affect her grandparental rights.

"In fact in this trial," said the judge, "all the issues involving everybody's relations to your grandchild are for another
day. Does that change your willingness to sign a release?"

"No," replied Joan Mack resolutely.

"I want to ask you, ma'am," said the judge, "has your son
ever asked you to sign releases?"

"No," she replied.

Then Shawn Meador asked if Darren had ever asked her
to cooperate with the financial settlement that was agreed in
January.

"He called me," she replied, "and asked if I could help
finance his position in a settlement. And I said, 'No.'"

It was late afternoon when Judge Chuck Weller announced he
was ready to rule; unfortunately, he said, somebody was not
going to like it.

"This is a terrible thing," he declared. "I can only pick
one side or the other and one of you has to lose."

Then Judge Weller ruled that the January 9 agreement
was binding on both parties, and Darren Mack must pay
Charla one million dollars, as previously agreed.

He then asked what needed to be done to resolve the outstanding custody issues. Shaw replied that his client wanted
a two-day trial and that Charla had refused to give him her

new address since she had moved out of Franktown Road in March.

"Is there a problem with giving an address?" asked the Judge.

"Yes," replied Meador. "Based on the history of this case, Charla is very uncomfortable with Darren knowing where she lives."

Then Shawn Meador asked the judge to order Darren Mack to start paying Charla immediately, as she was in dire straits.

"She hasn't had any money for months and months and months," Judge Weller told Mack. "Regardless of whose fault that is, she needs some sort of income stream. Well, does she receive periodic payment?"

"Your Honor," replied Mack, looking visibly agitated, "I've paid her sixteen hundred dollars a month, even though Mr. Meador has lied many times on the record in stating that I haven't."

Then, as his attorney looked on helplessly, Darren Mack lost control.

"I will give you bank records," he said, banging on the desk. "He lies over and over and over again. I have reliably paid about 40 percent of my income.

"I make $5,000 a month. I barely make enough to even live on, Your Honor. [Meador] lied in the first hearing, stating he never got checks from me. I will give you the canceled checks that went to his office. He just continually lies. I want you to know. If you want evidence in this case to what he says, I will refute almost every single thing he's said in here."

"Sir," replied Judge Weller, "if I had ruled in your favor, right now, whether or not she would be saying it loud, she would be thinking very similar thoughts about either me or your counsel or you. It's not nice not to get the decision, and so I'm not disputing what you say at all. I'm just saying that it's imperfect when you come into a courtroom. I mean, sometimes you get a judge, sometimes you get a jury. If you don't like the decision, you get to go forty miles south of here (to the appeal court)."

"Your Honor, but there's lies," replied Mack emotionally, pounding the table with his fist. "Look, we're not talking about your decision. Your decision's your decision. You have to make a decision. I'm talking about he keeps lying to you over and over."

Then, pointing directly at Charla and Shawn Meador, he raged, "They lie, lie, lie! How many times has he told you I have not paid? I'm behind? She's only got three hundred? Hasn't got a dime? I will show you records that will refute this and this may be perjury. He has lied so many times I can't tell you."

"Well, you should talk to your attorney about what he thinks is the appropriate thing to do about that," the judge told him.

"Well, you're asking about money," said Mack emotionally. "She's getting sixteen hundred dollars a month."

At the end of the hearing, Leslie Shaw demanded to know Charla Mack's new address, threatening to legally compel her to release it.

"Are we going to litigate whether Mr. Mack is entitled to know where his child's living," asked Shaw, "other than Mail Boxes Etc.? We've checked that location."

"Your Honor," said a visibly emotional Charla, speaking out for the first time, "can I say something about that?"

"Yes, ma'am," said Judge Weller.

"So, first of all, I feel that our daughter should be in her father's life, and I have volunteered to drive her. Well, since I've moved I've been doing most of the driving, so it isn't an inconvenience for him. But you know he's hired a PI [private investigator] who tried to date me through Match.com and other things."

She then described how Darren had refused to allow the alarm company, ADT, to take his name off the contract after she became concerned about him coming around. And she had to hire ADT to change the alarm systems for her own protection.

"And there have just been things," Charla sobbed. "And I have a commitment that he knows where [Erika] lives when the divorce is over, but he gets so angry and so worked up that I just don't feel comfortable right now [with him] knowing personally where I live.

"It's not about Erika. It's really about me. And I just would like to wait until the whole thing's resolved."

Judge Weller said there were several options available to her: she could either apply for a temporary protection order against domestic violence, or she could obtain permission from the secretary of state to use a fictitious residential address in upcoming family court proceedings.

"Just to be clear," said Charla, "it's not about Erika."

"As a general rule," the judge replied, "it is absolutely fair for a father to know where his child is all the time."

"I see," she said.

"I'm going to give you thirty days to pursue one of those two remedies," Judge Weller told her. "And if you don't obtain a fictitious address or an order from a court issuing a temporary protection order against domestic violence that gives you the authority to withhold your address, I'm going to require that you provide your address."

"But the protection order, then, would mean that he would have to stay a certain [number of] feet away, right?" asked Charla wiping her eyes.

Then Leslie Shaw interrupted, saying his client would agree, without any admission of wrongdoing, not to go anywhere near Charla's home.

"Does he agree not to have a private investigator tap my phones," asked Charla, "or go into my computer system and things like that?"

"That is not happening," replied Shaw as his client shook his head. "Mr. Mack is telling me he is not involved in any such activity. There's no evidence before the court of that. Let's make it easy. Mr. Mack will agree not to go near the house. Mr. Mack will agree not to go in the house. These people e-mail each other all the time. I have e-mail streams that are going on at one, two in the morning. They are in contact with one another regularly."

Then the judge asked Shawn Meador if they could fashion some sort of agreement in which Charla would feel comfortable giving out her new address.

"Okay," replied Meador after conferring with his client, "Mrs. Mack would disclose her physical address [if] Mr. Mack would agree that, with the exception of pickup or drop-off of his daughter, he would not go within a hundred yards of the property. That he would not have an agent go within a hundred yards of the property. That he would not hack into her computer or phone line . . ."

"Why is it one way, Your Honor?" shouted Darren Mack. "She's already sent viruses in my computer."

Judge Weller told Mack that if he wanted a similar agreement about Charla dropping off Erika at his condo, he would not be opposed to it.

"We were just looking at her request for the moment," he told him. "Your lawyer said he wanted to know the address; I came up with an option."

The judge then asked both attorneys to quickly draft an agreement between the parties.

"Here's the words that we propose," said Shaw. "That, starting immediately, neither party shall come within a hundred yards of the residence of the other except for the purpose of picking up or dropping off their minor child at the time of the custody exchanges. Further, neither party shall, personally, through agent, electronic means, or any other fashion, invade that residence telephonically, electronically, or by Internet."

"Or by agent go within a hundred yards of the house," added Judge Weller. "His mother can't start cruising her house."

Judge Weller then asked how they currently transferred

Erika's custody. Charla replied that they did it at school, but if there had been a time factor, she had driven her.

"So you've been driving to his house anyway?" Judge Weller asked.

"Yes," Charla said, "and picking her up and driving her so it wasn't an inconvenience for him."

"The language that's just been placed on the record and assented to by both sides is the order of the court," the judge told them. "Are you prepared, ma'am, to give your address now?"

"Yes," said Charla. "It's 2680 Alder Bridge Court, Reno, Nevada 89521."

"Is there any other thing that we can do today?" the judge asked.

"Not that I can think of, Your Honor," said Shaw.

"Thank you, Your Honor," said Charla.

"Good luck to you all," said Judge Weller, rising from his chair to leave the courtroom.

On his way out of the courtroom, Darren Mack locked eyes with Judge Weller, making him feel highly uncomfortable.

"He gave me this withering glare at the end of the proceedings," Judge Weller recalled. "A look of death."

CHAPTER TWENTY-ONE

"We're Not Going to Take This Anymore!"

After the hearing, Darren Mack embarked on a covert campaign of harassment against Judge Chuck Weller. He went online and logged into MapQuest, tracking down where the Judge lived with his wife, Rosa, and their two daughters. And then he took out an ad in the *Big Nickel* free newspaper want ads section, stating the judge's wife was auctioning off a valuable Harley-Davidson motorcycle at 7:00 a.m. the following Saturday. The ad, which was anonymously paid for in cash, gave the judge's home address, his phone number, and even directions to his house.

Darren also tried to hire someone to follow the judge to try and prove he was corrupt.

After being turned down by the local television stations, he found an alternative way to get his message out there. He had arranged to be interviewed by radical Libertarian William Wagener for his *On Second Thought* Web TV show.

The last week of May, Darren Mack drove Garret Idle and Michael Small to his cousin Jeff Donner's house in Moraga, California, where the interview would take place.

"We all met up in front of his cousin's house," recalled Idle. "We met William Wagener and then we went into the backyard to do the interview, as it was a beautiful day."

After setting up the lights and attaching a microphone to Darren Mack's lapel, the interview began.

"All right, this is William Wagener, *On Second Thought* TV. We're here at an undisclosed location in northern California with Darren Mack."

Wagener first asked Darren Mack to explain his situation to viewers.

"I was married to somebody," he began, "who I didn't know at the beginning has undiagnosed severe personality disorder. And then I struggled with it for years through . . . both physical and mental abuse."

Mack said that it was only after being stricken with spinal meningitis, caused by all his marital stress, that he had decided to get a divorce.

"I was taking care of her," he said, "giving up the high majority of my income, supporting her in a very nice house, taking care of all her bills. And then the judge got involved."

He claimed that Judge Weller had listened to false statements and allegations, holding him in contempt when he had insufficient funds to meet an order.

"And that's when Judge Weller started wielding his iron mallet," Mack continued, "and started threatening me with jail. Pushing me. Extorting me."

He claimed that at the January 9 settlement conference Judge Weller had used "intimidation and extortion," threatening to put him in jail if he didn't pay one and a half times his income for spousal support.

"That is the kind of justice that I had to face in front of Judge Weller," he declared. "Actually, it doesn't even come up in America for me. For me, this is probably what people felt in Nazi Germany, where things started to slide very subtly, and then all of sudden you find yourself being whisked away to concentration camps. That is the family court system, [and] my experience of it under Judge Weller reminds me much more about what I studied in school about Nazi Germany."

Wiping his eyes, he described losing everything in the divorce. He said he had already spent hundreds of thousands of dollars in legal fees and would be "completely broke" and "destitute" when he finally emerged from bankruptcy.

"This is a woman who came to me with a $20,000 debt and married me, lived like a queen, and is now walking away with more than what I have and bankrupting me," he said bitterly.

Then, taking a deep breath, Darren Mack declared that the time had come for patriotic action instead of mere words.

"So my ultimate point of what I'm trying to get across," he said, "is that it's time to take a stand. It's time to not let this tyranny go under wraps [and] keep it quiet.

"Somebody has to stand up! If our forefathers in 1776 stood by and just kept quiet and [hoped] maybe England would go away, we'd be sipping tea right now."

"I agree," said Wagener.

"At what point do we stand up to this absolute unconstitutionality and state, 'We're not going to take this anymore?' Where do we draw the line? That's the real point that I'm trying to get across.

"It takes us having the courage to step up like our forefathers did back in 1776 against the tyranny of England, because there is no difference; . . . [in fact,] this is even worse than what happened [with] England.

"We have to stand up because it is us the people and it's stopped being *us* the people and started being *them* the government, and the judges and specifically in this case Judge Weller, to rally his tyranny and his money-motivated campaign contributors. You need to stand up. I'm taking the risk of a life—all of us need to take this risk and stop this kind of injustice. So that's my last statement."

Earlier, as the equipment was being set up before the interview, Darren Mack and William Wagener casually chatted during the sound check.

Mack told the host that he believed that family judges had far too much power, calling the system "legalized Mafia."

Wagener agreed, saying, "The bottom line is it's a criminal enterprise [to] rape, pillage, and plunder. You're actually better off to murder your spouse and then plead insanity and be out in seven years. You'll have your kids, you'll have what you want."

At 7:00 a.m. on Saturday, May 27, a procession of tough-looking bikers started arriving at Judge Weller's house, looking for the Harley-Davidson auction advertised in the *Big Nickel*. One by one they rang the front doorbell, to the horror and astonishment of the judge's wife, Rosa.

"I'd gone to the courthouse because I had some paperwork to do," recalled Judge Weller. "My wife called me at 7:30 and told me all these bikers were knocking at the door, wondering where the auction was. It was intimidating."

The judge immediately alerted the police and Washoe County Court security, asking them to investigate. The Washoe County Sheriff's office later visited the *Big Nickel* offices, but there was no trace of who had placed the fake auction ad, as it had been paid for anonymously in cash.

Over the next week, Judge Weller and his family were woken up numerous times late at night by their pet dogs barking at an intruder.

"I thought there was something going on," said the judge.

Darren Mack told Charla he had no intention of ever paying her the million dollars as Judge Weller had ordered. She described the explosive face-to-face encounter to Shawn Meador, in a June 6 e-mail.

"He screamed at me, 'I don't care how the judge rules, you will get no money out of me! So what do you think about that?'" she wrote.

"I replied calmly, 'I don't know, how does jail sound to you?' Then I walked away. He ignored me from then on."

Soon afterward, Charla flew to Los Angeles, spending a few days with her best friend Laura Cunningham.

"She was depressed," recalled Cunningham, "because she felt that she was never going to get out."

The first week of June, investigators believe, Darren Mack decided to finally solve his divorce problems by murdering Charla, Judge Chuck Weller, and Charla's attorney, Shawn Meador. The always-methodical businessman sat down at his kitchen table, drafting out a to-do list on a yellow legal pad:

DAN .. TAKE ERIKA TO JOAN	*EQUIP*
HELEN .. APPT SHAWN MONDAY SOMETIME	BUSHMASTER 223 + CLIP
CHEROKEE .. ~~JORY~~ [DM] SIDE WINDOW DOWN	FLAK VEST
OTHER .. COREY DRIVEWAY	BLK VEST
GARAGE DOOR OPEN JORY SIDE	USAS 12 + CLIPS
END PROBLEM	45 + CLIPS
PUT LEX IN GARAGE/ LOCK HOME	40 CAL + CLIPS
PARKING GARAGE—IF YES	243 + AMMO
ATTORNEY OFFICE	22 RIFLE + AMMO
	OBTAIN
	○ FILING BOX

On the third item down, he crossed out his son Jory's name, initialing it as he was used to doing in business.

On Wednesday, June 7, Darren Mack arrived back from a brief business trip to Las Vegas with Palace's assistant manager, Mark Stone, and started putting his murderous plan into action.

His first move was to have Dan Osborne drive him to Reno Airport so he could pick up a Ford Explorer SUV. Osborne thought that strange, as Mack normally drove a Jeep Grand Cherokee and a Hummer H2.

Darren Mack rented the silver 2006 Ford Explorer from Budget rent-a-car at 2:52 p.m. using his American Express card. He rented it until Saturday, but later extended the rental three days, until June 13.

Soon afterward, Darren Mack logged on to a fathers' rights Yahoo! group he was active in called Redress2@yahoogroups.com, posting an angry diatribe against Judge Weller and Shawn Meador entitled: "Justice for Sale."

> *It is not only in Las Vegas that attorneys are playing with a stacked judicial deck. Judge Chuck Weller is criminal in his conduct on behalf of his contributing attorneys in Washoe County, (Reno) Nevada. We have done research and in ten out of ten cases we have researched where a contributing attorney was involved, they were got more than they even asked for to the extent of criminal conduct being allowed by the attorneys.*

> *We have a term [for] all the people who were stupid and believed in justice and didn't hire a contributing attorney, and the saying in Weller's courtroom is: "Justice for Sale."*

That Friday was the last day of the school year, and Charla Mack was on luncheon duty at the Mountain View Montessori School, where she sometimes volunteered. After school broke up, Charla took Erika to play in the park with some of her friends.

"We talked about what we were going to do for the summer," recalled Ann Mudd. "My daughter was going away to summer camp for three weeks, so [Charla] said we'll have to get together and have a glass of wine and picnic."

Later that afternoon, Charla brought Erika home, where she would be staying until Monday morning, when Darren was scheduled to take over custody. It would be their first exchange outside school since signing the new agreement forbidding either one from physically being within a hundred yards of the other's property.

Early on Saturday morning, Darren Mack called Charla, saying it was important that they talk on Monday morning when she brought over Erika. He refused to elaborate, making her suspicious.

She then asked if he was planning to secretly tape their conversation to use against her in a custody hearing. Darren vehemently denied it, saying that they would talk outside so he wouldn't be able to use a tape recorder. He kept repeating how it was important that they talk and was very insistent.

That night, Charla called her friend Jacqueline Ross, who she was meeting at 9:30 a.m. on Monday morning, right after dropping Erika off with her father.

"She was terrified and shaking," said Ross, "because he wanted to see her Monday morning. He had said he wanted to talk about the settlement and she was scared to death."

Ross then came up with a plan, so Charla would not have to deal with her estranged husband.

"I said, 'Give Erika a little kiss,'" she recalled. "Open the door, let her out, and drive off. You don't have to stay and talk to him. Just say, 'I can't. I've changed my mind.' You don't have to get out of the car.

"So that was the plan when we got off the phone Saturday night. Unfortunately it did not work out."

A few miles across town, Darren Mack was over at Alecia Biddison's house for a romantic dinner date.

"We had a traditional family night at the house," she recalled, "and he stayed the night."

Over a barbecue, they discussed spending Father's Day together the following weekend at Alecia's home. They planned to celebrate with Erika and Alecia's little son, Brandon, as they had decided to go to the next step in their relationship and meld their families.

"We were making plans for Father's Day weekend," said Biddison, "to spend it together with our children. We had made some decisions. We were transitioning our relationship. And we felt it was appropriate at that point in time to spend some time with our children together and see how that worked."

She remembers Darren being upbeat and optimistic that night about overturning Judge Weller's recent ruling. For he had hired yet another new lawyer to handle the appeal in the supreme court.

"He had an appeal he was filing," she said, "that would potentially stop all the proceedings and reverse some of these decisions that Judge Weller was making."

Over dinner, Darren invited Alecia to go shooting the following day, and she agreed.

Darren Mack stayed the night at Alecia's house, leaving early the next morning to return to Fleur de Lis and collect the rifles and ammunition for the shoot. Then, back in his condo, he e-mailed Alecia to thank her for dinner, saying he had had "a wonderful experience" the night before.

Several hours later, Darren Mack loaded his rifles into the back of his Jeep Cherokee. He drove north on Route 445 to the Pyramid Highway in Sparks, where he met Alecia Biddison and Palace managers Eric Maiss and Mark Stone, who were joining them for the shoot.

"We all loaded up the cars and drove out to a place where people routinely go shooting," said Biddison, "and did a little target practicing."

Darren Mack and his two employees were firing AR-15 rifles at exploding targets from the standing position, while Alecia Biddison used her personal Glock 35 40 handgun.

According to Biddison, Mack, who was an expert shot, failed to hit the long-range target that day. Eventually they ran out of exploding targets, so everyone quickly gulped down their water and soda so they could shoot at cans.

That evening, Darren Mack called Dan Osborne on his cell phone to ask a favor. Osborne was cleaning out the new apartment that he was moving into the next day when he received the call.

Darren explained that Charla was bringing Erika over at 9:00 a.m. the following morning and asked if Dan could take Erika over to Joan Mack's house, as Darren had errands to run. Osborne said that would not be a problem, as he was staying over at the Fleur de Lis condo that night before moving all his stuff out.

That apparently innocent telephone call—the very first item on Darren Mack's to-do list—would set in motion a chain of horrific events that would shake Reno to its very core.

PART TWO

CHAPTER TWENTY-TWO

Bloodlust

Darren Mack got up early Monday morning, putting on a T-shirt and jeans. At around 7:00 a.m., he came out of his bedroom, telling Dan Osborne he was going out to run some errands. Then he drove out to Truckee, stopping off at his mother's house on the way home.

On his return, detectives believe, Darren Mack began executing his to-do list. First he parked his gold Jeep Cherokee across the street, outside his cousin Corey Schmidt's town house. He moved the rented Ford Explorer SUV into his double garage, leaving an empty space. Then he placed two .243 hunting rifles with ammunition and a pair of binoculars in the rear cargo area. He had also packed a green Andiamo suitcase with $37,000 in $100 bills as well as spare clothes and other things he would need when he had finished what he had set out to do.

At 8:30 a.m., Dan Osborne returned from walking Rusty and noticed the rented Ford Explorer in the garage and the Jeep Cherokee across the road in Cory Schmidt's driveway. One of the garage doors was also open, so he began carrying his belongings downstairs through the garage and into his car.

Inside the condo, Mack was finalizing his plans. He had previously printed up MapQuest directions to Shawn Meador's law office and checked Judge Weller's court schedule on the official family court Web site, ensuring that the judge would be in chambers that morning.

At around 8:45 a.m., Darren Mack came out of his town house, confirming Osborne would take Erika over to her grandmother's house after Charla arrived with her. As they were talking, Corey Schmidt backed his BMW convertible out of his garage, stopping off for a brief chat on his way to work at Palace Jewelry and Loan.

"Darren was standing on his driveway next to Dan Osborne," he recalled, "and I talked to him real quick. 'How's it going, Cuz? What's going on? Not too much.'"

Then Mack promised to move his Jeep Cherokee out of his driveway.

"I go, 'That's fine, whatever,'" said Schmidt. "And then I just said, 'All right, man, I'll see you at the store later on. Bye, Cousin.' And I drove off."

Earlier that morning, Charla Mack had telephoned Laura Cunningham in a panic. Darren's Saturday call had greatly disturbed her, and she had become increasingly worried about his true intentions.

"I talked to her before she left to drop off Erika," said Cunningham. "She was concerned because she'd gotten a phone call from him, wanting to discuss things. She thought it was very strange, as he never wanted to talk to her. She said, 'What do you think this is about?'"

Laura warned that he was probably going to secretly tape-record their conversation as ammunition against her at the upcoming custody hearing. So she advised Charla not to get out of her car under any circumstance, sending Erika out if he wanted to talk to her and then drive off to avoid a confrontation.

After the call, Charla dressed Erika and prepared her lunch, putting it in a Tupperware container. She then packed all the clothes the child would need for her three-week stay with her father. Finally she dressed, putting on a red shirt and blue Gap sweat pants, brushing her long hair, and doing her makeup.

Just after 9:00 a.m., Charla, Erika, and their pet dog, Sparkles, left the Alder Bridge Court house for the three-mile drive north to Darren Mack's town house. It was a bright, sunny day with temperatures already in the seventies and little traffic on the side roads.

At precisely 9:20 a.m., Charla's silver Lexus pulled up at the front gates of the Fleur de Lis complex and was photographed by surveillance video. The attendant on duty, Brian Doebrick, asked her name and who she was visiting for the sign-in sheet. Charla replied she was "the estranged wife" who had come to see Darren Mack in Unit 1006.

The bewildered attendant then opened the electronic gates, waving her through. A few moments later Charla pulled up in front of 1006 Fleur de Lis, where Darren was chatting with Dan Osborne in the garage.

As soon as he saw her, Darren came out of the garage and walked over. He opened the Lexus passenger side door, gently lifting his daughter out of the car. Then Charla got out and came over to talk to Darren.

She strolled over to Osborne, whom she had never met, shaking his hand in a friendly manner.

"Then she turned around to get some stuff for Erika," Osborne recalled, "and Darren said, 'We're going to go upstairs.'"

Darren Mack left Erika and Dan Osborne watching television, investigators believe, and retrieved a brown bag with a large knife in it that he had previously left at the top of the stairs. Then he walked back down and into the garage.

Later, using forensic evidence and blood spatter patterns, detectives would carefully reconstruct what they think happened next.

When Darren Mack came downstairs, Charla was waiting for him in the driveway. Somehow he lured her into the garage, as she would have been wary about going in alone.

Once inside, investigators believe, Darren Mack pulled out a large Gerber double-edged dagger—used by the Army for close combat—and attacked her from behind.

Perhaps Charla screamed in terror as Darren threw her onto the garage floor. He began lunging at her neck with the knife. Instinctively, Charla crossed her arms to protect her face, sustaining stab wounds to her hands, left wrist, and inner arm.

The diminutive 120-pound woman desperately fought for her life, but didn't stand a chance against the six-foot, two-hundred-pound champion bodybuilder. As she desperately kicked out at her attacker, one of her shoes came flying off. But he was relentless in his ferocity, stabbing her lower legs and the back of her neck.

Dan Osborne's pet dog, Rusty, was so upset by Charla's screams that somehow he climbed out of the Honda, running into the garage barking. When Darren saw the large, powerfully built bull mastiff-Labrador mix come in, he thought Rusty was going to attack him.

Darren finally plunged the hunting knife deep into his wife's neck, severing the left carotid artery carrying the blood from her heart to the brain. The blade cut through her esophagus, almost slicing her trachea in half.

He then brutally placed his knee on the right side of Charla's head, using his full weight to pin her down on the cold cement floor as he watched her die.

Later he would describe how Charla was gurgling and gasping for air as blood spurted out of her gaping neck wound onto the garage walls.

Darren Mack brutally stabbed Charla seven times, but the deep wound to her carotid artery was the one that killed her. It bled into her trachea, making her cough up blood and leaving her unable to breathe.

It would have taken between three to five minutes for Charla to lose consciousness and finally die as her soon-to-be ex-husband pinned her head to the ground.

When he was satisfied Charla was dead, accomplishing

the "END PROBLEM" item on his checklist, he wrapped the bloody knife in a towel. Then he closed the garage door as Rusty, who was covered in Charla's blood, fled yelping up the stairs and into the house.

Darren Mack came upstairs like a ghost, a large bath towel wrapped around a cut to his hand. He passed within a few feet of Dan Osborne and Erika as they were examining Rusty's bloody fur. Then, without a word, he went into his bedroom and closed the door.

"His head was down," Osborne would later testify. "He had a kind of a weird look on his face. He went into his room."

After seeing his friend's bizarre behavior and Rusty covered in fresh blood, Osborne grabbed Erika and left through the front door without going through the garage.

Once inside his bedroom, investigators believe, Darren Mack undressed, took off his bloody clothes, and dressed his hand wound. He put the empty Gerber dagger sheath and his belt in a closet along with his clothes soaked in Charla's blood.

He then took a shower to wash off Charla's blood before putting on some clean clothes.

After redressing his hand wound, Darren finished packing his green Andiamo suitcase with a change of clothes and toiletries. He had decided to go to Mexico after completing his remaining task.

Then he phoned his longtime friend Mike Laub, a prominent Reno attorney.

"He told me had an altercation with Charla," Laub later testified. "He killed Charla."

Mack went back into the garage and dragged Charla's lifeless body across the cold cement floor to the back, leaving a trail of blood in her wake.

Sticking to his to-do List, he then opened the garage door and walked out into the bright sunshine. He got inside Charla's Lexus, grabbing the keys with his right hand and turning on the ignition, leaving a mixture of blood, hers and his, on the keys. He then drove her Lexus into the garage, turning off the engine and tossing the bloody keys onto the passenger seat.

He cracked open the back window so Erika's dog, Sparkles, could breathe. He also took Charla's cell phone and put it in his pocket, leaving the brown Trader Joe's bag that had contained the knife on the passenger floor.

Darren got in the Ford Explorer, putting the knife he had used to murder Charla in the back before reversing the car out of the garage and into the driveway. Then he moved his Jeep Cherokee out of Corey Schmidt's driveway and into the garage and closed both doors.

At 10:03 a.m., Darren Mack's rented Ford Explorer was captured on the Fleur de Lis security video leaving his town house. Three minutes later, he called the management office, saying it would not be necessary to clean his residence that day.

"He asked me not to have the [cleaning lady] come by to do the cleaning," recalled the complex's assistant manager, Lisa Carpenter. "I remember him being a little bit rushed but calm and collected. He asked me how I was doing . . . [and said] have a nice day."

Fifteen minutes earlier, Dan Osborne had left the Fleur de Lis complex, turning right into Wilbur May Parkway. He had noticed that Charla Mack's Lexus was still parked where she had left it, but now both garage doors were closed and there was no sign of her.

"Erika was freaking out," Osborne recalled. "There was blood on the dog. I was trying to get her to a safe place."

After briefly stopping off at a pond to wash the blood off Rusty, Osborne headed toward Erika's grandmother's house across town.

Then suddenly his cell phone rang and Darren Mack was on the line.

"He asked me to meet him at Starbucks," said Osborne, "so he could see his daughter."

Osborne nervously told Mack he knew that Starbucks and headed there. But a few minutes later he realized he had missed it as he was about to hit the 395 freeway.

"So called Darren back and asked where it was," said Osborne. "He told me . . . so I turned around and went to that location."

When he arrived, Osborne drove into the parking lot to find Darren Mack waving him down. As they got out of the car, Osborne noticed Mack had changed his shirt. He did not ask what had happened back at the house, as he was too scared.

"[Darren] looked at me and said he wanted to talk to Erika," Osborne said. "And I said, 'OK.' I knew that he carried a gun and I wasn't going to say anything for the safety of both myself and Erika."

Then Mack calmly told him to go into Starbucks, so he could have a few minutes alone with his daughter.

"He asked me if I wanted anything from Starbucks," said Osborne. "I said no. He asked Erika. She said, 'Yes, I'll have a lemon bar.' And he said, 'Can you get me an iced tea?' and I said, 'Sure.'"

Then Mack gave his friend some money, sending him off into Starbucks while he remained outside with Erika.

Later Darren Mack would explain that he wanted to talk to Erika, as it might be the last time he ever saw her. He told her that he loved her and not to believe anything that she might hear about him later on.

About ten minutes later, Osborne came out with the lemon bar and iced tea, handing Mack the change.

"He hugged Erika," Osborne recalled, "gave her a kiss, and said, 'Okay.' We put her in the car and I said, 'I'll see you later,' and drove off."

Dan Osborne then drove to Joan Mack's house on Ambrosia Drive, Reno, and dropped off Erika. He then took Darren's mother to one side, saying Darren had done something bad to Charla, and he was calling the police.

CHAPTER TWENTY-THREE

"I've Been Shot!"

After kissing his daughter good-bye, Darren Mack headed toward downtown Reno. Detectives believe he originally intended to stop off at Shawn Meador's law offices at 6100 Neil Road but changed his mind at the last minute.

Instead, he drove to the Galleria Garage at 135 North Sierra Street. Previously he had scoped it out, discovering it offered a perfect unobstructed view of Judge Chuck Weller's third-floor chambers, 170 yards away across the Truckee River. It was the same office in the Mills Lane Justice Center where he and Charla had first met the judge nine months earlier.

On the way there, it is believed he disposed of the bloody Gerber knife and Charla's blood-soaked clothes.

Then, at 10:38 a.m., Darren made the first of seven cell phone calls over the next eighteen minutes. He called his personal assistant, Cindy King, several times, asking her to renew the Ford Explorer rental agreement. He also called his life coach and landlady, Carol Kelley.

At 10:42 a.m., Mack's silver Ford Explorer was captured by surveillance cameras entering the Galleria Garage, going up to the fifth floor, and parking in a space by the south wall.

For the next few minutes, Darren Mack carefully set up his equipment in the back of the SUV. He loaded his .243

bolt-action rifle with ammunition, focusing his high-powered binoculars on Judge Weller, who was chatting with his administrative assistant in his chambers.

It was a beautiful day, with perfect conditions. Although his target was the equivalent of almost two football fields away, it did not present too many problems to the experienced marksman—who was nicknamed "the Doctor" for his surgical shooting precision.

At 10:55 a.m., Landon Mack called his brother's cell phone. He was concerned something was wrong after learning that Dan Osborne had brought Erika over to their mother's house.

When Darren answered, Landon asked if everything was okay.

"Hey, now's not a good time," his brother replied. "I'm not having a good day. I'll talk to you later."

After hanging up, Mack got back behind the wheel and started the engine. Then, at 10:56 a.m., he made a three-point turn, reversing into the parking spot so the back hatch of the Explorer was facing the Mills Lane Justice Center.

Two minutes later, he raised up the glass hatch. He picked up the .243 rifle, training its telescopic sights on Judge Weller, who was standing by his bookcase.

At 11:05 a.m., with the judge firmly in his crosshairs, Darren Mack pulled the trigger.

Half an hour earlier, Judge Chuck Weller had disrobed after finishing up his last family court hearing of the morning. It was his first day back from vacation, and he had gone into his chambers to catch up on court business with his young administrative assistant, Annie Allison.

Around 11:00 a.m., Allison was called to the front counter to handle a query about an upcoming family court hearing. On her way out of the office, she remembered something she needed to tell the judge about a lunch date.

Judge Weller was standing by the window, straightening out his bookcase, and they started talking.

Suddenly there was a loud pop and a blinding flash of light, and everything went into slow motion.

Judge Weller felt a painful burning in his chest and grabbed it. Initially he thought his cell phone must have exploded in his shirt pocket, before remembering he did not have it with him.

He looked down and, to his horror, saw blood gushing out of his chest through the now exposed flesh.

"I've been hit!" he screamed at his terrified assistant, who was already running out of the office. He dropped to the floor, glimpsing a hole through the window. The judge started crawling over to the door, staying near the ground, realizing the shot had come out of the second window and the assailant could be preparing to fire off another round.

Then Judge Weller coolly took an "inventory" of himself.

"I knew that I had been shot," he later explained, "but I didn't know if I was okay or not. I didn't know if there was a bullet in the wall of my heart, and that if I moved I was going to bleed out. I didn't know what the situation was.

"I was conscious. My fingers moved. My arms moved. My legs moved. I knew I was bleeding. I knew that I had more than one hole in me and I didn't know if I was going to die or not."

Suddenly he remembered the vicious Internet postings attacking him, fearing that his wife and children could now be in danger.

"Call my family! Get them out of the house!" he yelled to Allison, who was now in the hallway.

Annie Allison had initially thought Judge Weller was being dramatic and overreacting.

"I thought a fluorescent bulb had burst," she remembered, "and then my ears started to pound and hurt. Then I realized this was not fake."

Terrified, she ran out of the chambers, colliding with Sergeant Tim O'Connor of the Washoe County Sheriff's office, who had come to investigate what was going on.

"She ran past me screaming," he said. "The first words that I could hear were 'Gunshots! Judge Weller's been shot!'"

Sergeant O'Connor and another deputy drew their weapons and went into Judge Weller's office, assuming the shooter was in there.

"When I opened the door," said O'Connor, "Judge Weller was crawling out on his belly. He said, 'I believe I've been shot' . . . [H]e had blood on his face and on his glasses. So we grabbed him and pulled him out and let the door close behind him."

Judge Weller told Annie Allison to call his wife and tell her to leave their home immediately with their daughters. So Allison dashed into the reception area, where deputies were trying to get everyone away from the windows.

"One deputy was trying to shoosh me away," she remembered, "and I said, 'I have to make a phone call!' And she said, 'No, you do not.' And I ripped myself out of her arms and slid under a desk and grabbed her phone."

She then called Judge Weller's house and his youngest daughter answered. Allison asked her to get her mother, and a few seconds later Rosa Weller came on the line.

"I said, 'Get the girls and get out of the house,'" said Allison. "'Chuck's been shot. I think he's okay, but get out of the house.'"

A deputy pulled her out from under the desk, snatching the phone away. Allison was then taken down a back stairwell to the first floor, where terrified court staff had started to gather.

Somebody told Allison that she was bleeding.

"And then I started to touch my neck," she said. "I was stinging all over and it felt like I had been stung by bees in my hip and in my neck."

Officer Stafford and Sergeant O'Connor burst into Judge Weller's chambers in tactical stance, uncertain if there was a shooter inside.

"We were fully anticipating to encounter an armed

combatant in his office," O'Connor later testified. "We opened the door. Stafford was beneath me. I stood above him."

The office was covered in glass from the hole in the second window, and O'Connor saw that the shot had come from the direction of the Galleria movie theater and garage.

To their horror, they realized that there was a dangerous sniper on the loose in downtown Reno.

The sergeant radioed the court dispatch center.

"I notified our court control," he said, "that we had a shooter on the outside of the building and to call in the SWAT team. We didn't know whether this person was going to continue trying to shoot at pedestrians, judges, or anyone. We had to locate this individual."

Meanwhile, Judge Weller was lying in a third-floor hallway, badly injured and bleeding heavily.

"There were deputy sheriffs swarming with guns drawn," he recalled. "One ran into my office and was looking for a shooter. And I told him, 'No, it came from outside.'"

While the deputies were busy evacuating everybody from the third floor, Judge Weller borrowed a cell phone and called his wife.

"I told her that I had been shot," he said. "They were already out of the house and driving away. And I told her to go to the airport—just drive somewhere and not even say [where] on the telephone—because I didn't know what the circumstances were. I was just telling her to go away, just disappear until this is sorted out. I was wondering if it would be the last time I would ever speak to her . . . would I ever see my two children again."

After the call, Judge Weller lay on his back with his shirt open as Deputy William Wilhoyte administered first aid with two paramedics who had arrived.

"There was a lot of blood on Judge Weller's upper left shoulder," said Wilhoyte. "There were two major injuries that I saw there, two separate holes, and the medics asked me if I could apply pressure to these wounds, which I did."

While the paramedics were getting an IV started, the deputy told Judge Weller that he would be okay.

"He was very very cool," said Wilhoyte. "He seemed to be able to answer all of their questions coherently, concisely. He was probably calmer than I was."

While Judge Weller was being put on a gurney to be taken to the hospital, Deputy Wilhoyte asked if he had any idea who might have fired the shot.

The judge said they should look for a "Daryl Mack," meaning Darren Mack but getting the first name mixed up with a recently executed convict.

"I just confused it," Judge Weller explained later, "It was the same last name. I'd just been shot. I was losing a lot of blood. And then they took me away on a gurney down the prisoners' elevator and whisked me away to the hospital."

As Judge Chuck Weller was being taken away in an ambulance, Reno police detective John Ferguson arrived at the Mills Lane Justice Center. He interviewed Annie Allison, who was in the process of having bullet fragments removed by medics.

"She provided me with a basic understanding of what happened inside the room, what was going on at the time the Judge was shot," said Detective Ferguson.

The detective, who had already been assigned to the courthouse to head up the investigation, did not know if the sniper was still out there or how many shots had been fired.

"Normally, in a sniper situation, you have the first shot that breaks the window," he explained. "The next shot is the one that is supposed to kill the person."

The detective needed to know if Judge Weller was the sniper's target or if there was a madman out there just shooting from the rooftops.

"There are just the infinite possibilities of who would be pissed off at a judge," said the detective, "especially in family court."

Detective Ferguson asked Allison if Judge Weller was having any problems with anybody.

"She [mentioned] Darren Mack," he said. "She named a couple of other people, but Darren was one of them."

After Allison was taken away on a gurney, Detective Ferguson took the elevator up to the third floor. He wanted to examine Judge Weller's chambers and ensure that the crime scene was being preserved.

He found several Washoe County deputies standing guard outside the judge's chambers, which had been cordoned off with police tape.

After being given the all-clear, Detective Ferguson went inside to examine the second window's pane, where the bullet had entered. The double-pane window was almost completely gone, with glass scattered all over the inside.

"The shot had come outside to inside," he explained. "There was a small, almost triangular-shaped piece of glass that appeared to have a bullet strike."

There were also numerous small yellow-colored bullet fragments covering two of the walls.

In a bookshelf on the south wall, bullet fragments had entered the metal spine of a book's binding, ripping through the pages.

Using the fragment's trajectory, Detective Ferguson deduced that the bullet had come from a southerly direction. As he looked out of the remains of the window, the most logical place seemed to be the Galleria parking garage, directly north across the Truckee River, which had an unobstructed view of Judge Weller's office.

CHAPTER TWENTY-FOUR

Sniper

Just after 11:00 a.m., Reno police detective Ron Chalmers Jr. was typing a report at his desk, when the three-beep emergency alert sounded. It was immediately followed by a police radio report that a sniper was on the loose at the Mills Lane Justice Center.

"I'm part of the SWAT team," said Detective Chalmers, "so when I heard the report, I envisioned somebody who's gone to high ground, randomly shooting at people."

As Detective Chalmers dashed out of his office to his car, he feared another Texas school tower shooting like the August 1966 massacre when former marine Charles Whitman slaughtered sixteen people and wounded thirty-two others during an on-campus shooting rampage.

But as he drove the few blocks across town to the justice center, he learned that a judge had been shot and was down.

"So I raced to the scene," he recalled. "Fortunately for us, in our investigation the sniper had fired through glass, which helped us to determine a couple of the most likely locations he had fired from."

The Galleria parking garage had already been identified as a possible location; so had the nearby thirteen-story Palladio Condominium, still under construction.

At 11:30 a.m., Detective Chalmers reached the parking garage and downtown Reno was in chaos. A three-by-five-block area had been closed off and was swarming with scores of heavily armed police officers. A police helicopter circled overhead, as the entire downtown area was cleared. Dozens of people abandoned their cars on Second Street, hiding in various businesses and restaurants.

All three Reno courthouses were in lockdown, with about two hundred people nervously waiting inside the buildings. The Reno Police Department was setting up an emergency command post at West Second and Sierra streets to coordinate the sniper search.

"I threw on my heavy SWAT vest," said Detective Chalmers, "and my helmet and rifle. Then we began searching those two buildings for the shooter."

For the next ninety minutes, Detective Chalmers and the other SWAT team members searched the garage for the sniper, sneaking in and then combing through it floor by floor.

Then, at noon, the SWAT team left the garage, scurrying across Sierra Street to start searching the Palladio.

Two trained K9 dogs also checked for a possible explosive device under Judge Weller's car but found nothing. A few blocks away, SWAT officers burst into the Riverside 12 movie theater, ordering thirty stunned patrons outside while they checked the seating row by row.

"We searched the parking garage and then the condominium tower," said Detective Chalmers. "After that, I figured the shooter was gone."

After leaving the Galleria parking garage, Darren Mack had headed west on Interstate 80, toward Sacramento. He threw out Charla's cell phone by the side of the freeway, just west of the Robb Drive exit. But the phone was still working and over the next few hours several of her concerned friends would call.

Later, Reno police were able to track his route through

various Sprint towers, as he was carrying his Treo smart-phone. At 11:10 a.m., he made a call that was picked up by the UNR cell tower, just a few blocks away from Palace Jewelry and Loan on North Virginia Street.

At 11:19 a.m., Darren called his first cousin Jeff Donner in Moraga, California, where he had filmed his *On Second Thought* TV interview. Mack said that if anything happened to him, he must tell the world "the true story" about judicial injustice.

But before Donner, sixty-three, could get him to elaborate, Darren Mack hung up. And when his cousin called back, there was no answer.

At 11:25 a.m., Mack made another call, which was picked up by a tower at Verdi Township/West Truckee Meadows. A few minutes later the Sprint tower at the Boreal Mountain Ski Resort intercepted another.

News of Judge Weller's shooting spread around Reno like wildfire. Garret Idle was working in his real estate office at about 11:46 a.m. when he learned about it.

The first thing he did was call Darren Mack with the news.

"I got on the phone with Darren," said Idle. "I said, 'Hey, Darren, I just heard that Judge Weller got shot.' And he sounded very calm, saying, 'I'm busy right now. I can't talk but I'll talk to you later.' OK, fine. And that was the last time I ever spoke to Darren."

As Deputy Sheriff William Wilhoyte loaded Judge Chuck Weller's gurney into an ambulance, he ordered the driver to turn off the sirens and flashing lights for the short drive to Washoe County Medical Center.

"We didn't want to provide a target for anyone who may be shooting at the court or trying to take a shot at the judge," he later explained.

Once they arrived at Washoe Medical Center, Wilhoyte had another deputy go out and carry out a cursory check of the emergency entrance area.

"When we felt safe, we moved the judge from the ambulance," said the deputy sheriff, "and took him directly into the trauma room."

Once in the trauma room, the hospital staff laid the wounded judge on a table and cut all his clothes off. Then, after giving him oxygen, they began a barrage of tests.

While the doctors were working on him, Reno police detective Shanna Wallin-Reed arrived to interview the judge.

"There were doctors and nurses surrounding him," she recalled. "It was clear that he had some injuries to his chest area."

Detective Wallin-Reed asked Judge Weller who could have shot him. As one of the nurses lifted the oxygen mask off his face so he could speak, the judge said, "Daryl Mack," adding that he was the presiding judge in Mack's "high-dollar" divorce and custody case. He also told the detective that he suspected that Mack was responsible for negative Internet postings against him as well as a hoax advertisement about a motorcycle in a local publication.

The detective called her superior, Sergeant Randy Saulnier, telling him what the judge had said. He told her to go back and clarify if the judge had really meant Darren Mack. Judge Weller confirmed that he had.

He was then wheeled into the operating room, where doctors found five entry wounds where bullet shrapnel had pierced his chest. There were also wounds on the back of his left arm, abdomen, left knee, and right hand. All the wounds were between one and five centimeters, and there was a large piece of shrapnel embedded in his lower left flank.

Surgeons carefully removed the fragments, sending them to a police laboratory for forensic testing. It took forty stitches to close up the wounds, and one piece of shrapnel was buried so deeply in the judge's chest that doctors left it in.

Corey Schmidt was working at Palace Jewelry and Loan when all hell broke loose in downtown Reno. There were police swarming everywhere and loudspeaker messages ordering everybody to stay inside because of a sniper.

"There was a frenzy going on," Schmidt recalled. "I was on the phone with Joan Mack at the exact time they said there was a judge shot. And I go, 'I hope it was Weller.' I said this jokingly but Joan had already spoken to Dan Osborne and she said, 'Is Jory there?' I said yes. Then she said, 'Can you send him here?'"

After sending Jory home to his grandmother, Schmidt called Darren Mack's cell phone to see what was going on. It went straight to voice mail. Corey then left to go to a doctor's appointment.

"I told my doctor, 'There's something weird going on, man,'" Corey said.

At around 1:30 p.m., the SWAT teams were finally called off, as the shooter was obviously long gone. After taking off his bulletproof vest, Detective Chalmers checked in with his Reno PD robbery/homicide boss, Sergeant Randy Saulnier.

"He told me, 'We just got a call and somebody has given us some information about Darren Mack,'" Chalmers recalled. "'I need you to go back to the station and start looking up Darren Mack, and see what you can find.'"

After leaving Joan Mack's house, Dan Osborne had dialed 911 to report his suspicions. He told a police dispatcher what had happened at Darren Mack's condo, saying he believed his friend had done something terrible to his estranged wife.

"I asked if they were going to call me back," said Osborne. "They said, 'No, you call us back in about twenty minutes, and we'll let you know what's going on.'"

After the call, several uniformed patrol officers were sent to Unit 1006 at the Fleur de Lis complex for a "welfare check." But after no one answered the front door, they left, seeing nothing suspicious.

By then Dan Osborne had arrived at his new apartment

and dropped off Rusty. A few minutes later he received a call
from a friend named Toni Lackey, who had just seen a news-
flash about Judge Chuck Weller's shooting. Lackey used to
work for Darren Mack at Palace as a jeweler, and was aware
of his contentious divorce.

"I knew how much Darren hated the judge," she recalled,
"and that he was furious with him, so I called Dan and said,
'Did you know the judge was shot?'"

Osborne then told her what he had witnessed earlier at
Fleur De Lis, and his fears that Darren had murdered Charla.
He said he had already called the police, but they had not
been very forthcoming.

At about 1:05 p.m., Lackey called 911 herself and was
eventually put through to Reno Police Department robbery/
homicide detective David Jenkins. Lackey told the detective
what Dan Osborne had told her, saying she believed Mack
had harmed his wife before going downtown and shooting
the judge.

Ten minutes later, Detective Jenkins arrived at Toni
Lackey's house on Humboldt Street in Reno to interview Dan
Osborne, who told him what he had seen.

"I was concerned," recalled Detective Jenkins, "that a seriously injured person might have been inside the residence in
the complex."

So he asked Osborne and Lackey to accompany him to
Darren Mack's residence, to point out exactly what had happened and where.

On his way to the Fleur de Lis complex, Detective Jenkins called his colleague Detective Ron Chalmers and asked
him to meet him there.

"I'd come back to the station and had started [researching]
Darren Mack," said Chalmers. "Dave Jenkins called me and
said, 'Hey, this does not sound good. I need you to meet me
down there.' And I said, 'Well, I think I know where you're
going,' because I'd pulled [Mack] up on the computer."

Although Darren Mack had no criminal record, Detective Chalmers had a "very bad feeling" as he jumped in his

police car. On the way over he called his children, just in case something bad was to happen.

"I raced down there with the lights and sirens on," he said. "It had started to occur to me that [Judge Weller] was an intended target: [the shooter was] lashing out at the judicial system. I don't know what we're in for here: this is a man who just potentially shot at a judge."

As Reno detectives were racing toward his residence, Darren Mack crossed the state line into California, arriving at Sacramento International Airport. At 1:57 p.m., he drove his rented Ford Explorer into the parking garage and received a time-stamped receipt.

Days earlier, Darren had purchased an airline ticket to Mexico, but police believe he now panicked after seeing the heavy cable TV coverage of Judge Weller's shooting in the terminal, realizing he had already been named as a suspect.

"I don't think he estimated that he would get national media," said lead detective Ron Chalmers. "I think that's when he changes his plans and decides to drive to Mexico, so he does not have to show ID."

At 2:30 p.m., Darren Mack drove out of the garage, paying the parking charge with his Palace Jewelry and Loan corporate American Express card. Then he headed south toward San Diego and the Mexican border.

CHAPTER TWENTY-FIVE

"He Killed My Baby!"

At 2:15 p.m., Detectives Ron Chalmers and David Jenkins met outside the front gate of the Fleur de Lis complex. Dan Osborne directed them to Darren Mack's unit, and Jenkins parked outside.

During the drive over, Osborne had told Detective Jenkins further disturbing details of that morning. He described Charla parking her Lexus SUV in front of the condo and one of the garage doors being open. But half an hour later, when he had fled with Erika, her vehicle was gone and both garage doors were closed.

After telling Osborne and Lackey to wait inside his car, Detective Jenkins walked up to the garage, observing three small drops of blood on the concrete driveway outside.

"I saw several stains that I believed [were] blood," said Jenkins. "So it increased my anxiety level."

The detectives were now concerned that someone was inside the garage. Jenkins knocked on the front door and, after getting no answer, called Reno police headquarters for the phone number of the residence.

"We tried to call into the residence several times," Chalmers recalled, "and got the answering machine."

After Darren Mack's greeting finished, Detective Jenkins left a stern message: "Darren! This is the Reno Police Department, and we're here to check on the welfare of someone inside. We need you to pick up the phone or come outside."

Getting no response, the detectives decided to go into the house in case someone was injured. They radioed for uniformed police backup.

"I'm thinking maybe he's barricaded himself inside," said Detective Chalmers. "We recognized the potential of bad things."

Dan Osborne gave the detectives the numeric code to open the garage doors. After entering it on the keypad, the left garage door slowly opened, revealing a silver Lexus with something moving around in the rear cargo area.

"I could see movement," Detective Chalmers said. He stepped back, reaching for his gun. "Somebody was in the car. I didn't know what, and I'm yelling out, 'Let me see your hands!'"

After a few moments, the detectives' eyes adjusted to the dark, and they realized that it was Charla's German short-haired pointer, Sparkles.

Meanwhile, Detective Jenkins crouched on the ground, peering underneath the Lexus.

They cautiously proceeded farther into the garage, seeing Darren Mack's gold Jeep Cherokee parked alongside the Lexus to its left. There was a large trail of smeared blood going across the front of both vehicles and underneath the Jeep. The tires of both vehicles were covered in blood.

Then, as they came closer, they saw the body of a small woman lying facedown in front of the Lexus in a large pool of blood. Her right arm was pulled across her face, as if she had been trying to defend herself.

"She's just lying at the front of the garage," Detective Chalmers stated. "You could see the large blood trail smear leading to her body.

"She had a very severe incised injury to the left side of her neck. It was a very gruesome cut and caused a significant amount of damage. It was very nasty, clearly a very violent and effective cut.

"I recall specifically that she had one [green] shoe on. She was wearing those plastic Crocs. And one had fallen off. I remember a towel being laid against her. Laying on her."

Detective Jenkins checked for any signs of life.

"I reached out and felt the exposed skin of her ankle," he said. "The skin was noticeably cold to the touch. The next thing I did was try and manipulate that ankle a little bit to see if it moved freely. Rigor mortis was present, which is an [indication] of death."

Detective Jenkins watched Charla's chest for any signs of breathing, but there were none. Finally he checked her pulse before concluding she was dead.

The detectives now decided to go into the condo. Dan Osborne had told them that Darren Mack was an avid hunter with plenty of firearms, and they feared he had barricaded himself inside.

"We could see the large blood trail where her body was dragged," Chalmers explained, "and we could see that this Jeep that Mr. Osborne had told us was Darren's vehicle [had] pulled over the blood. I'm thinking, *He's barricaded himself inside here,* because clearly his car's been pulled in over the blood."

At 3:00 p.m., Jenkins radioed police headquarters to request that a SWAT team be dispatched to the Fleur de Lis complex immediately.

"Our concern was for Darren," said Detective Chalmers. "Is Darren hurt inside as well? Is he holed up in there and [does he want] to shoot it out with us, the police? What is he doing? We don't know."

A few minutes later, Reno Police Department SWAT team leader Detective Jerry Burkey arrived. Within seconds, half a dozen members of his team had joined him. On his way over, Burkey had been briefed that they were going to enter the second-floor condo through the garage and to expect trouble.

Burkey led his heavily armed SWAT officers into the garage, where they carefully negotiated the way around Charla Mack's bloody body.

"We had to step over her to gain access to the condo," he later said. "We were very careful with our footing [so as] not to disturb any possible evidence. Then we made entry through [a single swing] door into the condo."

Detective Burkey led his team through a short hallway and up the stairs into a living room. After searching it, Burkey provided cover for other officers as they searched the two bedrooms and bathroom lying off the hallway.

"We did a very slow tactical [search], given the circumstances," said Detective Chalmers, who went with them.

During the sweep, Reno police sergeant Mike Lessman entered Darren Mack's master bedroom. On the floor he found an assortment of explosive materials he immediately recognized as ingredients commonly used in manufacturing bombs.

When Detective Chalmers inspected the en suite bathroom, he noticed a large color photograph of Darren Mack flexing his muscles in the Mr. Nevada contest.

"It was right above his toilet," Detective Chalmers said, "so literally as he's peeing in the morning he can look at himself in his Speedos, flexing. That was one of the first indications to me that this person is obviously very egotistical."

Landon Mack was at his mother's house when a SWAT team burst in to see if Darren was hiding out there. His 2006 Hummer 2 had already been found parked nearby.

"They wanted to see what we knew," said Landon. "I mean, I don't know what's going on. Where's my brother? Maybe he's in a ditch somewhere."

Alecia Biddison was on a business trip in California, when she first learned of Judge Weller's shooting from a friend who had seen it on television.

"What came into my mind was *This is unbelievable. I've got to call Darren and tell him*," she recalled.

But when she couldn't reach Darren on his cell phone, Alecia sent him a text message saying, "Judge Weller's been shot! Call me."

"I made every effort to try and contact Darren," she said, "because I was beside myself, thinking, *Oh my gosh. I can't believe this has happened.*"

Later that day, Biddison was listening to Reno talk radio station KKOH, when she learned Darren Mack had been named as a person of interest in the shooting.

She panicked, making three calls to the Reno Police Department. Detectives would later claim that she told them she was scared of Darren Mack and needed protection. But she would vehemently dispute that, explaining she feared becoming a suspect after going target shooting with Darren the day before.

"So there was a decision made to call a friend of mine who was a local sheriff and ask him, 'Well, what do I do? Am I a suspect? Do I go home?' " she said.

At 4:00 p.m., after ascertaining that the sniper's bullet had come from the Galleria parking garage, Detective John Ferguson crossed the Truckee River to inspect it. He was joined by forensic investigator Victor Ruvalcaba, of the Washoe County Sheriff's Office, who came from photographing Judge Weller's office before it was forensically processed.

Ferguson and Ruvalcaba then walked the garage floor by floor, observing that both the fourth and fifth levels offered clear, unobstructed views of Judge Weller's third-floor office.

Ruvalcaba attempted to measure the distance to Judge Weller's office using a laser meter, but it was too far to get a reading. Later that day he returned with better equipment, measuring the distance at just over 170 yards.

On their way out, Detective Ferguson arranged to get copies of all the garage surveillance camera videotapes made between 9:00 a.m. and 11:00 a.m. that morning.

When Charla Mack failed to arrive for their 9:30 a.m. meeting, Jacqueline Ross was not unduly concerned. Charla was often late for appointments, sometimes forgetting to show up altogether.

"She was under a lot of strain," Jacqueline explained. "It wouldn't have been unlike her to do something else and call me, saying, 'I've forgotten.' I mean it wasn't a big deal, her not coming over."

But several hours later, after hearing a radio report that Judge Weller had been shot, she knew instinctively that Darren was responsible and had probably murdered Charla:

"I walked into my husband's business office in the house and I said, 'Holy shit, Darren fucking shot the judge!' He goes, 'What?' I said, 'Darren shot Judge Weller. I can't find Charla anywhere. She's dead!' And he said, 'You're kidding.' And I said, 'No.'"

As Charla had given her a spare set of keys to her new house, Jacqueline decided to drive over and see if she was there. On her way there Ann Mudd called after hearing about the shooting: she was concerned that Charla was not answering her phone. Jacqueline said she was on her way to the house and would keep her posted.

When she arrived at 2680 Alder Bridge Court, there was no sign of Charla. So she let herself into the house and began searching it room by room, not knowing what she would find.

"I checked all through it," Ross remembered, "knowing that at any moment I was going to turn a corner, enter a room, and there would be her dead body covered in blood. It's what I was sure I would find."

After finding nothing unusual, she got in her car for the ten-minute drive back to her house. She turned on the radio and heard a report that an unidentified female body had just been found. She immediately knew it was Charla and pushed her foot down hard on the accelerator.

She got pulled over by the police for speeding and started questioning the officers about Judge Weller's shooting and the body that had been found.

"They wouldn't answer any questions," she said. "They let me off and did not give me a ticket, which kind of confirmed everything that I knew."

Back at home, Jacqueline called Laura Cunningham in Los Angeles, giving her the news that Judge Weller had been shot and Charla was missing. Cunningham immediately called Shawn Meador's secretary, as Charla had told her a call had been scheduled that morning between Meador and Darren Mack's attorney, Leslie Shaw.

"The secretaries always cough up," said Cunningham. "I knew that Charla had absolutely talked to her attorney that day about it. So if she was somewhere, they would have talked to her. And she put me on hold and was gone a long time. And she came back and said, 'I'm really not supposed to tell you this, but Charla was found dead this morning.' So that's how I found out and I was very alarmed and I was concerned about our safety."

Soon afterward, Charla's mother, Soorya Townley, learned the tragic news in California.

"My mother calls me trembling and crying," Charla's half brother Chris Broughton later told *Dateline NBC*, "and says, 'Are you sitting down?' And she says, 'He killed my baby! He killed my little girl! He killed her!'"

At 4:00 p.m., police shut down Reno Airport. All airline departures were delayed and passengers were ordered back to the gates as armed police searched the entire airport. Wanted fliers with Darren Mack's photograph were distributed to all of the airport's 2,600 workers.

By this time reporters were descending on Palace Jewelry and Loan, looking for any information on Darren Mack. Police had now officially named the pawnbroker as a person of interest in Judge Weller's shooting, but had still not identified the body found in his garage as his wife, Charla.

Inside, Corey Schmidt had decided to keep the store open, instructing his staff not to give any interviews.

"I was running the store," he said, "and the next thing you know there were all kinds of video news cameras. I went down and I told everybody, 'We have no comment.'"

Finally, Schmidt decided to close up, coming outside and locking the front door to a flash of press cameras.

"I said, 'Hey, we don't have any comment,'" he recalled, "'because we really don't know what's going on. We don't. Nobody knows.'"

At 4:30 p.m., Reno deputy police chief Jim Johns held a televised press conference at police headquarters. He told reporters that the police wanted to question Reno businessman Darren Mack in connection with that morning's sniper shooting of Judge Chuck Weller. Johns said that they also wanted to talk to him about a murder in his condo, but still refused to release the victim's name or relationship to Darren Mack.

"The suspect," said Deputy Police Chief Johns, "is known to have access to firearms and had recent dealings with the judge and court."

Police were called to the homicide at 3:00 p.m., he told reporters, adding that it was possible Judge Weller, who was now in "a critical condition," was shot prior to the murder.

After interviewing Dan Osborne and Toni Lackey back at police headquarters, Detective David Jenkins met with Washoe County deputy district attorney Elliott Sattler to prepare a search warrant for Darren Mack's Fleur de Lis residence.

At 5:45 p.m., they swore out a search warrant affidavit in front of Justice of the Peace Edward Dannan. Under Sattler's questioning, Detective Jenkins said he had probable cause to believe Darren Mack had murdered an "unidentified female adult." He said they urgently needed to search Mack's condo to identify the victim and look for materials that might have been used to build an explosive device.

Jenkins told the justice of the peace that Dan Osborne had called the Reno Police Department several hours earlier to report his suspicions "that a female had been seriously injured or killed" and voicing his concern that Darren Mack was "at large and posing a risk to the community."

The detective outlined what Osborne had told him about Mack's "very contentious divorce" and the strange events he'd witnessed earlier at Mack's condo.

At 5:56 p.m., Justice Dannan officially authorized the warrant to immediately search Darren Mack's residence.

Late in the afternoon, Reno police investigators arrived at Darren and Charla Mack's former residence at 5350 Franktown Road to gather evidence. The huge, rambling house was now vacant except for a few pieces of furniture and a couple of items hanging in a closet.

But when an investigator stepped into the master bathroom, he stopped in his tracks.

On a mirror the words "SO LONG. GOOD RIDDENCE" [sic] were scrawled in blue paint.

Just after 7:00 p.m., Detective David Jenkins arrived at Darren Mack's condo with Washoe County forensic investigators Victor Ruvalcaba and Lisa Harris. And for the next eight hours they processed the garage and upstairs residence.

Investigators first set up yellow numbered police placards identifying the various bloodstains leading into the garage. Investigator Harris then photographed the entire garage with Charla's bloody body and the two vehicles inside.

While the investigators were processing the murder scene, Detective Jenkins examined Charla Mack's Lexus.

"I could see what appeared to be small bloodstains," he said, "both on the seat and some paper on the front seat of the vehicle. A Lexus key and key fob appeared to have been covered in blood."

Detective Jenkins also saw a bloody fingerprint on the key, easily visible to the naked eye. He placed it in a forensic envelope for laboratory testing.

"There were several . . . blood transfers on the driver's side of the vehicle," said Jenkins, "specifically on the side molding of the driver's door, the door handle, and the steering wheel. Those stains were initially photographed . . . and then swabbed by crime lab personnel."

Both vehicles were then removed from the garage and more photographs were taken of the body and the trail of blood leading to it.

The two forensic investigators began taking Q-tip swabs of the three reddish-brown stains on the cement driveway outside. Inside they swabbed numerous other suspected bloodstains covering the floor and walls, some of them obviously coming from the pads of a dog.

Investigator Harris also collected the green sandal found by the victim's head, carefully placing it in a manila envelope for later fingerprint and DNA testing.

When they had finished outside, the forensic team entered the residence, swabbing large bloodstains on the doorknob and banister going upstairs. As they proceeded into the living room, Detective Jenkins impounded a Budget rent-a-car envelope and contract for a 2006 Ford Explorer that were lying on a table.

He then walked into the master bedroom, finding an empty black Gerber knife sheath on the floor of Darren Mack's walk-in closet. Meanwhile, Detective John Ferguson searched another bedroom, finding several boxes of .223- and .243-caliber rifle bullets strewn around the floor. He also found an empty rifle case with a purchase receipt in Darren's name for a .223 Bushmaster rifle equipped with laser sighting.

Detective Jenkins then went into the kitchen, where he found a Dell desktop personal computer.

"Near the computer," he said, "were numerous printed e-mails and other computer-generated documents which referenced Judge Weller."

The detective also found several documents and handwritten notes by Darren Mack with allegations of Judge Weller's corruption and bias against him. Nearby, investigators found a printout of MapQuest directions to Judge Weller's house.

At around 4:00 a.m., the investigators finally left the condo, posting a uniformed police officer outside.

That night the Reno sniper story went national when MSN-BC's Rita Cosby featured it on her top-rated show *Rita Cosby Live & Direct.*

"It's an all-points bulletin which is taking place right now for an intensive search for a sniper who may be tied to two violent crimes today," Cosby told viewers.

A recent photograph of Darren Mack was shown.

"This man," Cosby continued, "could be responsible for shooting family court judge Chuck Weller. He's [also] a suspect in a killing at a Reno apartment."

Reno Police Department spokesman Steve Frady was interviewed on the phone but refused to release the identity of the murder victim until family members had been notified.

"Right now we're seeking Darren Mack as a suspect," he said. "Mr. Mack is a local businessman; he has been in the community quite a while."

While investigators searched his condo, Darren Mack had already crossed the border into Mexico. After leaving the Sacramento Airport parking garage, he had driven south on Interstate 5 toward San Diego. During the five-hundred-mile journey, he monitored the news bulletins on the fast-developing events back in Reno. He also played a *Learn in Your Car* Spanish CD he had brought along to help him in Mexico.

Sometime around midnight, Mack's Ford Explorer crossed the San Diego border into Tijuana without any trouble with border patrol. He then drove seventy-miles south to Ensenada, where he pulled into the Cinema Star parking garage near the bus station. He bought a $40 long-term ticket, giving the name of Tim Nichols and telling an attendant that he was going on a cruise and wanted to store it for a month.

Then, taking only his green Andiamo suitcase, his PalmPilot cellular phone, a change of clothes, and around

$40,000 in cash, he walked to the bus station. He bought a first-class bus ticket to La Paz using the name Steve Santini.

In the early hours of Tuesday morning, Darren got on the bus and fell asleep as he began the twenty-hour journey south through the desert to the tip of the Baja Peninsula.

CHAPTER TWENTY-SIX

Manhunt

Early Tuesday morning, Detective Ron Chalmers typed out Darren Mack's arrest warrant for suspected murder with a deadly weapon. It went out on a National Crime Information Center (NCIC) bulletin, alerting law enforcement from coast to coast that Mack should be considered armed and dangerous.

Then the Reno Police Department issued a press release naming Charla Mack for the first time as her husband's suspected murder victim.

It read: "An arrest warrant was issued early this morning for Darren Roy Mack on one count of murder with the use of a deadly weapon in the death of his estranged wife, 39-year-old Charla Mack, whose body was found Monday afternoon at an apartment at 9900 Wilbur May Parkway, where Darren Mack had reportedly been living. Family members were notified of her death late Monday evening."

The warrant stated that the five-foot-eleven-inch suspect, who weighed between 190 and 220 pounds, was also wanted for questioning in the shooting of family court judge Chuck Weller.

Reno police asked to anyone with information about Judge Weller's shooting, Charla Mack's homicide, or Darren Mack's current whereabouts to contact them immediately. They also appealed to anyone seeing a silver 2006 Ford Explorer with the California license plate number 5POR272, which Mack was known to be driving, to immediately call 911.

"The Reno Police Department is continuing to follow leads through Secret Witness tips," read the release, "as well as those developed in the investigation, including information that may indicate the shooting of the judge and the death of Charla Mack were planned in advance by Mack."

At a press conference that morning, Reno deputy police chief Jim Johns said Mack had access to multiple weapons.

"The definition of a sniper," Johns told reporters, "is the application of deadly force from a distance. This individual was a sniper."

Washoe County district attorney Richard Gammick, who had known the fugitive for many years, also addressed the media. He confirmed that a warrant had been issued for Mack's arrest on a count of murder with a deadly weapon.

"Before anybody even asks," he told reporters, "that has the potential—and I'll say that several times—it has the potential of being a death penalty case under the state laws. I'm not saying it is a death penalty case. It's way too early in the ballgame."

That morning's edition of the *Reno Gazette-Journal* carried full coverage of one of the most sensational days in Reno history. With the banner headline "Police Link Judge Shooting With Homicide; Suspect Still Missing," the fast-moving story dominated the entire newspaper.

"Police were looking for a Reno businessman," it began, "after a family court judge was wounded by a sniper shot Monday morning in his Reno Justice Court Office, causing terror in downtown Reno and freezing workers in their buildings."

The story said police were hunting for Darren Mack, who was also a suspect in his wife Charla's homicide.

Then, using family court records, it detailed the Macks'

troubled divorce case in Judge Weller's courtroom, which had ended in murder and the first Reno courthouse shooting in nearly half a century.

"[It's] a tragedy and an outrage," declared Nevada supreme court justice Robert Rose. "It is a slap against lawful authority and an attack not just against a judge but against everyone. The shooting of a judge, who was dedicated to helping citizens resolve their disputes, is one of the most despicable and cowardly acts imaginable."

At 9:00 a.m., Washoe County assistant medical examiner Dr. Katherine P. Raven, began an autopsy on Charla Mack's body at the Washoe County Coroner's Office. Also present were several Reno police detectives and other investigators.

First, forensic investigator Lisa Harris photographed the body before removing brown paper bags from Charla's hands and feet, that had been attached at the crime scene to protect any trace evidence. She then took post-mortem fingerprints and palm prints and collected samples of blood and other bodily fluids. Laboratory tests would later show that no drugs or alcohol were present in Charla's body at the time of her death. Investigator Harris then removed Charla's red shirt and blue sweatpants and underclothes, impounding them as evidence.

Dr. Raven then began the autopsy, which was photographed at every stage. The medical examiner found at least six deep stab wounds, including a particularly brutal one to the left side of the neck, by the collarbone, almost slicing off Charla's head. The dagger wound had hit her spinal cord, severing the carotid artery, the main pathway between the heart and the left side of the brain.

"It cut the left carotid artery in half," Dr. Raven explained. "It also cut the esophagus, which is the deepest structure. The esophagus is where we swallow food; it goes down to our stomach. And it also cut completely in half the trachea, or windpipe, where the air goes down."

The assistant coroner also observed a stab wound to

Charla's right forearm and another to her elbow. There were other knife wounds to the inside of her arm and left side of her back.

In addition, Dr. Raven found numerous defense injuries, showing that Charla had fought for her life.

"You can imagine that someone is putting their hands up to protect themselves from a sharp instrument like a knife," said Dr. Raven. "So the knife would come and hit that part of the arms, and that's what we're seeing here."

Then Harris carefully photographed how Charla's right arm was pulled across the right side of her face, showing a stab wound and several scrapes and abrasions to her elbow.

"It's consistent with a defensive wound," said Dr. Raven. "It's in the same position on the back of the arms, like someone puts up their arms to defend themselves."

The doctor also observed a vicious stab wound to Charla's lower right leg, going in one side and coming out the other. This wound showed how desperately Charla had tried to kick her attacker after being taken to the garage floor.

Furthermore, Dr. Raven found extensive blunt force trauma injuries to the right side of Charla's neck, both legs, and her upper left arm. There was bruising as well as abrasions on Charla's face, ear, and jaw area that could have been caused by a punch or a kick.

"A lot of things can cause a BFI [blunt force injury]," said the doctor. "Anything from a table to the floor to a blunt instrument. Hands would be considered blunt."

Dr. Raven counted at least six and possibly seven stab wounds to Charla Mack's body, although the one that had killed her was the one to her neck, which had almost severed it. She determined that Charla had suffered a long and agonizing death.

"Death is rarely immediate," the doctor explained. "The main artery going to the brain was cut in half. So it's going to . . . bleed out rapidly but it won't be immediate. It'll probably take several minutes."

Charla's windpipe had also been severed, so she would

no longer have been able to breathe. And the heavy bleeding from the stab wound to her carotid artery had leaked through her trachea and into her lungs, making her cough up blood.

Dr. Raven determined that it would have taken between three and five minutes from the stab wound to the neck for Charla to die. She would have been choking on her own blood until she finally lost consciousness.

"The manner of death is homicide," wrote the coroner in her autopsy report.

Although all three Reno courthouses remained closed on Tuesday, the rest of the city was slowly getting back to normal. Corey Schmidt opened up Palace Jewelry and Loan, and attempted to carry on with business as usual.

"I was the front man at the store," he explained. "I was the one that was defending the family, telling the people to leave when they were coming in [and] saying bad stuff [like] 'Is this the place where the guy offed his wife and shot the judge?'"

Charla's father, Jan Sampsel had quit his job at Palace, after learning of his daughter's death.

Under these trying circumstances, Schmidt utilized all his experience as a Carnival Cruise director to motivate his other employees, who were concerned about their future.

"You've got to keep your head up and try and keep morale up," he explained, "and to be honest with you, you try to keep sales up."

While Schmidt was minding Palace, Landon Mack hired the high-profile Las Vegas defense attorney David Z. Chesnoff, fifty-one, to bring his brother back to Reno alive. There was already a $2,500 bounty on Darren's head from the Secret Witness program, and his family were concerned that his life was in danger.

After signing on a retainer to represent Darren Mack, Chesnoff, whose previous celebrity clients included Leonardo Di Caprio, Shaquille O'Neal, and magician David Copperfield, telephoned prominent Reno attorney Scott Freeman, inviting him to come aboard.

"Mr. Chesnoff called me at about 11:00 and asked me to cocounsel the case with him," said Freeman.

The popular attorney, who has his own Sunday afternoon television show called *Lawyers, Guns & Money*, had first met Darren Mack in the early 1990s, when he had offered legal advice on a pawn issue.

Over the years, they occasionally met socially, as Freeman's son attended the same school as Jory Mack.

But initially there was little Chesnoff and Freeman could do except inform the Washoe County District Attorney's Office and the Reno Police Department that they were now representing Darren Mack.

So they began giving interviews to the national media, hoping their new client, wherever he was, would learn he had legal representation and keep his mouth shut.

As he recovered from his wounds at Washoe County Medical Center, Judge Chuck Weller learned of Charla Mack's murder. It only made him even more concerned for his family, who were now under heavy armed guard at the hospital.

On Tuesday morning, Annie Allison, who had been released from the hospital the previous afternoon, arrived for an emotional visit.

"The judge actually called me and asked me to come down and see him at the hospital," she remembered. "And he was attached to all sorts of IVs, and he just gave me a big hug and said he was so sorry. He was weak. You could tell he was in a significant amount of pain."

That afternoon, from his hospital bed, Judge Weller dictated a statement for the media.

"I would like to thank everyone, for the outpouring of support in the last twenty-four hours for me and my family," it read. "I am especially grateful to the emergency medical personnel and the fine people at Washoe Medical Center for their work in saving my life."

A few hours later, Judge Weller was released from hospital and went into hiding. He was taken to a Reno hotel, where he and his family were placed under twenty-four-hour heavily armed police protection.

That night the Darren Mack story dominated the national news. The dramatic murder of Charla Mack by her handsome multimillionaire husband Darren was big news in itself, but the attempted assassination of a family court judge took it to a whole new level.

The top-rated *Nancy Grace* show on CNN Headline News led off with it that night.

"In twenty-four hours one judge shot in his chambers and a woman dead," Grace told her television audience. "What is the latest on the investigation? What has become of Darren Mack?"

Reno deputy police chief Jim Johns was interviewed by phone for the latest developments.

"Darren Mack is in the wind," he said. "We currently have an arrest warrant out for him, charging him with the homicide of his wife, Charla. She was that body that was originally reported."

Then Grace asked exactly how she was killed.

"We're holding that close as we go through the investigation," he said. "But I can tell you she suffered multiple stab wounds to the upper chest."

Deputy Chief Johns was also interviewed on Rita Cosby's show *Live & Direct* on MSNBC.

"Jim," she asked, "any sightings? Any idea where he could be?"

"We don't have any specific location," replied Johns. "We have multiple leads come into the department. We would encourage anyone who thinks that they do see him to make sure they call the Reno Police Department, because we're willing to track down these leads wherever they may go."

CHAPTER TWENTY-SEVEN

Hiding Out in Paradise

Early Tuesday morning, Darren Mack's bus arrived in La Paz, Mexico. From there he headed straight for the Meliá Cabo Real beach and golf resort, a three-hour drive away in Cabo San Lucas. It was a place he knew well, as he had spent nine days there the previous November at a Utopia swinging convention.

After checking in under a false name and paying cash, Darren went to his room and put all his money in the safe. Then he turned on the satellite television news to update himself on developments in Reno.

He went downstairs to the front desk, asking an employee named Germain to make a local phone call for him. He explained that since he had not used a credit card, his room phone had not been switched on. Germain agreed to dial the number, and Mack tipped him.

At around 2:00 p.m., Darren Mack put on his sports clothes and went to the gym for a workout. Virginia Delgadillo, a beautiful twenty-year-old blonde resort employee, was on duty at the resort's health club when Darren Mack came in. She remembered how he looked her up and down, making her blush.

"He was handsome," she later told *Reno Gazette-Journal*

reporter Martha Bellisle. "He had big muscles. I remember his arms."

When she said that he must sign in as a guest to use the health club, he was hesitant. But eventually he scribbled an illegible name and made up a room number.

Then he stripped down to shorts and a tee shirt, and started working out in front of the full-length mirror.

"But he was looking at me all the time, looking at me in the mirror," Delgadillo recalled.

Soon afterward, Chad Ruff, a United Airlines pilot on a one-night layover, walked in with another crew member. He saw that the only other person in the tiny gym was a tall, muscular dark-haired American who was lifting weights.

During his workout, the pilot couldn't help but notice the man, who was dressed in a tee shirt and shorts.

"The gym was lined with mirrors," Ruff said, "so at any given direction you were looking at the whole gym."

Then the man moved to the elliptical machine next to the treadmill the pilot was using. A few minutes later a beautiful, petite Asian-looking woman wearing skintight spandex pants and a tiger shirt walked in, going straight up to the man on the elliptical machine.

"They had a conversation," said Ruff. "I could not overhear [it]."

The man got off the machine and left the gym with the woman, heading off in the direction of the hotel rooms.

At around 3:00 p.m., Ruff returned to his room for a shower. As he was getting dressed, he turned on the Fox News Channel, where news anchor Shepard Smith was discussing the Darren Mack story.

"I wasn't paying too much attention," Ruff later testified, "but I did look at the mug shot and it struck me . . . I had seen that person."

He recognized the photograph of Darren Mack as the man he had just seen in the gym. So he decided to go and find the man for another look, to make absolutely sure.

"I went down to the pool," Ruff recounted, "and I observed the man with the female that had been in the gym with him."

The couple were sunbathing at the pool bar, casually chatting away over cocktails, the man wearing Speedos and the woman a sexy bikini. Ruff walked by them several times, trying to be as inconspicuous as possible.

"I was now paying closer attention," he explained, "and making little notes to myself."

For the next hour he hung around the pool before the couple left to go back to their room.

"Then I went back to my room and watched the Fox News Channel again," said Ruff. "They profiled the [Darren Mack] case again . . . and I became more sure that this was definitely the person they were profiling. I paid a lot more attention on the second time they talked about the case. I studied the photograph."

The pilot went to Cabo San Lucas to report his Darren Mack sighting to police. But unable to find any Federales, he returned to the resort to try and find Mack again.

The World Cup was taking place, and most of the hotel guests were in the bar, watching the Brazil-Croatia soccer match.

"I went down there hoping maybe I would see him again," said Ruff. "I never did."

The next morning he left the resort and flew to Denver, Colorado. As soon as he cleared customs, he telephoned Reno Police Department, reporting that he had seen Darren Mack at the Meliá Cabo Real beach and golf resort.

But by the time the FBI arrived at the resort to investigate, Darren Mack was long gone.

CHAPTER TWENTY-EIGHT

"The Police Are Going to Kill Him!"

At 8:00 a.m. on Wednesday morning, the Mills B. Lane Justice Center reopened for the first time since the shooting. And for the next few days, the sole topic of discussion in the hallways was security and how to improve it.

"We are trying to get back to normal," court administrator Darin Conforti told the *Reno Gazette-Journal*, "but that's a relative term when you've been through what we've been through."

One hour later, Detective David Jenkins swore out another search warrant to go back into Darren Mack's condo. The first search had involved evidence pertaining to Charla's murder, but now investigators wanted to carry out a broader sweep, looking for any evidence relating to Judge Weller's shooting. In the affidavit, Detective Jenkins said that during the previous search he had observed several boxes of ammunition for firearms in a bedroom and knew that Darren Mack owned a .223 Bushmaster, which was now missing.

An unnamed witness had also told police how Darren Mack had tried to hire him to follow Judge Weller, looking for evidence that he was corrupt. The witness had described Mack as "extremely frustrated" and "at the end of his rope."

Later that day, Soorya Townley arrived in Reno to bury

her daughter and take care of her granddaughter. Now sixty, Soorya had quit her job at an alcohol recovery center in Malibu, California, to move to Reno.

"I quit my job the day after Charla was murdered," she explained. "I had to stay in motels while arranging the funeral, looking for a place to live, still in shock."

Soorya was soon joined by her son, Chris Broughton, who would help her make funeral arrangements once the Washoe County Coroner released Charla's body, pending the results of toxicology tests.

"Erika was in massive emotional trouble," said Soorya, "floating along a river of shock and horror. And I was determined to do anything and everything I could to save her."

At 2:00 p.m., Detective Jenkins arrived at the Fleur de Lis complex to execute the second search warrant. Accompanying him were Detectives John Ferguson and Shanna Wallin-Reed. Forensic investigator Lisa Harris was also there to take photographs and impound evidence.

They fanned out through the condo, searching for any evidence to tie Darren Mack to the courthouse shooting.

Detective Wallin-Reed went through the front door and up a flight of stairs, turning right into Erika's bedroom, with its child's bed inside.

"There [were] some handguns laying there," she later testified. "There [was] ammunition."

The detective then impounded a green box of .243 ammunition, which had some rounds missing. The investigators were looking for a rifle that would fire .243 bullets like the ones believed to have been fired at Judge Weller. But all they found was a receipt for a Bushmaster rifle, made out in the name of Darren Mack and dated May 12, 2006.

Detective Wallin-Reed then came out of the bedroom, turning left down the corridor to the long kitchen. At the far end was a breakfast nook, where she noticed several pads and documents scattered on and underneath a table.

"There were just numerous papers," she recalled. "Hand-written, computer printed, e-mails. Just all kinds of different papers and books."

After donning plastic gloves, the detective looked through them, searching for anything concerning firearms, Judge Weller, or family court corruption.

"I collected anything that was consistent with what we were looking for," she said. "Ultimately [I] took them back to the Reno Police Department so I could look through them even closer."

While Wallin-Reed was sifting through the papers, lead detective Ferguson was searching Darren Mack's master bedroom. Just inside the doorway he found a black corduroy IBI Global bag, and on the carpet were more boxes of ammunition and firearms.

The detective then opened up the bag and found Mack's extensive research on Judge Chuck Weller, including notes about donors who had contributed to his election. Also in the bag was a yellow notebook detailing a Plan A and a Plan B.

Detective Ferguson discovered two printouts of MapQuest.com directions, made on February 18, 2006. One was the route to Judge Weller's private residence and the other to Shawn Meador's home.

While detectives were searching inside Darren Mack's condo, police divers searched two ponds on the Fleur de Lis complex near Mack's condo for the murder weapon and bloody clothes.

"We were searching those ponds for evidence," Sergeant Russell Pedersen of the Washoe County Sheriff's office explained. "Nothing was found."

On Wednesday afternoon, the group Nevadans for Equal Parenting distanced themselves from Darren Mack, condemning his actions. The father's rights group, whose meetings Mack had regularly attended, issued a statement on its Web site offering prayers to Judge Weller and Charla Mack.

"Nevadans for Equal Parenting condemns the violent and

senseless crimes which have occurred this week in Reno," read the statement. "We hope if any good can come of this tragedy, it will be that we take a close look at the current situation in our courts, and hopefully make positive changes."

Later in the afternoon, the FBI issued a federal warrant charging Darren Mack with unlawful flight to avoid prosecution. And the Reno Police Department warned small airports to be on the lookout for Darren Mack, who had a student pilot's license.

Reno police also appealed for any women who might have hooked up with Darren Mack on Internet dating sites to contact them immediately.

Producers from Fox TV's top-rated *America's Most Wanted* (*AMW*) had also arrived in Reno to prepare a segment on the Darren Mack case, to air the following Saturday. They met with Reno police, who fully briefed them on the investigation. Darren Mack's photograph had already been posted on the *AMW* site and was generating hundreds of tips.

"This is the highest profile and labor intensive investigation," explained Reno police lieutenant Ron Donnelly. "Mack is resourceful and has connections and really could be anywhere."

At 7:40 p.m., a team of volunteers from Washoe County Search and Rescue were searching the shoulder and median of Interstate 80—near the cell phone tower that had last picked up Darren Mack's Monday calls—when Charla Mack's black cell phone was found lying by the side of the freeway west of the Robb Drive exit. It was then taken away to the Washoe County Crime Lab to be processed.

That night at their home in Moraga, California, Jeff Donner and his wife, Marsha, held an emotional press conference appealing to their cousin Darren Mack to give himself up. Talking to reporters from his back garden, where Mack had given his *On Second Thought* interview, Donner revealed

Mack had called his cell phone at precisely 11:19 a.m. on Monday, just minutes after he had shot Judge Weller.

"His comments were brief," said Donner, on the verge of tears, "and his message to me was 'Please, if anything happens to me, please make sure that the true story about the injustices that are going on in that courtroom get out to the media and to the public.'"

Mack had then "disengaged" before Donner could ask any further questions.

Donner was asked his reaction to Charla's murder and the judge's shooting, coupled with the fact his cousin had called him right afterward.

"I was really shocked," Donner replied. "I mean, this is not a violent man. If he is in fact responsible for this, it is totally out of character and it is simply an example of someone that has snapped."

Then Donner's wife, Marsha, told reporters that she was still not convinced that Darren was the guilty party.

"After that phone call," she said, "my first inclination was that something was going to happen to him, that Charla was going to hurt him. And it is public record that she had many, many times attempted to hurt him. We believe that all the speculation about the knife—it may even have been her knife. She had a restraining order. What was she doing there? So we're very confused about the actuality of what really happened."

The Donners were then asked if they had a message for Darren Mack in the event that he saw the interview.

"If Darren is listening," said Jeff Donner in a breaking voice, "if he's watching, we love him. We care about him. And we'll do anything to assist to bring him in. My concern is that he's going to get cornered someplace and the police are going to kill him.

"Obviously he's on the run, and I'm begging him that if he's listening to this, please contact us. He knows he can trust us. We will do anything to help him. We want to save his life. He's at least entitled to a trial."

CHAPTER TWENTY-NINE

A Smoking Gun

On Thursday morning, seventy-two hours after Darren Mack's murderous rampage, there were still no leads as to his whereabouts. Since Monday, Reno detectives had been working twenty-four-hour shifts, tracking down thousands of tips from the public.

"It was really one of *the* most chaotic cases," said lead detective Ron Chalmers, "especially with the national media attention. We'd been running around the clock. I remember literally having to take my work cell phone in the shower with me because it would not stop ringing. The phone was ringing off the hook nonstop."

The most promising lead so far was that someone had used a Palace Jewelry and Loan credit card at a Sacramento Airport garage at 2:30 p.m. on Monday, and detectives were examining the surveillance video.

Detectives Chalmers and John Ferguson had been appointed joint lead detectives in the investigation.

"We worked it together," said Chalmers. "But John is a computer guy and really into the technical stuff, so he spent a lot of time tracking down the e-mail address that Darren started sending e-mails from."

Over the first couple of days, the Reno Police Department was flooded with leads from the public, which went nowhere.

Early on, there was a report that Darren Mack had been arrested at an airport, which turned out to be groundless. But when Mack's new attorney, Scott Freeman, heard the rumor, he immediately faxed Reno police, saying his client Darren Mack had invoked his right to remain silent.

"Which was not entirely accurate," said Detective Chalmers, "because he had not been arrested."

Nevertheless, later that day Freeman gave an interview to Reno's NBC affiliate KRNV-TV, saying he was "waiting and hoping" that Darren Mack would get in touch soon. There was a plan already in place for his client to surrender to authorities.

By now, Detective Chalmers had reviewed surveillance video from both the Fleur de Lis complex and the Galleria parking garage, for sightings of the distinctive 2006 Ford Explorer Mack was believed to be driving.

He identified the suspected vehicle leaving Mack's condo, before the meeting with Dan Osborne at Starbucks.

The fifth-floor parking garage surveillance video was even more damning.

"[I] observed a light-colored 2006 Ford Explorer enter the parking garage and park along the south wall of the fifth floor . . . at approximately 10:42 am," Chalmers later wrote in his search warrant affidavit. "The driver of the 2006 Ford Explorer repositioned the vehicle by backing it into a parking stall against the south wall, so that the rear of the vehicle would be facing the Mills B. Lane Justice Center, at approximately 10:56 am. The rear glass hatch of the 2006 Ford Explorer is observed being lifted at approximately 10:58 am. At approximately 11:14:45, the glass hatch is closed. The driver then exits the parking garage."

At 10:00 p.m. on Thursday, investigators returned to Unit 1006 of the Fleur de Lis Complex to continue their search. This time they concentrated on the garage, removing a section of the east wall that had a clear bloody palm print.

The famous Reno Arch stands in the shadows of Palace Jewelry and Loan
(Courtesy: John Glatt)

Charla Mack's photograph was shown to the jury at Darren Mack's trial
(Courtesy: Press Pool Video)

Darren Mack's jewelry and loan store, which was started by his parents in the middle of the last century
(Courtesy: John Glatt)

Darren and Charla Mack were regulars at the Fantasy Girls strip club, located in a mall in a seedy part of Reno
(Courtesy: John Glatt)

Darren won fifth place in the 2002 Mr. Reno Body Building Championship *(Courtesy: Phil Pape)*

The grand entrance to the palatial Fleur de Lis complex in one of Reno's most exclusive areas *(Courtesy: John Glatt)*

Darren Mack's luxurious Fleur de Lis condominium, where he stabbed Charla to death in the garage *(Courtesy: John Glatt)*

Darren delivered a passionate attack on the family court system on a web TV show, just days before he exploded into violence *(Courtesy: Clark County Court Exhibit)*

Fathers' rights campaigner Garret Idle helped Darren Mack amass evidence to try and discredit Judge Chuck Weller

(Courtesy: John Glatt)

Darren Mack's "To Do" list, laying out in advance how he was going to murder Charla and then go after Judge Weller *(Courtesy: Reno Police Department)*

Charla Mack was captured on video arriving at the Fleur de Lis to drop off Erika that fateful morning

(Courtesy: Clark County Court Exhibit)

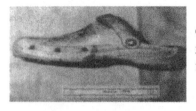

Charla's blood-soaked sandal flew off, as she desperately fought for her life
(Courtesy: Clark County Court Exhibit)

The bloody key to Charla's Lexus SUV was later found with Darren Mack's thumb-print *(Courtesy: Clark County Court Exhibit)*

The front entrance of the Galleria parking garage, where Darren Mack headed after killing Charla
(Courtesy: John Glatt)

The unobstructed view Darren Mack had of Judge Weller's third-floor office from the parking garage, 170 yards away across the Truckee River
(Courtesy: John Glatt)

Judge Weller was rushed to hospital after the sniper attack in critical condition, where he was photographed
(Courtesy: Clark County Court Exhibit)

A weary Darren Mack was photographed by Reno police after he surrendered in Mexico

(Courtesy: Clark County Court Exhibit)

Joan Mack during her son's murder trial *(Courtesy: Press Pool Video)*

Darren Mack's mug shot after his arrest for Charla's murder
(Courtesy: Reno Police Department)

Darren Mack's loyal girl-friend Alecia Biddison remains his staunchest supporter
(Courtesy: Press Pool Video)

Darren Mack's younger brother Landon financed Darren's million-dollar defense
(Courtesy: John Glatt)

Washoe County Court
(Courtesy: John Glatt)

Clark County special prosecutor Robert Daskas delivered a moving opening statement at Mack's trial
(Courtesy: Press Pool Video)

Veteran Reno defense attorney Scott Freeman makes a point during his dramatic opening statement
(Courtesy: Press Pool Video)

Judge Weller was subjected to a brutal cross-examination during the trial
(Courtesy: Press Pool Video)

Darren Mack with his Las Vegas-based defender David Chesnoff
(Courtesy: Press Pool Video)

Judge Douglas Herndon presided over the complicated murder trial, with its many twists and turns
(Courtesy: Press Pool Video)

Charla's younger half-brother Christopher Broughton was in court every day of the trial
(Courtesy: Press Pool Video)

Darren Mack showed little emotion during his murder trial
(Courtesy: Press Pool Video)

Defense attorney William Routsis was hired by the Mack family to get Darren a new trial, after Darren decided to change his guilty plea *(Courtesy: Press Pool Video)*

Darren Mack at his sentencing
(Courtesy: Press Pool Video)

Charla's devoted mother Soorya Townley, addressing the court during sentencing, reduced many to tears
(Courtesy: Press Pool Video)

Darren Mack was sentenced to the maximum of life in prison, and will be eligible for parole when he is eighty-three years old
(Courtesy: Press Pool Video)

Then forensic investigator Lisa Harris went upstairs to test the two sinks in Darren Mack's master bedroom for any sign of blood. She put a piece of tubing down the sink as far as it would go, before drawing the water into a sterile syringe. Then she took further samples from the shower and another sink.

Detectives also impounded Darren Mack's Dell XPS desktop computer, miscellaneous papers from the hallway closet, as well as his address book, a Reebok duffel bag, and six CDs found on a kitchen counter. They also seized one box of Remington .243 ammunition, twenty-eight boxes of various .223 ammunition, and fifty-eight loose .223 cartridges, four empty rifle cases, a Buck knife with sheath, one Case brand knife with sheath, and a folding knife.

They took various yellow legal notepads and e-mail printouts from the bedroom, a Sony Handycam video recorder and a Sony Cybershot camera, and a CD labeled "Alecia" and dated 1/13/06, that was found in the master bedroom.

Charla Mack's Lexus and Darren's Jeep Cherokee were now at the Washoe County Crime Laboratory, awaiting forensic testing. That afternoon, under a court-ordered search warrant, Washoe County forensic investigator Dean Kaumans began processing them.

He first carried out a visual examination of the Cherokee, looking for any signs of blood. Several areas on the exterior had stains resembling blood, but the only positive result he got was from the bumper area, which he swabbed for further DNA testing.

Investigator Kaumans also seized items inside the vehicle, including a number of red-stained tissues; a Safari Club International (the world's largest big-game hunting organization) exhibitor badge bearing the name Darren Mack; and six packets of McCranie's Red Flake tobacco.

The investigator then moved on to Charla Mack's Lexus SUV, on which he found more traces of blood.

"There were areas on the driver's front quarter panel," he later testified, "that had discoloration. Those were tested and produced a positive result for presumptive blood."

Although this test did not conclusively prove it was human blood, samples were taken away for further testing at the DNA lab.

Kaumans then swabbed red stains found on the steering wheel, the armrest of the driver's door, and the emergency brake. On the front seat he discovered Charla's black Coach purse with her Nevada driving license and credits cards. In the rear were photocopies of checks for child support and alimony dated May 22, 2006. They were both made out to her and signed by Darren Mack, with red stains on the back.

Still in the ignition, he found a key ring with five keys and a leather fob.

"I removed that," Kaumans remembered, "and saw that there was also a red staining on that set of keys. There was possibly a fingerprint on one of the keys. I [photographed] the keys so the fingerprint would not be destroyed.

Back at the Reno Police Department, Detective Shanna Wallin-Reed began to process the numerous printouts and papers taken from Darren Mack's kitchen. She was particularly interested in a yellow legal pad found on the kitchen table.

On the sixth page she saw some kind of to-do list in Darren Mack's neat handwriting.

"That really stood out to me," she recalled. "I found it most relevant."

Right at the top of the list was the name "Dan," and it also mentioned him taking "Erika" to "Joan." Then, in a eureka moment, halfway down she found the words "End Problem."

Thinking this might be the smoking gun, Wallin-Reed excitedly called in the other detectives and showed it to them.

"That was huge," lead detective Ron Chalmers recalled. "I thought if we have any issue with first-degree murder before, we don't now. Clearly this is premeditated, preplanned out. I mean, he wrote out this beautiful list of things to do for us."

Detective Chalmers chuckled, noticing how Mack had even initialed a mistake on the third item down about his son, Jory.

"He made an error on the to-do list," said Chalmers, "and then mark[ed] it out and initialing it—DM. I think he's just a creature of habit and used to do it in the pawnshop. So clearly that was a nice piece of evidence."

On Friday morning, Joan and Landon Mack were in Washoe District Court, attending an emergency custody hearing for little Erica Mack. Armed guards were posted outside the closed-door family court hearing, where Darren's new attorney, Scott Freeman, was representing the Mack family.

Also at the hearing were Charla's mother, Soorya Townley, and half brother, Chris Broughton. There was great tension between the two sides.

At the end of the brief hearing, juvenile court master Cindi-Elaine Heron gave Joan Mack temporary custody, as she had been involved with Erika since birth. Soorya was given "liberal" visitation rights.

Outside the courtroom, Soorya's hastily appointed custody lawyer, Egan Walker, refused to discuss what arrangements had been made for the child.

"Our focus," said Walker, "is trying to calm the hurricane that's blowing around this child."

Later, Scott Freeman complained to Reno *Journal-Gazette* reporter Martha Bellisle that Charla's half brother Chris had tried to intimidate him after the hearing, making as if to shake his hand and then asking, "How does it feel to defend a murderer?"

Around midnight, Alecia Biddison sent an e-mail to her boyfriend, Darren Mack, appealing to him to return to Reno.

"I said to him, 'Please come home,'" she said. "And he wrote back and said, 'I'm working on it.' And that was it."

CHAPTER THIRTY

The Martyr

After a couple of days relaxing at the Meliá Cabo Real beach and golf resort, Darren Mack moved on. Between workouts and enjoying the five-star resort's bars and restaurants, he had been carefully monitoring cable TV coverage of the search for him.

"As soon as I turned on the TV, they were talking about how they were going to execute me," he would later explain.

So he checked out of the resort, taking a three-hour taxi ride back to La Paz, costing around $150 before the tip.

In La Paz, investigators believe, he stayed at an anonymous boardinghouse for a couple of days, waiting for the next Baja ferry across the Sea of Cortés to the town of Mazatlán.

As a fugitive in Mexico and unable to speak Spanish, Darren Mack was becoming increasingly uncomfortable with his situation. Although he had carefully planned out Charla's murder and Judge Weller's subsequent shooting, he had given little thought to the problems of being on the run in a country where he did not speak the language. He was also worried about carrying around nearly $40,000 in cash, realizing he was an easy target for Mexican gangsters.

His only previous experience of Mexico had been at top-of-the-line resorts, where everyone spoke English. But now he was becoming increasingly alienated and began contemplating giving himself up and facing the consequences back in America.

On Friday, June 16, he brought a 770-pesos ($71 U.S.) first-class ferry ticket to Mazatlán. Although he would not have had to show his passport, he would have had to pass through an X-ray machine, so he would not have been carrying any weapons.

Then, at 3:30 p.m., he departed La Paz for the eighteen-hour crossing on an ancient Dutch-built ferry. Traveling first-class, Mack enjoyed a private cabin with a shower and flush toilet.

At 9:00 a.m. Saturday, the ferry docked at the terminal at Mazatlán, the country's largest commercial port. Few paid any attention to the handsome, dark-haired American wheeling a green Andiamo suitcase behind him.

At 9:20 a.m. Reno time on Saturday, June 17, Washoe County district attorney Richard Gammick received a lengthy, rambling, often incoherent e-mail from someone named Kerry Warlburg. It was sent from exposingcorruption@hotmail.com and its subject was "Darren Mack's Surrendering Himself."

Investigators believe that Darren Mack had sent the e-mail, using a fictitious name to cover his tracks. The Internet service provider (ISP) was later traced to Mexico.

A cover note, purportedly coming from Warlburg, read: "A very good friend of mine D. Mack called me and asked me to send you this message. I am deeply troubled by what has happened but I told him I would do it. He also asked me to send it from his account, so I am sending it from this address."

Darren Mack began by telling the district attorney he trusted him, knowing him to be one of "the finer of men." He said he understood Gammick would have to convict and then execute him, and had already forgiven him.

"If he agrees to my conditions," wrote Mack, "he will get no resistance from me."

He then invited Gammick to become "my partner" in

exposing corruption in the family court system, bringing the "criminals," Judge Weller and Shawn Meador, to justice.

"I will be executed and soon become a statistic," he wrote, "but what can be accomplished here is to spark a change and stop the ongoing destruction of . . . the family court industry. Then this tragedy will not be for [nothing]."

He laid out his conditions for surrender:

1   I will surrender only to Richard Gammick and who he wants to bring. I trust him. I am unarmed and will go peacefully.

2   I would like Mel Laub and Mike Laub to accompany Richard not as my attorneys but as my friends if they will come.

3   I will ask for the death penalty and want it agreed on prior to surrender. Even though I was defending myself from yet another attack from Charla I am sure everyone [will] want someone to really pay for this. On another note if I would have wanted Weller dead he would have been. I wanted him alive to have his corruption exposed and to get out what is really coming to him as well as the criminal Shawn Meador.

4   I want to see my family and children if they will see me.

5   Since I am stipulating to the death penalty I want it done in 1 year so that I have time to have the truth of what has happened to me and others told.

6   I want a private cell until my execution.

7   I want access to a computer, printer and internet along with being able to see a writer regularly.

8 *I want no prison and in exchange I will not play*
the game and appeal etc. A deal is a deal.

9 *I want your word that you will support the truth*
getting exposed. Nothing more and nothing less.

He then instructed the district attorney not to reply directly but post his answers to each of his conditions of surrender on the Legal Reader Web site blog.

"One other thing is so he knows this is real," wrote Mack, "tell Richard that I have been donating pearls and fur coats for the last number of years to the Boys and Girls Club."

When the e-mail arrived in his in-box, the district attorney failed to notice it, as he did not recognize the name Kerry Warlburg. It would be another forty hours until Darren Mack's next attempt to make contact.

Later that day, Joan and Landon Mack finally broke their silence, inviting *Reno Gazette-Journal* reporter Martha Bellisle into their home for an exclusive interview. But they refused to address Darren's role in either Charla's murder or Judge Weller's shooting, limiting the questions to how the family were surviving its ordeal. Joan Mack also supplied a favorite family photograph of her and Darren, taken during happier times.

As Sunday was Father's Day, the Mack family interview was front-page with the headline, "Father's Day Fugitive—Suspect's Mother Describes Relatives in Shock, Disbelief."

"Darren Mack's mother and brother are living by the minute," it began, "but staying strong for the children, to protect them and offer them as normal a life as possible."

The Mack matriarch credited friends, family, and the Reno community's support for giving them the strength to carry on.

"I've been in shock," she tearfully told Bellisle. "We just have to put one foot in front of the other and pray. Lots of prayers. We hope everybody can pull this for the best interest of the children."

Asked if they had heard anything from Darren since he went on the run, they said they didn't even know if he was still alive.

Finally, Joan Mack thanked the Reno community for supporting her family in its time of need, saying nothing had prepared her for all the outpourings of love and support they had received.

That night, *America's Most Wanted* led off with the Darren Mack story, with host John Walsh appealing for any information on the dangerous millionaire fugitive. After the show, the Reno Police Department switchboard was inundated with leads, which would take many days to check out.

CHAPTER THIRTY-ONE

"Meet Me in Mazatlán"

On Monday, June 19—one week after he was shot—Judge Chuck Weller started catching up on court business. But with Darren Mack still at large, the judge and his family were still under heavily armed guard.

"They had moved us to a local hotel," said the judge. "There was a SWAT team outside the door and the doctors came to the hotel. The level of protection was like nothing I had ever experienced."

After all the adverse publicity about Darren Mack declaring bankruptcy a year earlier, Palace Jewelry and Loan issued a press release to set the record straight. It emphasized that for the last year the company had been under the "sole management" of Joan Mack; it was not in bankruptcy; and it would continue to operate as normal.

"In these difficult times for the Mack Family," read the statement, "as well as Palace and its employees, the Palace appreciates the continued support from its friends, customers, partners, vendors and the community."

Charla Mack's body had now been released by the coroner's office and taken to the Mountain View Mortuary, in readiness for the planned funeral the next day. Charla's father, Jan Sampsel, was paying, and her family spent Monday, at the funeral home, trading emotional stories with her friends.

Reporters waited outside, and at one point Soorya came out and showed pictures of Charla and Erika, giving a brief interview.

"It's such a nightmare," she told the *Reno Gazette-Journal.* "I never imagined something like this would be happening."

Then she showed Martha Bellisle a framed picture of Erika dressed as a fairy, posing in a Walt Disney–type magical flower garden with butterflies hovering around her.

"This was the fantasy world they had," said Soorya sadly. "This is the direct opposite of what Darren has now created for his daughter."

At around midday, Darren Mack's close friend Melvin Laub called Richard Gammick's office and was put through to Gammick's administrative assistant. Laub, a Reno attorney, informed her that Mack would be calling the DA to discuss his recent e-mail and terms of surrender. The assistant then gave him Gammick's cell phone number.

A few minutes later Darren Mack called the DA's cell from Mexico.

Richard Gammick had just left Harrah's Casino when he received the call on the way back to his office.

Mack asked if he had received his e-mail, but Gammick knew nothing about it.

"I told him to call me back in ten minutes, give me a chance to get back [to my office] and see what you are talking about," Gammick recalled.

After hanging up, the DA went straight back to his office, alerting the FBI.

Then, a few minutes later, Darren Mack called back, announcing he would surrender and not fight the death penalty as long as he was executed. Gammick told him it was too early to make that decision and they should take things one step at a time.

Then, according to the district attorney, Darren Mack confessed to murdering his wife and shooting the judge. Unfortunately the ten-minute call was not recorded.

"Darren Mack advised me that he had in fact killed his wife, Charla," said Gammick, "and that he had in fact shot Judge Weller. [He said,] 'I killed my wife, but it was in self-defense. And I shot Judge Weller, but you know if I wanted him dead, he would be dead.'"

The DA asked Mack to resend the e-mail and then call back after giving him a chance to read it.

Over the next hour, the FBI and Reno police strategized with the district attorney, in readiness for Darren Mack's next telephone call. FBI agents planted a recording device on Gammick's phone under the federal wiretap authority.

At 2:30 p.m., Richard Gammick's phone rang and an FBI agent turned on the recording device. It was Darren Mack calling from a public phone on a Mazatlán street, using a phone card.

"Darren," said Gammick. "I grabbed the wrong line—you there?"

"I'm here," replied Mack. "Did you get the e-mail?"

The DA said he had found it and now had a printed copy on his desk in front of him.

"Okay," said Mack. "Well, there is one more thing . . . some access to the media. But I'm not going to fight for myself, but I do want to fight this battle."

Gammick said that was okay, but first he wanted to go through each of his conditions of surrender, telling him where he stood on them.

"I thought we [could] just walk through them," he said casually. "Do you mind if I put this on speakerphone so I can write?"

Mack said that was fine, so the DA turned on the speakerphone. Now all the investigators could hear the call, allowing them to provide input through scribbled notes.

Gammick said he did not have a problem with having Mike and Mel Laub there with him at the surrender. But he could not guarantee that he would be seeking the death penalty.

"That one I cannot answer for you at this time," he told Darren. "We've got laws that have to be met. I cannot promise you we're going to get you the death penalty."

"That's fine," Mack replied. "I just want it to be on the record that I'm not going to fight that."

Gammick said they should take it one step at a time, and although he was charged with Charla's "open murder," he had still not been charged in Judge Weller's shooting.

"I can guarantee you," said Gammick, "the judge and Shawn Meador are very much alive."

"I know they are," Mack said flatly.

Then Mack said he wanted a private cell with a computer and Internet access, so he could give media interviews. The district attorney said that might pose a security problem and he would have to consult with the sheriff.

"Would you?" asked the fugitive. "Would you give me your word you'll fight for it for me?

"I will give you . . ."

"[I'm] not saying that you can get it done," Mack interjected, "but that you'll support that."

"I can give you my word," replied the DA.

"Listen, I trust you, Richard, you're one of the only people in the government right now that I trust."

"I will give you my word," Gammick repeated, "I will definitely check into it. I will ask if it can be done. I've got one thing I want from you on this, though. Everything that you are printing or going to be put out or you are sending out, I get a copy of it."

"No problem," Mack replied. "All I want to do is just to expose what's happening to people in this thing called a family court industry that's destroying people . . . I'll get into the whole story when we have more time."

Then Gammick asked what he had done with the Ford Explorer he'd escaped in.

"I'm dying to figure it out," he said. "Where the hell is the car?"

"Um . . . ," replied Mack guardedly, "I will give you the keys to the car when I meet you. I'd like to meet you Thursday."

"Okay, if that's what we've got to do," said the DA. "You just got me dying because we've been looking for that car and can't find it."

"I know you are," said Mack smugly.

The district attorney then said they had to discuss how Darren was going to surrender, noting that there were some security concerns and it must be peaceful.

"Nobody'll get hurt," replied Mack. "I'm completely unarmed. You have my word on it. You've known me long enough to know that I wouldn't do anything to ever hurt you or anybody around you or any police officer."

"Well," the DA replied, "I didn't expect the thing to happen last Monday, either, buddy."

"I understand," said Mack. "You know you have my word as much as you can trust it at this point. I'm unarmed. There'll be nothing but a peaceful surrender. All I ask is the same thing. I don't want to have my teeth bashed in. I don't have a problem if you want me to lay down and have them frisk me and do everything you want. Have a sharpshooter sitting on me. I don't care. All I'm saying is I'm going to come in peacefully, otherwise I wouldn't be calling you. I could stay away for a long time."

"Well, I can guarantee—" Suddenly there was a loud beep on the line.

"What's that?" asked Mack suspiciously.

"Are you there?" replied the DA. "Okay, I can guarantee you a couple of things: one, I'll be there; two, you will be treated exactly the way you asked to be treated. So if you're cool, everything is mellow, you will not be manhandled. You will not be hurt. If you go nuts on me, then they're going to—"

"I won't go nuts on you," Mack replied. "You have my word."

"You swear?"

"I wouldn't, Dick. I wouldn't be calling you if I was going to. I mean, I would just stay underground."

"All right," said the DA, "I understand that. I got you. We'd have fun looking for you. I'll tell you that."

"This phone card is going to just go out," said Mack excitedly. "So you got just, like, twenty-two seconds."

"Thursday. When and where?" said Gammick.

"Meet me in Mazatlán, Mexico. I will call you at noon Mazatlán time and tell you where I'll meet you."

A couple of minutes later, Darren Mack called back with a new calling card.

"Sorry," he said.

"Okay, I got Mazatlán, Mexico," said Gammick, "at noon on Thursday. How do we connect here?"

"I don't know," replied Mack. "You got a cell phone that will work in Mexico?"

The district attorney said he doubted his phone would work but would find one that would.

"Why don't you give me until tomorrow to get that arrangement made," he suggested, "and then you tell me when you want me to be here, and call me back here at the office and I can give it to you then."

Then Gammick said that if he didn't hear anything else, he would see Darren on Thursday noon in Mazatlán.

"How many airports are there?" he asked.

"I have no idea," replied Mack.

"Okay. I understand," said the DA. "I've one of my guys sitting here who's working on this who says there is one there. I've never been there. So we'll be in at the airport noon Thursday and go from there."

"Okay," agreed Mack.

"Don't get weird on me here," said Gammick, "like back in the back brush hills. Down in the canyons and crap like that."

"No, no, no, no. I'll do it in public. You've known me long enough," said Mack conspiratorially, "other than the incidents that happened the other day, that I'm not . . . I mean why would I do . . . I can't even think of a reason why I would do anything other than what I'm offering to do."

"Now you're sounding like the Darren I know. So I'm pretty good with that, okay."

Mack then repeated that he would never hurt any members of law enforcement accompanying Gammick to Mexico for the surrender.

"Those guys are all heroes in my book," said Mack, "so I don't have anything against any one of them and I don't want any of them hurt."

Then the DA asked if he should bring along recording equipment so Mack could be interviewed on the flight back to Reno.

"Yes, I want to talk," said Mack. "I don't want to have lots of recording stuff. I want to talk."

"We will need to get all this recorded at one time," Gammick told him.

"Yeah, I don't have a problem, but I just want to talk to you. And I don't care if you want to bring somebody from the press."

Then Gammick asked what expectations he had in terms of the media.

"My expectation is to be able to be interviewed by the media," he replied, "as soon as possible when I get back."

"Okay," said Gammick, "I guess I'm getting a trip to Mexico Thursday, huh?"

"You are."

"Good."

Then Mack asked him to keep everything low-key when he surrendered, so it would not become a "big hubbub."

Gammick assured him that as long as he was "mellow and cool," that's the way it would go down.

"I understand," said Mack. "Listen, if I'm a whacko and get all whacked out, then you do what you have to do."

"You don't sound like you're doing that to me," said the DA. "Just be cool; everything will go cool."

"Everything will be cool, I promise."

"All right."

"Super."

"All right, it's beeping again," said Gammick as the calling card ran out. "So we'll see you."

"Okay."

"Bye."

"Bye."

After hanging up, District Attorney Gammick and the investigators discussed their next move toward getting Darren Mack back on American soil.

"So we began dealing with that," said Detective Ron Chalmers. "It was obvious he hadn't talked to his attorney. He began to negotiate a surrender, clearly not knowing that he had an attorney hired for him. He clearly had not talked to his family and very obviously he had not talked to anyone."

Although Scott Freeman had asked the detective to inform him if and when Darren Mack made contact, Chalmers did not, knowing Freeman would order his client to invoke his right to remain silent.

CHAPTER THIRTY-TWO

The FBI's Most Wanted

On Tuesday, June 20, the FBI officially placed Darren Mack on its list of the top ten most wanted fugitives. His photograph was now posted on the FBI Web site, listing him as a five-foot-eleven-inch, 190-pound bodybuilder with "access to all types of weapons."

FBI director Robert S. Mueller III warned that Darren Mack should be considered "armed and dangerous."

At 10:25 a.m., Darren called Richard Gammick's office again after receiving a message that the DA wanted to finalize arrangements for his surrender. The investigative team had decided not inform the Mexican authorities in order to avoid any unforeseen extradition problems. An FBI special agent was on hand to offer advice during the call.

"We've been doing some brainstorming here," Gammick told the fugitive, "and I'm sure we're on the same sheet of music. There's no way in the world that we want to notify the Mexican authorities when we're coming in and what we're up to. There's no way in the world we want the Federales to get their hands on you if we can help it. I imagine you're in the same boat."

"Right," agreed Mack.

Gammick then said they had decided that he should give

himself up at a U.S. embassy, saying he had several suggestions of ones for his approval.

"Well, let me give you a different city that I'm close to," said Mack.

"All right go."

"It's Puerto Vallarta."

"Okay," said the DA. "Does Puerto Vallarta have a consulate?"

"Okay."

"So you want to plan on that?

"Yeah, that's fine," said Mack, "but what do I do, just go to the consulate gates?"

"I've got one of the federal guys here that does this stuff with me," said the DA, " 'cause we're trying to get all of this planned out."

Then, at the apparent prompting of the special agent, Gammick suggested the surrender take place at the U.S. consulate in Guadalajara, three hundred miles south of Mazatlan.

"They're inland a little further," he explained, "but if you want to do Puerto Vallarta, we're going to need to call them and get all the details [of] exactly what needs to be done. Can you call me back?"

Mack said he could, and asked the DA to call his two friends, Mel and Mike Laub, and see if they would come to Mexico too.

"I can't reach anybody," Mack complained.

Gammick said that he did not have room for both brothers, although Mike was "scheduled" to come along.

"Hang on, hang on," Gammick said, apparently receiving another instruction from the FBI agent. "I did have another question for you. Is there any chance that you can get back across the border to the United States?"

"Um, I don't know," replied Mack. "Coming back through is probably a little bit more challenging [than] getting out."

"Do you have fake identification or anything, or are you using yours?" the DA asked.

"Well, neither one."

"Neither one? That wasn't the answer I was looking for," said Gammick. "You don't have any ID with you?"

"Well . . ."

"I don't care what it is."

"I'm not using any ID."

"Okay, well, I just want to know, if you had fake ID, if you could get across the border."

"No, I can't," said Mack. "I don't have fake ID."

Then Mack said if he was going to give himself up in Guadalajara, they'd have to postpone the meeting, as it would take him longer to get there.

"I have to figure out a way to get there."

"Okay, and Puerto Vallarta you could make Thursday at noon still?"

"Yep."

"Okay. Call me back in two hours, would you?" said Gammick.

"I will. All right, bye."

At 1:00 p.m., a private funeral service was held for Charla Mack at the Mountain View Mortuary on Reno's west side. In honor of the solemn occasion, Palace Jewelry and Loan closed for a few hours so employees could attend.

Soorya Townley and her son, Christopher, came with Charla's daughter, Erika. Also there were Darren Mack's mother, Joan, his brother, Landon, and cousin Corey Schmidt.

"So we were going to her funeral," said Schmidt, "the same day that Darren was put on the FBI top ten most wanted. It was just difficult. We all went there and I mean we all loved Charla too. It's tough."

Teams of TV crews and reporters arrived to cover the funeral but were kept one hundred yards away from the mortuary by heavy security.

The one-hour service, entitled "Celebration of Charla's Life," was attended by an estimated five hundred mourners.

"It was a full house," said Laura Cunningham. "It was terrible."

Charla's ex-boyfriend Mark Phillips went, later telling a reporter that the service and ensuing reception had been positive.

"People shared the memories that stood out in the years that we knew her," he said. "I spent time with [Erika]. Everyone was making sure that she was surrounded by family."

At the same time that his wife was being laid to rest, Darren Mack bought a $55 bus ticket for the two-hundred-mile journey south along the coast to Puerto Vallarta. That night he made the eight-hour journey to the scenic resort town to give himself up.

Back in Reno, co–lead detective John Ferguson and his team were trying to locate Darren Mack through e-mails and various postings to his favorite Internet sites. Since going on the run, he had been blogging on various judicial rights sites under the name "Mark." And DA Gammick had posted a special contact cell phone number for him to use on the Legal Reader site.

Investigators were desperately trying to pinpoint Darren's location from the ISPs he was using, while closely watching the Legal Reader Web site. They were also monitoring his "Toomuchfun" MySpace page, which he was regularly checking into.

"We were doing a lot of stuff to determine where he was," Detective Ferguson explained. "There was a way we could watch [the Legal Reader site] in real time and see who was posting, and then go to that particular post and go into the record of what ISP it came out of. Once we started looking at the ISP stuff, we knew how he was traveling and we had a pretty good understanding of where he was."

Detectives tracked down many of the "Mark" postings to the same ISP, working closely with FBI agents in Mexico to run it down.

"We had two thoughts," said Detective Ferguson, "that it was either an Internet café that he was going to, or a hotel.

We had a kind of general area, so we basically just pulled up all the hotels and started asking them what their ISP was."

And with all the heavy media coverage and his picture everywhere, investigators were certain he would avoid luxury resorts, where he could easily be spotted again.

"I don't think he was [in] the resort crowd," said Ferguson. "I think it was probably the little dive hotel that might have an Internet connection in the lobby."

Detectives also attempted to build up a picture of Darren Mack's day-to-day life in Mexico and where he might be hiding out. They theorized he had not thought out his escape plan quite as well as his to-do list.

"What's he going to do?" asked Detective Ferguson. "He had a bagful of money but doesn't speak Spanish, so you can't blend into the background. He was a pretty good-sized guy, so you're not going to blend in that way. The only thing I think was probably to his advantage is that his skin was a bit darker, so he could probably pass as someone with a Mexican mother and an American father—as long as he didn't open his mouth."

While the FBI and Reno Police Department searched for Darren Mack, forensic investigators were carefully building the case against him for when he was caught. Latent print examiner Ronald Young, of Washoe County's forensic science division, had been busy studying photos of latent fingerprints found on the bloody ignition key belonging to Charla Mack's Lexus SUV. And he had identified a thumbprint belonging to her husband.

His colleague Suzanne Harmon, a senior criminologist, examined swabs of blood taken from Charla's clothes, her Lexus, Darren Mack's Jeep Cherokee, and the yellow pants Dan Osborne had been wearing the morning of the murder.

She analyzed swabs taken from three different areas of the Lexus ignition keys and fob, obtaining positive results for blood on all of them. There was also blood from the Lexus's exterior driver's door and steering wheel.

The forensic criminologist analyzed the pants that were removed from Charla's body at the autopsy.

"It was heavily stained with blood," Harmon would later testify, "and additionally there were numerous animal hairs . . . possibly that of a dog."

She also found blood on the driveway leading up to Mack's garage as well as inside above a light switch and on a dead bolt on the door leading into the residence. They traced a bloody trail going up the stairs, with positive results from swabs taken from banisters, the kitchen door, as well as by a mirror and on shower door handles in the master bathroom.

In another laboratory in the forensic science division's DNA section, scientist Jeffrey Riolo examined numerous blood samples taken at the murder scene. Using a known DNA reference standard from Charla Mack, Riolo found traces of her DNA on Dan Osborne's pants where his dog, Rusty, had rubbed up against him.

He analyzed samples taken from the blood-coated Lexus keys, finding Charla's Mack's DNA mixed with another DNA profile, too weak to identify.

Charla's DNA was also found in blood samples taken from the garage, on a chair in the upstairs living room, and in the master bathroom.

CHAPTER THIRTY-THREE

Surrender

By the time he arrived in Puerto Vallerto, Darren Mack had somehow learned he had legal representation back in the United States. He had already spoken to Scott Freeman and David Chesnoff, who had ordered him to stop talking to Richard Gammick.

"He told us," recalled Chesnoff, "that he could explain why what happened with the judge happened."

On Wednesday, June 21, Joan and Landon Mack flew to Las Vegas with Scott Freeman, meeting David Chesnoff for a conference call with Darren to discuss his surrender. Several days earlier, Landon had given Freemen a $30,000 payment on his retainer.

That afternoon, Darren Mack telephoned David Chesnoff in his office.

"He told me in a telephone conversation that he wanted to come back and face the death penalty," the defense attorney said. "I thought that was a little insane."

Then, in the middle of the conversation, Joan and Landon walked in with Scott Freemen.

"When we arrived," said Landon Mack, "Chesnoff was already on the phone with my brother. The first thing Darren said was 'Thanks for finding these guys.'"

Darren wanted to know whether he was going to surrender to Richard Gammick and the FBI or to his new attorneys.

"Darren then proceeded to address the two conditions of his return,"·Landon said. " 'Does everybody in the room agree that Freeman and Chesnoff will use all their legal power and connections to see that Erika is placed with my mom [Joan Mack] or my brother [Landon] or both?' "

The other condition was that when the case eventually went to trial, he would get to tell his story to the jury.

"Then Darren canvassed the room," said his brother, "and once again all the parties agreed."

At around 6:00 p.m. they called Richard Gammick to finalize Darren Mack's surrender.

"We were preparing to go to Mexico," said Gammick, "and on the line was Scott Freeman and David Chesnoff."

Gammick asked Darren Mack if both attorneys were now legally representing him; Darren replied that his family had hired them.

"And I said, 'No, that's not the question,'" said Gammick. "'Are these people representing you?' At that time David Chesnoff broke in and said, 'Are we your lawyers?' And he said, 'Yes, you are.'"

Darren Mack agreed to surrender at 8:00 a.m. the following morning Puerto Vallarta time (which is an hour behind Reno time), at the American consulate in Puerto Vallerta.

"It would basically be a safe haven for everyone involved," explained Gammick, "and then we could just go ahead and pick him up there."

But arresting Darren Mack wouldn't be so simple, as they would soon find out.

At 7:53 p.m. that night, a rambling blog appeared on the Legal Reader Web site under the name "Mark," who purported to be a friend of Darren Mack. Reno police were monitoring the posting, which was sent from the IP address 201.121.174.67, assigned to Latin America, the Caribbean, and Mexico:

Here is the real numbers as given to me in documents by Darren himself. . . . I saw the real financial and bank records myself.

The order said:
44,000 income
15,000 income taxes that no-one remembered that had to be taken out.
Remember income taxes
_____

29,000 left after taxes
10,000 spousal support as per Weller's order
_____

19,000 left after spousal support
14,000 all those items that were listed on that order by Weller but not put into dollars. Just the 2 mortgages were 9,000 a month. I have seen the bank records.
_____

5000 left after paying all the bills ordered to be paid by Weller.
849 child support for one child
1000 child support to the previous wife for another child
_____

3151 left after child support
6000 in interest payments and other expences [sic] that Weller did not address in his order but had to be paid. Can't tell the bank Weller said I don't have to pay.
_____

-2849 left after bills that must be paid that Weller did not address.
15000 a month for attys fees to fund a war that he tried to settle many times rather than go BK.
_____

-17,849 left after attys fees. Remember Darren has yet to spend $1 on rent, food, gas, car, support one

child full time that lived with him and one child that lived with him half time.

6000 a month for all the above. Darren had a minus cashflow of $-23,849 per month

based on Judge Weller's order. Live with that for 2 years!! And see if you need to file BK. Get a grip people.

So here it is in simple form Weller. A man making $44,000 a month to pay $61,849 before he got $1 to live on himself and to take care of his children when they lived with him. You make your own conclusion of fairness.

Remember criminals like Charla's atty Shawn Meador and brought and paid for Judges can make anything look reasonable in court docs. The real test is how does it play out when you have to write the check and balance the checkbook. Don't be fooled by the surface level BS. I have seen the bank records.

Posted by Mark at June 21, 2006 07:53 PM

At 8:30 A.M. Thursday morning, when Darren Mack failed to show up at the U.S. consulate in Puerto Vallarta, law enforcement ratcheted up the pressure on him. The Reno Police Department immediately called a press conference and issued a release, updating the media on the investigation.

Reno police chief Mike Poehlman and Washoe County DA Richard Gammick shared the platform at the news conference, which was carried live by all Reno TV stations. The flamboyant sixty-year-old district attorney wore a Reno Rodeo–style shirt and a large gleaming silver belt buckle, and seemed to be enjoying the spotlight.

Behind them on the wall was a large map of Mexico, with Mack's suspected flight path highlighted.

"Darren Roy Mack, wanted in the murder of his estranged wife, Charla, and for the sniper shooting of Reno family court judge Charles Weller on June twelfth," said Chief Poehlman, "today failed to turn himself in to a U.S. consulate in Mexico at Puerto Vallarta at 8:30 this morning. Earlier this week, Mack contacted DA Dick Gammick by telephone and expressed a desire to surrender."

Chief Poehlman told reporters that Mack was believed to be using the names "Darren Stone" and "John Smith," and had last made contact the previous night at 6:00 p.m.

"He is believed to have been in the Mazatlán and Puerto Vallarta areas of the west coast of Mexico this week," the chief said. "There was a credible sighting of Mack in Cabo San Lucas on June the fifteenth. And we believe he had also been in La Paz on June seventeenth on the Baha Peninsula. Our belief is that he has a large sum of cash with him."

Chief Poehlman appealed to the public to continue to be on the lookout for the silver 2006 Ford Explorer SUV with California license plates that Mack was believed to be driving.

"I would emphasize," he said, that "we consider Darren Mack to be armed and dangerous. He did not follow through with an agreement that he had made with us and the DA to surrender himself this morning. That only leads us to believe he's gone off in a completely different direction and changed his mind.

"We believe when he left he was armed and had sufficient weapons, so somebody traveling to Mexico in that area, if they've seen his picture and they think they see him, notify the Mexican authorities."

Then a reporter asked DA Richard Gammick how Mack had gotten in touch with him.

"He called me Monday," said the DA, "and as far as we are able to determine, he was still [in Mexico] as of yesterday evening. He would not tell me where he was at. I picked up that information through conversations from places we were supposed to meet."

Gammick was asked how Mack's no-show would affect any future negotiations.

"If he does call me back again," said the DA, "we're going to have a little discussion about his credibility. And I'm going to have a heart-to-heart with him to see where we're going to go."

Detective Ron Chalmers explained that after Darren Mack failed to surrender, investigators changed strategy.

"We obviously turned up the heat significantly on Darren," said Detective Chalmers. "I understand that, based on our release, the Mexican authorities began setting up roadblocks and doing a lot of stuff around Puerto Vallarta."

It had been agreed to tell the media that Mack was carrying a large amount of cash on him.

"If you're Darren Mack," said Chambers, "you've got to think that Mexico's not the place you want to be when everyone knows you've a lot of money."

After failing to give himself up, Darren Mack decided to take his case to the American people. He contacted Fox News host Greta Van Susteren, trying to arrange a live interview that night on her top-rated show *On the Record*.

"I have a story to tell and a difference to make," he told her in one of his many e-mails. "They want me as the sacrificial lamb. They want the pleasure of executing me . . . People have to understand that condemning any act in response to . . . divorce court . . . is like condemning us now for using violence with Osama [bin Laden]."

Van Susteren initially believed the e-mail to be a hoax, but the sender was so persistent, she finally invited him to call her.

"He did . . . many, many times," she later wrote in her blog. "You have no idea how many calls I received from him. Yes, my voice mail is now full."

The calls made certain "unusual" demands that had to be complied with first, and Van Susteren decided not to pursue the interview.

But at 7:00 p.m. that night, two hours before she was due to go on the air, the TV host received a call from a Reno detective who had somehow learned Mack had been in contact with her.

"I said I did not believe this to be true," said Van Susteren. "The detective seemed to have a different opinion . . . and asked me to call her if I heard from the fugitive Mack."

At the same time he was e-mailing Greta Van Susteren, "Mark" posted another incoherent message on the Legal Reader Web site:

> *This is just one order. The first financial order that was posted in just one of 20 or more things that were Nazi like against Darren. By the way anyone who understands the law would know that he couldn't appeal until the entire case was finished including custody and the divorce decree issues. . . . It is my understanding that he was in the middle of an emergency writ but those are very rarely used.*

> *They make up rules and they are the umpires so when they are crooked like in this case one has absolutely no chance at coming out without being robbed broke, put into BK, jailed, extorting the people around you, and then kidnapping your children. This is one place where one has no constitutional rights and that is in the 4 walls of the divorce court. It just legalized organized crime.*

> *It was not just with Darren but read fatherunite.org and you will see hundreds of stories of the crimes that divorce industry are inflicting on mostly men throughtout [sic] this country. They are plain out crimes. Read*

them and weep for crimes being waged against mostly men in this country.

Posted by Mark at June 22, 2006 11:11 AM

Soon afterward, a Reno Police detective and an FBI agent contacted the San Francisco headquarters of the Legal Reader, asking questions about Darren Mack.

"They both thought Mack might have been posting comments to this Web site," said John, the site administrator, "and that he might be continuing to monitor the comments on this site."

John told the detectives exactly how to monitor who was accessing the site in real time using a Site Meter. That was the last he heard from law enforcement.

That afternoon, Scott Freeman found Darren Mack a Mexican lawyer, in the event there were any extradition proceedings arising from the death penalty. And throughout the day Darren Mack was in contact with his attorneys, who had now taken charge of the terms of his surrender.

Finally, at 5:00 p.m., Freeman and David Chesnoff were ready to negotiate Darren's surrender with Richard Gammick without their client's further involvement. But by the time they reached a deal, the U.S. consulate had closed. So it was decided that Mack would give himself up in the lobby of the Marriott Hotel at midnight.

So he could easily be recognized, Freeman and Chesnoff promised to instruct their client to wear a red California Angels baseball cap.

FBI special agent Steven J. Kling arrived early at the Marriott Hotel to take charge of Darren Mack's midnight surrender. The former border patrol agent, who had worked many fugitive cases in his career, had no jurisdiction to make an arrest in Mexico. So he had previously contacted the Mexican immigration authorities, arranging for agents to come to the Marriott and make the actual arrest.

At 11:30 p.m., special Agent Kling was staking out the front entrance from the Marriott lobby when Darren Mack casually walked in, half an hour early. Kling immediately recognized the fugitive from his wanted poster.

Mack walked toward him wearing a blue and orange long-sleeved shirt and jeans and pulling his green two-wheeled suitcase. He looked tired and unshaven as he walked past the main check-in desk, turning left down a hallway toward the toilets. Then he stopped in front of a bank of public pay phones and called Scott Freeman back in Reno for last-minute instructions.

Special Agent Kling then phoned the Mexican immigration agents, saying Mack was early and he would keep him under observation until they could get there.

"I walked by him on the pay phone," said Kling. "I went into the bathroom briefly, stayed there a minute or two, and came out. He was still on the pay phone."

The agent walked past Darren, finding a vantage point in the lobby to observe him; he was still talking on the phone. A few minutes later he hung up and walked back into the lobby, stopping at the registration desk.

At that point, two Mexican immigration policemen arrived and came over to special Agent Kling, who pointed out Mack at the registration desk, talking to someone.

Then they all walked over and Special Agent Kling told Darren, "I believe we're the people you're looking for."

Mack smiled and gave himself up without a struggle. He was then escorted out of the Marriott front entrance to a white immigration van waiting outside. Special Agent Kling followed closely behind with Mack's suitcase.

After being searched for any weapons, Mack was handcuffed and driven away to a municipal jail in nearby La Juntas, ending the eleven-day international manhunt.

* * *

At around 1:00 a.m. on Friday morning, the van arrived at the drab concrete jail. At the front gate the immigrations officials got out of the van to identify themselves, leaving Special Agent Kling and Darren Mack inside.

Then, for the first time since his surrender, Mack spoke, expressing concern about his money.

"He told me that he had $37,500 in cash inside his suitcase," Kling later testified. "And he asked me who was going to remain with that suitcase during that evening. I assured him that I would take custody of his suitcase and his belongings."

Once inside the jail, Special Agent Kling telephoned Scott Freeman and put Mack on the line.

"I made sure he was all right," said Freeman, who had been anxiously awaiting news of developments in his office. "I monitored the entire process."

After the call, Mack said he was hungry, so the FBI agent drove into town to buy some food and then delivered it to Mack at the jail.

"There's not a lot of places open at that hour," Kling recalled. "We got some tacos at a taco stand, some bottled water, and soda."

After being processed, Darren Mack was placed in a cell away from the other prisoners. It was one of six lining a wall and there was a dirty tile floor for him to sleep on, as there were no beds, blankets, or mattresses in the jail. Outside the cell was a septic tank toilet.

At around 2:00 a.m., Special Agent Kling returned to his room at the Casa Magna Hotel in Puerto Vallarta. He immediately opened up Darren Mack's suitcase, counting the money inside.

"I was concerned about the money," he said. "It was $36,201. Every bill was a hundred-dollar bill except for the one-dollar bill."

During a cursory search of the case, Kling also found Mack's passport, driver's license, and credit cards, as well as clothing, shoes, and a bus ticket from Ensenada to La Paz in the name of Steve Santini.

* * *

Early on Friday morning, the U.S. ambassador to Mexico, Tony Garza, officially broke the news of Darren Mack's capture to the world in a statement released by the American embassy in Mexico City.

"The arrest of accused killer Darren Roy Mack," read the statement, "proves that criminals cannot find a safe haven on either side of the border."

PART THREE

CHAPTER THIRTY-FOUR

Going Home

At 7:00 a.m. on Friday, June 23, FBI Special Agent Steven Kling arrived at the Seguridad Publica Prisión in Las Juntas to collect his prisoner. Then Kling and a Mexican immigration agent drove Darren Mack in handcuffs to Puerto Vallarta Airport, buying him a breakfast burrito, coffee, and orange juice.

They then boarded a 9:48 a.m. flight on American Airlines to Dallas, ahead of the other passengers. The prisoner was handcuffed at the waist and sat between special Agent Kling and the Mexican immigration officer at the back of the plane, to avoid attracting attention. Kling placed Mack's suitcase, packed with the one-hundred-dollar bills, in an overhead compartment.

Throughout the three-hour flight, Mack drank water but said nothing.

At 11:00 a.m. Reno time, they landed at Dallas/Ft. Worth International Airport.

"When we got off the plane," said special Agent Kling, "we were met by the FBI detectives from Dallas and U.S. Customs agents at the door of the aircraft."

The media had been alerted, and as Darren Mack was escorted by two policemen through the terminal in handcuffs, a TV news crew followed.

"Anything to say?" asked a reporter.

"Not at this point," replied the prisoner as he was put into a police car to be processed through immigration and customs.

"We went to the customs secondary area," said Special Agent Kling, "which has holding cells and offices to interview people."

Kling then handed Mack's suitcase over to the Customs Service, and an agent counted the notes in front of him, verifying it was exactly $36,201. A few minutes later, the Dallas Airport Police Department formally arrested Darren Mack for the murder his wife, Charla. On the advice of Scott Freeman, who had a Texas attorney there as a witness, Darren remained silent.

Mack was then taken to Dallas County Jail, where he waived extradition.

While Darren Mack waited in a holding cell at Dallas/Ft. Worth International Airport before being brought home, Reno police held a press conference to announce his capture.

"Darren Mack was apprehended in Puerto Vallarta, Mexico, overnight," declared Reno police chief Mike Poehlman. "And this morning was flown to the Dallas/Ft. Worth International Airport, where he was arrested by the Airport Police Department on a warrant charging him with the June twelfth murder of his estranged wife, Charla Mack."

Chief Poehlman told reporters that Mack had peacefully surrendered to the FBI and Mexican law enforcement the previous night at a Puerto Vallarta resort. He then spent the night in a Mexican jail before being flown to Dallas, where he now was being held.

He explained that Reno detectives were now on their way to Dallas on Nevada governor Kenny Guinn's official state of Nevada jet, to arrange for Mack's state extradition home.

"Once though in Reno," said Poehlman, "Mack is expected to be arrested for the attempted murder of Reno Family

Court judge Charles Weller...the same day as Charla's murder."

Chief Poehlman then fielded reporters' questions.

"Was it him turning himself in, or was he about to be arrested?" asked a TV reporter.

"I think it's a combination," said the chief. "I believe, based on what we know, that he was aware that things were tightening around him with these checkpoints that the Mexican authorities were running, aggressively checking public transportation, etc. He obviously was following the media and your coverage that we thought he was in the area. The Mexican media had picked up on that and was beginning to also get that information out."

A reporter asked Richard Gammick if the death penalty had played a role in the previous night's discussions with Scott Freeman and David Chesnoff.

"They did raise the death penalty," the district attorney replied. "As I've said all along and will continue to say, it is premature to even address that subject. We will address it at the appropriate time under the Nevada statutes and under the law."

Gammick was then asked how his twenty-year relationship with Darren Mack would affect the case, with his office ultimately deciding whether or not to seek the death penalty.

"I owe my allegiance to the people of this county," he replied, "and this case will be handled just like any other murder case. And an attempted murder. We'll throw that one in too."

The DA was then asked if any deals had been made with Mack in return for surrendering.

"There are no deals," he replied. "We had some other discussions of a personal nature to him, and I'm not going to discuss those at this time."

Gammick announced that had recused himself from the case and would not be prosecuting Darren Mack. The case had been assigned to Washoe County deputy district attorney Elliott Sattler.

He was asked if there would still be possible conflicts of interest and whether an outside prosecutor would have to be brought in.

"Not at this time," replied Gammick. "I like to take it a step at a time. If there's a challenge made for conflict of interest with our office, then we'll definitely address that however it needs to be addressed. The death penalty will be addressed somewhere down the road. We'll look at all of it.

"We've worked very carefully to try to avoid as many of these legal issues as we can, but the attorneys on the other side are aggressive and I'm sure we're going to see challenges on just about every single thing that can possibly be challenged. And a few that can't be."

A few hours earlier, lead detective Ron Chalmers had received a call informing him that Darren Mack was now in custody in Mexico.

"And then we were scrambling to try and catch a flight to Dallas and back," said the detective. "And the governor's state of Nevada jet was going to be the fastest, so we jumped on it and flew to Dallas to extradite him."

Detective Chalmers flew to Dallas with his boss, Sergeant Randy Saulnier, and another homicide detective. When they landed they were met by the two officers from the Dallas Airport Police, who drove them to Dallas County Jail, forty-five minutes away.

"Darren was sitting there on a bench with a suitcase," Detective Chalmers recalled. "We talked to him. He didn't seem scared but just very, very melancholy. He seemed very unexcited."

The detectives tried to talk to Mack, but he seemed very hesitant and slow to answer their questions.

"I wondered if there was something wrong with him," said Chalmers. "I'd ask him a question and there would be a ten-second pause and then he would answer. Is this guy slow? He seems dumb."

So Chalmers asked Sergeant Saulnier, who had known Mack for years from training in the same gym, what was wrong.

"Randy told me that he's just being very careful," said Chalmers. "He's thinking about everything you're saying before answering. Scott Freeman had talked to him significantly and told him not to say anything."

But Darren Mack was concerned about his Palm Treo smartphone in his suitcase, asking Detective Chalmers to charge up the device so none of his contact numbers or other electronic information be lost. He also asked that the cell phone be given to Freeman as soon as possible.

The Reno detectives drove Darren Mack to Dallas/Ft. Worth International Airport in handcuffs, stopping off at a Taco Bell to buy him something to eat. On the way there Detective Chalmers handed the prisoner his personal cell phone, asking if he wanted to call his family to let them know he was okay. Mack said no, but he did want to call his attorney.

"So I said, 'Sure. No problem,'" Chalmers said. "There's definitely some tactics that you use, and as I happened to have Mr. Freeman's number in my cell phone, I dialed it for him. I go, 'It should be ringing.' And you could see Darren's face going, *Well, how do you know Scott's number? What's going on here?*

"Well, I know that he's a little bit of a conspiracy theorist . . . so I'm playing a little bit of a game with him."

During the brief phone call, Freeman reminded his client to remain silent, warning that law enforcement would attempt to make him incriminate himself.

"I told him that the most powerful tool we had in his case was the confidentiality between us," said Freeman.

It was late afternoon when they arrived at Dallas/Ft. Worth International Airport. Darren Mack was then taken aboard the governor's jet, where he was shackled and seated next to Detective Chalmers for the long flight to Reno.

"He was very very quiet and fell asleep," Detective Chalmers recalled. "When he woke up, I talked to him a little bit, asking questions about the case. Small talk. Trying to build up a rapport with him.

"Clearly my significant goal was to get him to confess and tell us what happened. To tell us the truth so we would know what the truth was: good, bad, or indifferent, the truth is what I work in."

In an attempt to relate to his prisoner, the detective told Mack about his own father, who is currently serving a life sentence for lewdness with a minor under fourteen, and about his brother, a former heroin addict who went to prison and then managed to straighten out his life.

"I treat people differently than probably most police officers who don't have that background," Chalmers explained. "I understand how their crimes affect their family. I understand their fears and their expectations. I don't cast stones."

From personal experience, Detective Chalmers told him what it was like having a father in prison, comparing it to what Mack's son, Jory, would have to go through.

"And I remember him breaking down and crying at some point while we were talking about his children," said the detective.

During their long conversation, Detective Chalmers also discussed Mack's stated mission to change the family court system at length.

"I told Darren, 'You know, I don't agree with how you went about it, but I've got to give you credit. You have drawn a lot of attention to the family court system . . . and you actually have the ability and the power at this stage of the game to maybe make a change. Right now you have America's ear.'"

While Darren Mack was flying back to Reno, Chris Broughton held an emotional press conference with his mother, Soorya Townley.

"I'm Charla Mack's brother," he told reporters. "Our family, as it was, has forever been destroyed by the barbaric and heinous acts of June the twelfth. We are greatly relieved that Darren Mack has been apprehended without additional senseless bloodshed. And we look forward to justice being served for my sister's murder and for the shooting of Judge Weller."

A reporter asked how the family felt, now that Mack had been caught after eleven days on the run.

"Nothing will bring my sister back," he replied, "so we are still in mourning and we are still in great sadness. However, we don't have to look over our shoulder for the rest of our lives."

At around 11:00 p.m. on Friday night, Darren Mack landed at Reno International Airport. He was then taken to the Washoe County Jail in an armored SWAT van, escorted by two Reno police cars. When they arrived, Detective Chalmers led Darren out of the van in handcuffs, past a line of reporters and photographers waiting outside the back entrance. Five armed officers with assault rifles stood guard as he was escorted inside.

"Darren," shouted one female reporter, "why did you come back to Reno?"

Inside the sheriff's office, Darren Mack was formally booked before being fingerprinted and photographed to see if there were any injuries to his body. At one point Detective Chalmers and a police photographer took him into a bathroom to examine him naked.

"He had a healing incised injury on the back of his upper left arm," recalled the detective. "And Darren said, 'What are you looking at?'"

Then Mack explained that a doctor had done it a couple of months earlier, as part of a medical procedure. Detective Chalmers breathed a sigh of relief, thinking that he was going to claim Charla had tried to stab him.

Outside the jail, Scott Freeman and David Chesnoff, who had flown in from Las Vegas, waited patiently as their client was being processed.

"I didn't have any control," Freeman recalled, "because they had him in custody. But I was right outside the front door of the jail and I told them, very politely, I would like to see him as soon they were done with that process."

It was after midnight when Darren Mack's two attorneys were finally allowed into his cell to see him. And for the next three hours Freeman and Chesnoff discussed his situation and their next steps.

"We established a rapport with him," Freeman recalled, "and talked about the case. It was pretty dramatic . . . because we only talked to him on the phone [and] it was his first time seeing us."

They also discussed his various defenses to murder.

"One of the defenses I spoke about was self-defense," said Freeman. "It came in the context of Charla being stabbed."

At that first meeting, Mack admitted killing Charla, but made no mention of being attacked by Charla.

On Saturday morning, Darren Mack was placed on a special suicide watch in a private cell at Washoe County Jail. After a few hours' sleep, he began to undergo a barrage of physical and psychological evaluations.

Around mid-morning, Scott Freeman arrived at the jail for another meeting with his client and to prepare him for his scheduled arraignment on Monday morning.

"Yesterday was surrender day," Freeman told reporters waiting outside the jail, "and today is meeting-with-the-lawyer day."

Asked about the Mack family's reaction to Darren's capture, Freeman said they were relieved he was safely back in Reno.

"The most important thing," said Freeman, "is that their son and brother is alive. They're grateful this ended peacefully."

CHAPTER THIRTY-FIVE

Raw Emotion

On Monday, June 26, Darren Mack appeared via a video link from jail for his arraignment at Washoe County District Court. Wearing a regulation red prison jumpsuit, Mack remained silent throughout the hearing, which was abruptly halted after Scott Freeman refused to acknowledge any charges against his client.

Then he told Justice of the Peace Edward Dannan that the case must immediately be moved out of DA Richard Gammick's office and Washoe County's Second Judicial District, because of a conflict of interest.

Freeman, who sat with his client at the jail, also declared that the eventual presiding judge in the Mack case must come from a judicial district different from Judge Weller's.

"The district attorney's office," said Freeman, "is a witness in this case and has an actual conflict."

The defender also claimed that every judge in Washoe County had been affected by the events of June 12 and could no longer rule objectively.

"We're just looking for a fair trial," he declared.

After the dramatic hearing, Deputy DA Elliott Sattler said he had been expecting a hard-fought battle and was not surprised by Freeman's challenge.

"I guess," he told *Reno Gazette-Journal*, "this would be the first shot across the bow."

District Attorney Gammick strongly denied any conflict and vowed to fight the defense challenge.

"Just because I've known Darren Mack as an acquaintance," he told reporter Martha Bellisle, "doesn't mean he isn't going to be held responsible for what he has allegedly done. If this was in family court against Judge Weller, I could see it . . . but you can't just do a blanket 'I don't like him.'"

A few hours later, David Chesnoff told a Las Vegas TV news reporter that his concerns went far beyond his client's "personal relationship" with Richard Gammick.

"There are other issues," he said, "based on what we believe are some conversations he may have directly had with our client, prior to our representation of him and after the alleged events which may make him a potential witness."

Chesnoff warned that he might have to petition the Nevada Supreme Court to get justice for his client.

After the arraignment was postponed, Scott Freeman met his client to discuss a defense strategy. At this second meeting, Darren Mack for the first time claimed that Charla had pulled a gun on him in the garage.

"He indicated to me that he had meditated on what we had talked about," Freeman recalled, "and described to me in fairly significant detail what had occurred in the garage. That included a gun."

Mack told his attorney that he had gotten rid of the gun in a Dumpster, along with his bloody clothes and the knife that had killed Charla. He said the Dumpster was on the intersection of California Avenue and Arlington, just a couple of blocks from his law offices.

"And he described how he had gone into the alleyway and he was trying to clean the blood off the gun and the knife, and he had some bloody clothes," said Freeman. "And he also said that while he was at the Dumpster, he cleaned out his car and threw the trash out . . . in this Dumpster."

After leaving the jail, Scott Freeman went to look for the Dumpster.

"There was no Dumpster," he said. "I had two concerns . . . that perhaps Mr. Mack was being less than candid [with] me, or, alternately, the Dumpster had been moved. So I decided to go with the Dumpster being moved as opposed to him being less candid with me."

On Tuesday, June 27, Judge Chuck Weller and Annie Allison held a thirty-minute press conference at the National Judicial College. Looking weak and in obvious discomfort, the fifty-three-year-old judge said his health was improving daily.

"It hurts a little bit," he told reporters. "I'm mostly okay. I'm just healing."

The judge, who was sitting in a chair, said the scars from the shrapnel wounds were still healing over and were very painful if he stood for long periods.

He said he and his family had breathed a sigh of relief after Darren Mack was captured, as they had been concerned for their safety while he was on the loose.

"I didn't know if the violence was over," he said. "There were a lot of sightings of the suspect."

Judge Weller described family court as "a place of raw emotion," but refused to say how he personally felt about his attacker.

"Mr. Mack is entitled to all of the protections that our system affords: due process of law, the presumption of innocence. The court system will appropriately deal with Mr. Mack."

Later that day, Alecia Biddison wrote a letter to Joan Mack, offering support and sympathy. It was a difficult letter to write, and Biddison had thought long and hard before putting pen to her personalized notepaper.

I wanted to take a moment out of my busy schedule to tell you about my friend Darren. I met Darren sev-

*eral months ago. He responded to a posting I had
placed on an Internet blog. You see, I too am a victim of
Washoe County's broken family court and judicial system. I have been working with Darren to expose possible corruption in the courts as well as to make changes
to repair the overall system. We were making progress.*

*I opened my heart, my home, and the lives of my
fourteen month old son and me to Darren because he
is a warm, passionate, caring, fun and family-oriented
man.*

*. . . There is no doubt in my mind that Darren is an
active and involved father, because it was with great
pride that he regularly shared his stories of his children and their accomplishments.*

*I was very much looking forward to the opportu-
nity to meeting each of you.*

*I wish you strength and courage during this very
difficult time. My prayers and love are with you and
your family. I hope what I have shared brings you some
comfort. I miss my friend.*

CHAPTER THIRTY-SIX

Conflicts of Interests

Late Wednesday night, Scott Freeman filed a motion in Reno Justice Court, demanding that Darren Mack's case be frozen immediately. It accused District Attorney Richard Gammick of unethical behavior for not disqualifying himself from the case because of his long-standing personal relationship with Mack. It claimed all charges had been filed "inappropriately."

The defender labeled the criminal complaint a "fugitive document."

In his motion, Freeman claimed that Gammick had lunched with Darren Mack on at least three occasions during which they'd discussed his divorce and problems with Judge Weller. And his many telephone and e-mail communications with Mack while he was a fugitive in Mexico had made the district attorney a witness.

The motion also claimed that Judge Weller's shooting had affected all Washoe County District Court judges, rendering them incapable of viewing the Mack case objectively.

"Boy, he's desperate, isn't he?" Gammick told the *Reno Gazette-Journal* after reading the defense motion. "I've made no secret of the fact that I'm an acquaintance of Darren Mack. He asked me if I knew some names of some lawyers who could help him out. I fail to see why that's an issue."

The following morning, Darren Mack's arraignment continued in Washoe County District Court. Once again Darren Mack appeared through closed-circuit television from jail with Scott Freeman and David Chesnoff standing on either side of him.

But despite defense objections, Justice of the Peace Dannan refused to delay proceedings, arraigning Mack and setting his preliminary hearing for July 11.

Soon after the surrender, lead detective Ron Chalmers received a telephone call from a prominent Las Vegas attorney. He claimed Darren Mack had unsuccessfully tried to solicit a mob hit man to murder Charla and a family court judge, even showing him a rifle he wanted used.

"The attorney called me and passed on that information," said Detective Chalmers. "We tried to interview the gangster, who I guess has legitimate mob ties, but he refused to answer the interviews. But I'm under the impression that was true and accurate, from a fairly reliable source."

Darren Mack soon adapted to life in Washoe County Jail. He had his own private cell, thanks to Scott Freeman's influence, and was receiving first-class treatment.

"Quite frankly," Freeman explained later, "I had some strong relationships with the jail, and they allowed him some special courtesies."

The wealthy prisoner was also given office space to work on his case. And over the next few weeks Freeman would bring in thousands of pages of discovery for him to read.

"He kind of had it set up like an office in some ways," said Freeman, "because he had a solo cell."

Another visitor was Alecia Biddison, and over the next few months they would grow even closer.

"It was a very emotional kind of reunion," she said, "seeing him again for the first time and realizing the full gravity of what had happened, and how life was never going to be the same again."

During the visits, where they talked on the phone separated by a thick Perspex window, she never broached the subject of Charla Mack's killing or Judge Weller's shooting.

"We had been forbidden to," she explained. "The attorneys had made it very clear that that was something that [we] were not allowed to talk about."

On Wednesday, July 5, District Attorney Richard Gammick recused his office from the Darren Mack case, asking Clark County district attorney David Roger to appoint a team of special prosecutors to take over. He conceded that it was because of his long relationship with the accused and the likelihood of being called as a witness.

"My relationship with Mack has caused shadows on the case," he admitted. "Now [that] we've eliminated issues raised so far, we can get to the facts of the case."

Gammick said that from then on, Las Vegas–based prosecutors would make all the decisions, including whether Mack would face the death penalty. And he pledged money from his own budget to help finance the high costs of bringing in a special prosecutor.

It was an early victory for the defense, and Scott Freeman applauded Gammick's decision.

"We are very pleased that Mr. Gammick took the time to review the issues and made an obvious self-examination in terms of his relationship with Mr. Mack, and made the correct and professional decision," he told the *Reno Gazette-Journal.*

Over the next few weeks, Scott Freeman and David Chesnoff plotted out a defense strategy for Darren Mack. Landon Mack had agreed to pay the attorneys $1 million and at least $200,000 in costs. By mid-July he had already paid them $135,000 to get the legal ball rolling. The Mack family was convinced they were getting Darren the best defense money could buy.

From the beginning, the defense dream team sought an insanity defense for Charla Mack's murder. To this end they hired two experienced investigators to build up the always difficult defense.

"This wasn't like a whodunit where we were trying to find the killer," Chesnoff later explained. "We were trying to work an investigation that related to the defense that I wanted, which was insanity, because I believed that what occurred with Mr. Mack and his wife in the garage was also a product of his delusions. The only way to defend the case, as far as I was concerned, was insanity. At least to the second count, there was no available defense. It wasn't like we were looking for another shooter."

The second week of July, Clark County District Attorney David Roger assigned his two top prosecutors to the Darren Mack case: Assistant District Attorney Christopher Lalli, chief of the criminal division, and Chief Deputy District Attorney Robert Daskas, in charge of the major violator's unit.

"We're treating this as if it was a case that happened in our own community," DA Roger told the *Reno Gazette-Journal*, adding that a committee would decide whether to seek the death penalty after the scheduled August 8 preliminary hearing. The eventual trial would still be held in Reno.

Within days of the special prosecutors' appointment, Detective John Ferguson prepared a PowerPoint presentation on the Mack case. As Robert Daskas was busy prosecuting a murder trial, the entire Reno investigation team traveled five hundred miles south to Las Vegas to conduct a briefing.

At their first meeting with the Clark County prosecutors, the Reno detectives walked them through the case with PowerPoint.

Throughout the presentation, Chris Lalli took copious notes on his laptop computer, and had previously prepared a list of questions for the detectives.

"Chris is very meticulous," Detective Ferguson explained. "When we sat down with him at that initial meeting, he had a whole listing of questions to ask, and he wanted to discuss strategies."

A week later, after Daskas had finished his trial, he and Lalli flew to Reno to view the two crime scenes firsthand. Detective Chalmers had managed to secure an identical condo to Darren Mack's in the Fleur de Lis complex so they could conduct a walk-through.

"It had the exact same floor plan," said Detective Chalmers, "just so they could get a good feel for what the layout was and where we found the evidence."

On August 1, Darren Mack's preliminary hearing was postponed a month, so the two new special prosecutors could digest all the discovery. A week later the defense team filed a petition, demanding that all Reno Justice Court and Washoe District Court judges be disqualified from the case and the preliminary hearing.

"We just want Mr. Mack to have a fair trial," Scott Freeman pointed out. "The judges are good judges, but they're also human beings."

The defense argued that, as Judge Weller's courthouse shooting had affected every judge in Reno, the Nevada Supreme Court must immediately assign an outside judge to the case. The petition stated that because Judge Weller had "a significant personal relationship" with his judicial colleagues, any local judge overseeing the Mack case would cast "a cloud over the proceedings."

CHAPTER THIRTY-SEVEN

"Paralleled Only by the Unabomber"

On Thursday, August 10, Darren Mack was led into a Washoe County probate courtroom in shackles. It was his first appearance in a courtroom since his last family court appearance in May. Once again he was arguing about his money, although this time it was Charla's estate that was seeking it.

Several weeks earlier, Soorya Townley had hired civil attorney Egan Walker to file a wrongful-death suit against her son-in-law on behalf of the Charla Mack estate. One of their first moves had been to file a motion calling for Darren Mack's Palace Jewelry and Loan pension plan—worth an estimated $750,000—to be frozen.

On Scott Freeman's advice, Mack had hired Reno civil lawyer Mark Wray to argue that it was not part of his late wife's estate and therefore could be used toward his defense.

Dressed in regulation red jail garb, his wrists and ankles shackled together, Darren Mack sat alongside his new attorney. Behind him sat his mother and Scott Freeman.

Wray told probate commissioner Lynne Simons that the federal Employee Retirement Income Security Act exempted Mack's pension from any claims from his late wife's estate.

"If a former spouse does not have rights to the plan," he told Simons, "a deceased spouse doesn't and the estate does not."

Egan Walker countered, asking Simons to issue a restraining order so Mack could not touch the money. He argued that his pension was no longer protected by federal law if he had murdered his wife and that the money should go to Charla's estate and heirs.

"While no factual determination has yet been made with regard to Mr. Mack's responsibility for the killing of his wife," said Walker, "he should not profit from her estate pending any such determination."

At the end of the hearing, Commissioner Simons froze the pension funds for thirty days, allowing both sides to file motions on whether the case should be heard by a federal court.

That same day, Judge Weller administrative assistant Annie Allison filed a civil lawsuit against Darren Mack, alleging she'd "suffered extreme shock, horror, terror and fear for her life." Seeking punitive damages in excess of $50,000, Allison claimed the trauma caused by the sniper attack had left her in distress and suffering recurring nightmares.

One week later, Judge Chuck Weller returned to Washoe County Family Court to a standing ovation from fifteen local attorneys.

"I'm back at work, and I'm happy to be back at work," he declared to a round of applause. "This experience has changed every aspect of my life . . . it's been a transformative experience."

On August 21, the new special prosecutor, Chris Lalli, filed a motion opposing defense attempts to remove all Washoe District Court judges from the Darren Mack case. But he had no problems with the defense recommendation that the Nevada Supreme Court select a judge from another county to make the final decision.

In his motion, Lalli revealed horrific new details of how Darren Mack had allegedly killed Charla in his garage.

"He stabbed her body repeatedly," read the motion, "striking her with a knife or sharp object on her leg, forearm, wrist and throat. The resulting injuries included the severance of Charla's left carotid artery, her esophagus and her trachea. He also inflicted injuries that resulted in blunt force trauma to large portions of her body."

Later in the motion, Lalli argued that there was no reason to exclude Washoe County district and justice court judges from the murder case. He argued that Judge Weller's "professional relationship" with his judicial colleagues was not grounds to disqualify them all.

On Tuesday, August 29, Senior Judge J. Charles Thompson ordered the next day's preliminary hearing to go ahead, ruling that it was too early to disqualify Washoe County judges from the murder case. At a special hearing in Las Vegas, Judge Thompson said he would probably call in a judge from another county to run the case if Darren Mack was sent to trial for Judge Weller's attempted murder.

"I believe that a reasonable person," ruled Judge Thompson, "having learned all the facts . . . might question whether or not the district court judges of the Second District would be entirely impartial when one of their own is a victim of such a serious offence."

Then Scott Freeman attempted to delay the preliminary hearing, filing an emergency motion that his client first undergo a mental competency evaluation. Attached to his motion were affidavits from two psychiatrists, Dr. Ronald Segal and Dr. Norton Roitman, who had examined Mack in jail to evaluate his competency.

"Dr. Segal told me," defender David Chesnoff would later reveal, "that Mr. Mack was among the most paranoid people he had ever interviewed, paralleled only by the Unabomber."

At 10:00 a.m. on Wednesday morning, Darren Mack was back in court, still uncertain if his preliminary hearing would go ahead. For Reno justice of the peace Edward Dannan must first decide if his competency should be evaluated.

Arguing that it should be, Scott Freeman questioned

his client's mental state, citing various conversations he and David Chesnoff had had with him since his surrender. But he refused to reveal any details, citing attorney-client privilege.

Special prosecutor Chris Lalli told Justice of the Peace Dannan that he was suspicious of the timing of the defense competency motion.

"This is not a ploy," replied Freeman. "This is a real issue."

After hearing the arguments, Justice of the Peace Dannan ruled against a competency evaluation, ordering the preliminary hearing to begin immediately.

The first witness was Annie Allison, who described Judge Weller's concern about Darren Mack's behavior after the May 24 family court hearing.

" 'That guy gave me the look of death,' " she said the judge had told her after the hearing. She also said he had believed Darren Mack had placed an ad for a Harley-Davidson in the *Big Nickel* paper, giving out his home address.

The next witness was Reno police detective Shanna Wallin-Reed, who revealed that a to-do list for Charla's murder and the subsequent shooting of Judge Weller had been discovered in Mack's kitchen. She then read out the list, laying special emphasis on the "end problem" item.

Then Dan Osborne took the stand, vividly describing what he had witnessed the morning of June 12, and Darren Mack's "weird" look after Osborne's dog came upstairs covered in fresh blood.

Reno police detective David Jenkins then testified about discovering drops of blood outside Darren Mack's garage. He described opening the garage door, and seeing Charla Mack lying facedown in a large pool of blood.

Finally, Washoe County assistant medical examiner Dr. Katherine Raven testified that Charla Mack had seven stab wounds, including several defensive ones.

After hearing all the witnesses, Justice of the Peace Dannan ordered Darren Mack to be held for trial on charges of

Charla Mack's first-degree murder and the attempted murder of Judge Weller.

The next day, Judge Charles Thompson officially disqualified all Washoe County judges from Darren Mack's upcoming trial. Five days later, Chief Justice Robert Rose of the Nevada Supreme Court appointed Clark County District Court judge Douglas Herndon to take charge of the Mack case. He made his decision after consulting with the defense and the prosecution, who had both recommended Judge Herndon for the job.

Based in Las Vegas, the forty-two-year-old Texas-born judge was appointed to the bench in January 2005 by Governor Kenny Guinn. A former chief deputy district attorney in the Las Vegas Special Victims Unit, Herndon became a prosecutor in 1991, after law school. During his career, he had handled all types of cases, including homicide, sexual abuse, and Internet crimes against minors.

Judge Herndon was well acquainted with special prosecutor Chris Lalli and defender David Chesnoff.

"I probably know Chris as well as David Chesnoff," said the judge. "We've been on the same team together, but we never tried a case together.

On Monday, September 11, a special panel was convened to decide whether prosecutors should seek the death penalty against Darren Mack. Under Nevada law, someone convicted of first-degree murder could be executed by lethal injection if one of fourteen aggravating circumstances could be proved, without any mitigating ones outweighing them.

After considering all the factors, the panel decided that Darren Mack would not face lethal injection if found guilty of Charla Mack's murder.

When Detective Ron Chalmers learned that Darren Mack was getting preferential treatment at Washoe County District Jail, he lodged an official complaint. This resulted in inmate

Mack being moved out of his private cell to share one with another inmate.

"He seemed to be getting special treatment from the jail," said the detective. "He did not have a cell mate. I said, 'Stop treating him different. Stick somebody in that cell with him.' Quite frankly, it's better for the investigation if he starts talking and the cell mate gets some information."

Then Scott Freeman was told to collect all the boxes and bags of case discovery and law books by a certain date or they would be destroyed.

"They had emptied his cell," said Freeman, "so I had to physically come and get it . . . and bring it back to my office."

On Wednesday, September 13, Darren Mack pleaded not guilty to charges of first-degree murder with the use of a deadly weapon, and the attempted murder of Judge Weller. As he was led into court with his wrists handcuffed to a large chain around his waist, he sadly acknowledged Joan and Landon Mack, sitting behind the defense desk.

During his arraignment, Mack did not utter a word, as Scott Freeman entered not-guilty pleas to both charges on his behalf.

The defense attorney then told Judge Doug Herndon that their client intended to challenge all charges. He also announced he would be appealing Justice of the Peace Edward Dannan's ruling, demanding that his client undergo a full competency evaluation before the case proceeded any further.

Judge Herndon then set a trial date for October 1, 2007, giving the defense three weeks to file a petition to dismiss the charges against Mack.

On September 29, Reno was swept up in another high-profile murder case after critical-care nurse Chaz Higgs was arrested and charged with the first-degree murder of his wife, Nevada state controller Kathy Augustine. Just before her death of a

suspected heart attack, Higgs had told a colleague that Darren
Mack had been "stupid" to kill his wife the way he had. Higgs
said he would never make the same mistake and would use an
undetectable drug instead.

CHAPTER THIRTY-EIGHT

Get "Macked"

On Monday, October 2, Scott Freeman filed a motion in Washoe County District Court claiming that the attempted murder charge against his client should be dismissed. He maintained that prosecutors had failed to present enough evidence and that Darren Mack should be given a full competency evaluation.

Freeman's motion stated that the prosecution lacked evidence showing that Mack had fired the shot at Judge Weller.

"It is equally as possible," it claimed, "that it came from a weapon discharged by someone other than Darren Mack. We know of at least three other people who are or were royally upset with Judge Weller and his rulings, one of whom allegedly has a 'personality disorder.' To conclude, even as a matter of probability, that Darren Mack attempted to murder Judge Weller is to engage in pure speculation."

Freeman's motion also said Justice of the Peace Dannan's refusal to allow his client to be psychiatrically evaluated was biased and should be overturned.

Ten days later, Senior Judge J. Charles Thompson disqualified all Washoe County District Court judges from handling any of the civil cases involving Darren Mack. Explaining this unprecedented move, Judge Thompson said he had applied the "same rationale" to the civil cases as he had with the criminal.

Two weeks later, Nevada Supreme Court Chief Justice Robert Rose assigned the seven civil cases to two judges from neighboring counties. Judge David Huff of the Third Judicial District was put in charge of the Charla and Darren Mack divorce case; a probate case involving Darren's first wife, Debra; the Charla Mack estate case; and Joan Mack's ongoing civil case against her late daughter-in-law for the return of a diamond ring and a Rolex watch.

Judge John Iroz of the Sixth Judicial District was assigned Erika Mack's custody case, and Annie Allison's damage suit against Darren Mack.

Darren Mack's civil attorney, Mark Wray, welcomed the appointments, so all the cases could now move forward.

"We've been in limbo since August in all these civil matters," Wray said.

On October 24, special prosecutor Chris Lalli filed a motion claiming Darren Mack was fully competent to stand trial.

"[The] defendant," his motion read, "has presented no evidence of hallucinations, delusions, history of mental disorder, attempts at suicide, time spent in mental health facilities or numerous witnesses of the opinion that he is incompetent."

Two weeks later, Charla Mack's estate sued Darren Mack for her wrongful death, seeking an unspecified amount of compensatory, special, general, and punitive damages. The nineteen-point civil suit filed by the estate's recently appointed administrator, Randal S. Kuckenmeister, accused Darren Mack of "viciously and brutally" attacking Charla Mack "without provocation or cause" and stabbing her seven times, ultimately causing her death.

"During the marriage," it stated, "Darren Mack was physically abusive of Charla Mack, causing [her] significant and substantial emotional and physical pain and suffering.

"Before Charla Mack died . . . she unsuccessfully attempted to defend herself, sustaining additional wounds and injuries in her effort to defend herself. From the initiation of Defendant Mack's attack on Charla Mack to the time of her death, [she] experienced sustained severe physical and emotional pain, suffering, disfigurement and anguish.

"Given the financial condition of Darren Mack and in light of the malicious, vicious, willful and deliberate nature of [his] fatal attack on Charla Mack, punitive damages should be awarded in the maximum amount allowed by law."

Four days later, Detective Ron Chalmers flew to Mexico, after Darren Mack's rented 2006 Ford Explorer was found abandoned at the Cinema Star long-term parking garage in Ensenada, about fifty miles south of Tijuana.

Detective Chalmers wanted to process the vehicle in Ensenada, before towing it back to Reno. So he brought along Reno police detective Scott Hopkins and forensic investigator Victor Ruvalcuba from the Washoe County Sheriff's Office to assist.

"He wanted to process the exterior of that vehicle," explained Investigator Ruvalcaba. "In addition, the authorities in Mexico had located a weapon in the car and he wanted to process [it] because it was believed . . . that they weren't going to release that weapon to us."

When they arrived in Ensenada, the Reno investigators went straight to the Mexico Federale office, where they were taken to a room where Mexican police had brought the contents of the Explorer.

A Federale opened a drawer and brought out a plastic bag containing a Desert Eagle handgun.

"They pulled it from a drawer," recalled Ruvalcaba, "and set it on a counter. It had been handled a lot prior to my receiving it."

The officer also handed him a nylon ankle holster with two magazines and ten cartridges, as well as some toll bills and a parking receipt from Sacramento Airport dated June 12, 2006. The Mexican police had also found twelve empty water bottles and cans of the energy drink Red Bull.

Investigator Ruvalcaba processed the gun for latent fingerprints but found none.

After impounding everything found inside the vehicle, the detectives were taken to another building, where the now dusty Ford Explorer had been towed. Then, after processing its exterior, the investigators went to the parking garage to photograph where it had been found.

They returned to the impound lot, placing the Explorer on a flatbed tow truck for the six-hundred-mile journey back to Reno.

"It was towed . . . to the border," said Ruvalcaba, who traveled inside the tow truck with Detective Chalmers while Detective Hopkins sat in the vehicle. "At [the border] it was transferred to a different tow truck."

When the Ford Explorer reached Reno after its two-day journey, it was taken to the Washoe County forensic investigation section (FIS) garage. There, the interior was tested for gunshot residue, the small particles emitted from the barrel of a gun or rifle after firing.

Investigator Ruvalcaba performed the gunshot residue test, placing strips of special tape on the interior cargo doors, posts, and window moldings. Then he dabbed the tape lifts on these surfaces, picking up any trace evidence.

"I had to ship out the gunshot residue kits," said Inspector Chalmers, "as we don't do that here locally, which ultimately came back positive that the interior of the car still, six months later and with him traveling six hundred miles to Ensenada, tested positive for gunshot residue. It only confirmed the fact that a shot had been fired from within that vehicle."

On Thursday, November 16, Darren Mack was back in Washoe County District Court wearing a smart white dress shirt, a tie, and black pants. His attorney had successfully petitioned Judge Herndon to let him wear his own designer clothes for all future court appearances.

Judge Herndon had flown in from Las Vegas for the hearing on the defense motion to throw out the attempted-murder charge for lack of evidence.

Special prosecutor Chris Lalli argued there was plenty of evidence to charge Darren Mack for Judge Weller's attempted murder.

"You have Charla Mack brutally murdered," he said, "and you have Judge Weller attempted to be murdered. What is the common thread there? The common thread is Darren Mack."

Judge Herndon then observed that many people are angry with family court decisions, but don't "go out and kill the judge."

He said he could not view the evidence "in a vacuum," but cumulatively it was enough for Darren Mack to go to trial for attempted murder and battery with a deadly weapon.

The judge then turned to the defense motion that the defendant should have been allowed to have a mental competency evaluation prior to his preliminary hearing.

Defender Scott Freeman argued that his client had been unfairly treated by the court after his surrender. He said that denying him a psychiatric evaluation was just one example of how the defense always "get Macked."

"The Mack case has taken on a life of its own," Freeman told the judge. "It is the Mack mode."

Judge Herndon upheld Justice of the Peace Dannan's ruling, saying it was reasonable. And without something concrete to suggest Mack suffered from mental health problems, the defense's claim of incompetency would not stick.

At the beginning of December, television crews from the CBS show *48 Hours* and *Dateline NBC* visited Reno to film segments on the Darren Mack case. The *48 Hours* team were also preparing a show on the Chaz Higgs case in tandem with the Mack one.

"I can't remember the last time we had two stories coming out of the same town at the same time," explained producer

Marc Goldbaum. "There are a lot of elements in the [Mack] case that I, obviously, thought made it a national story, beginning with the judge being shot."

Providing color and a unique perspective on the case, as a *48 Hours* special correspondent, was *Marie Claire* magazine writer Amanda Robb, who had gone to Reno High School with Charla Mack and Darren Mack's first wife, Debra. Robb's acerbic in-depth feature on the case had appeared in the December issue of *Marie Claire*, sending shock waves through the town.

"Fashion magazine *Marie Claire* should stick to what it does best," wrote *Reno Gazette-Journal* journalist Siobhan McAndrew in an editorial. "It should run articles on 'How Snacking Can Make You Skinny,' and 'Hot Tricks for Holiday Hair and Makeup.'

"When it paid a former local woman . . . to report on the Darren Mack case, it portrayed our city and the people who live here as obsessed with money and sex."

CHAPTER THIRTY-NINE

Preparing for Trial

That Christmas, Darren Mack remained behind bars at Washoe County Jail, preparing his defense for his criminal and civil cases. Scott Freeman visited regularly, updating him on how the defense case was going and raising his morale.

"I saw him on a weekly basis," recalled Freeman, "and sometimes I saw him with other people."

The fact that he regularly visited his client in jail, while his Las Vegas–based case partner David Chesnoff seldom came, led to some friction.

"Mr. Freeman complained regularly to me that I lived [in Las Vegas] and he got stuck with going every week," Chesnoff said.

From the beginning, Darren Mack's defense was an uphill battle, and his attorneys were concerned that the prosecution had damning evidence showing premeditation.

"Mr. Freeman and I made it clear to him," said Chesnoff, "that the state's prosecution was a premeditated prosecution and there were all sorts of additions . . . including having $36,000 in cash on him to escape. I thought escape suggested premeditation."

On January 2, 2007, Charla Mack's estate asked a judge to impose the $1 million divorce settlement that Judge Weller had ordered Mack to pay just prior to her killing. The estate's lawyer, Egan Walker, said that even though the divorce settlement had not been signed, it was still valid.

A week later, Darren Mack's new team of civil attorneys, John Springgate and Mark Wray, lodged an objection calling for the Mack divorce case to be dismissed on the grounds that Charla was dead.

"The undeniable evidence," stated their thirty-five-page petition, "is that there was no final enforceable agreement. The court should find as a matter of law that the divorce abated with the death of one of the parties and the case should be dismissed."

On January 23, the U.S. Senate majority leader, Harry Reid, backed a new bipartisan bill in Congress strengthening protections for judges, as a direct result of Judge Chuck Weller's shooting. The Democratic Nevada senator said he was making the proposed Court Security Improvement Act of 2007 a top priority.

"The urgent need for this legislation," he explained, "is especially important to the people of Nevada, where someone attempted to take the life of Judge Weller of Reno just this past summer. I am committed to fast-tracking this legislation—quickly passing this bill in the Senate and working with the House in order to get it to the president to become law."

Under the proposed bill, there would be new criminal penalties for anyone using personal information to threaten or seriously harm judges and their families. It would also provide federal money in all states for better security for all state and local courts.

On Tuesday, February 13, 2007, Alecia Biddison met Scott Freeman in his office to discuss her boyfriend's defense.

"During this short meeting," she said, "Mr. Freeman and I discussed the need for an immediate payment of $250,000 to fund expert witnesses [and] investigators and pay for continued work on the case."

One of the defense's main priorities was to have Darren Mack's highly damaging phone calls from Mexico to DA Richard Gammick declared inadmissible. In mid-April, Freeman and Chesnoff filed a motion in Washoe District Court claiming the district attorney had illegally recorded the telephone conversations while their client was on the run.

"It certainly is a felony in Nevada," read the motion, "to record someone without prior authorization."

As soon as he heard this, DA Gammick lashed out at the defense lawyers.

"It's a lie," he declared. "All of those conversations were made pursuant to a federal court order. I had a court order. They knew that. I told them."

The motion also accused Gammick of failing to inform Mack that legal representation had been arranged for him.

Asked to comment about the defense allegation that he hadn't informed Darren Mack that Chesnoff and Freeman had been hired to represent him, the district attorney refused to discuss it.

This pivotal motion also changed Darren Mack's plea on Judge Weller's attempted murder from not guilty to not guilty by reason on insanity. It asked that the murder and attempted murder be separated into two distinct cases and tried outside Washoe County. It claimed that the jury would be confused by the two charges if they remained in the same trial.

Lastly, the defense demanded that all the evidence taken from Darren Mack's condo should be ruled inadmissible, as investigators did not have a search warrant.

On May 16, special prosecutors Chris Lalli and Robert Daskas countered, claiming Gammick had a legal right under federal law to record the conversations. They maintained that Darren Mack had admitted his crimes to the DA before any calls were recorded and anyone knew he had a lawyer.

"Since no attorney-client relationship existed," read Lalli's motion, "during the period in which [Mack] contacted Gammick and confessed his crimes, Gammick could not possibly have violated any rules of ethics, which apply exclusively to communications with represented parties."

But the special prosecutors said the conversations were a moot point anyway, as they had no intention of introducing them at trial.

In a separate motion, Daskas vehemently opposed the defense motion to disallow any evidence found at the defendant's condo. He maintained that the Reno detectives had ample reason to enter Mack's home.

"Based on the presence of blood on the driveway," the motion stated, "and the information provided by [Dan] Osborne . . . the detectives believed there was a likelihood of a seriously injured person inside the residence."

The prosecutors also objected to splitting the two cases into separate trials, saying it would be "inappropriate."

"The relevance between the two events is obvious," wrote Chris Lalli.

A week later, the defense claimed DA Gammick had broken the law by talking to their client while he was a fugitive in Mexico.

"Quite obviously, Mr. Gammick took advantage of an individual who was so flustered that he was then willing to stipulate to the death penalty, even while claiming he acted in his own defense," read Scott Freeman's motion.

On Friday, June 1, Judge Doug Herndon ruled Darren Mack's recorded phone calls to DA Gammick inadmissible at trial. In a daylong pretrial hearing, the judge rebuked the district attorney for violating his prosecutorial code of conduct, by failing to inform Mack that he had legal representation during their June 19, 2006, phone call.

"There is no more prejudicial evidence," said Judge Herndon, "than Mr. Mack telling Gammick, 'I killed my wife.' To allow that in would be overly prejudicial. It would be manifest injustice to allow the statements to remain."

The judge also ruled that recording the phone calls had broken Nevada law, which requires a two-party consent, although he conceded that under federal law, which does not require the other party's consent, it was perfectly legal.

But the judge ruled against the defense in two other key matters. He refused to split the charges into two separate trials, finding that they were intertwined. He also accepted the prosecutor's contention that detectives had more than enough reason to enter Mack's condo.

Four days later, the Washoe County district attorney called a press conference. Standing on a podium in front of the seal of the state of Nevada, Richard Gammick criticized Judge Herndon's ruling, brushing off any suggestions of wrongdoing.

"I decided to have a little discussion," he began. "It's time to speak out on some of these issues on the Mack case and time to maybe get a little bit of the truth out."

He told reporters that just because the Mack family had hired attorneys, it did not mean Darren was covered by attorney-client privilege. He said that an attorney also could not invoke the personal right of a defendant to remain silent and not talk to detectives.

"Mr. Freeman tried doing both," he said angrily. "And he out and out lied."

He then handed out copies of a one-paragraph letter from the Northern Nevada Disciplinary Board finding he had not acted unethically and dismissing the matter.

DA Gammick also told reporters that Darren Mack had confessed to his crimes, during one of the phone calls from Mexico.

"Darren Mack advised me that he had in fact killed his wife, Charla," said Gammick, "and that he had in fact shot Judge Weller. That is [sic] the statements that the judge suppressed at a hearing Friday."

The Washoe County district attorney also questioned why Judge Herndon had disqualified the telephone conversations from being used at trial after the Nevada State Bar opinion had supported their legality.

"One thing I just absolutely do not understand," said Gammick, "is Judge Herndon made the finding that these confessions would be extremely prejudicial. No kidding. Confessions in murder cases normally are extremely prejudicial."

CHAPTER FORTY

"Keep Him Focused"

On Tuesday, June 12—the first anniversary of Charla Mack's murder—Third Judicial District judge David Huff ruled that Judge Weller's divorce settlement was fully enforceable, and ordered Darren Mack to pay more than $1 million to his late wife's estate. Mack now had to pay "Mrs. Charla Mack" $480,000 immediately as well as $500,000 over the next five years. He was hit with an additional $15,500 in arrears and support, and $6,500 from a Smith Barney account.

The judge also ruled that the diamond ring and Rolex watch—the subjects of Joan Mack's civil suit against her late daughter-in-law—should be returned to Palace Jewelry and Loan.

Later, after apparently consulting with his client, Mark Wray announced that Mack would appeal.

"She was only entitled to that [settlement] when she was alive," he told the *Reno Gazette-Journal*. "You have to ask the higher court to see if this is right. I don't think there's any precedence for that."

On June 28, Chaz Higgs was convicted in Washoe District Court of the first-degree murder of his wife, Kathy Augustine, by injecting her with a paralyzing drug. Two days earlier, he had tried to commit suicide for the second time since her death.

The critical evidence that Higgs had killed the former Nevada State controller, jurors later said, was his statement that Darren Mack had mistakenly used a knife to murder his wife instead of an undetectable poison.

The following day, the jury imposed a life sentence on forty-three-year-old Higgs, with the possibility of parole in twenty years.

While preparing for his murder trial, Darren Mack settled into a comfortable routine. He was optimistic that he would win his case and soon be back to his old life in Reno.

"Usually I get up and do some yoga," he later explained. "And then I meditate, study, and then there'll be a little time to come out and mingle with other people. There's a television in the dayroom where we get to come out for [recreation]."

The genial prisoner had few problems making new friends with the other inmates. He was even using what he had learned at his Landmark Communication courses to help some of the other prisoners.

"I consider [Darren] a true friend," said Washoe County Jail inmate David Shelton. "He has not only helped me through these hard times in my life emotionally, but also spiritually."

Another fellow inmate, named Hamilton, described Mack as a "magnet to kindness."

"I just wish me and Mack could have met under different circumstances," he said. "He's a very down-to-earth guy, with a personality that is very kind and likable."

Darren also became friends with a pre-op transsexual named Richard "Cynthia" Murphy.

"At first when I met Darren I was kinda intimidated by him," she said. "Darren has always treated me like a person. If I needed something, he would give [it to me], or if I needed someone to talk to, he'd lend an ear."

Mack spent hours each day poring over law books to gain a firm grasp of the case.

"I'm learning quite a bit," he explained. "I've spent tons of time studying the case law and . . . studying the statutes."

The first week of July, Scott Freeman hired Kemp Shiffer to come onboard the defense team. The fifty-four-year-old licensed private investigator had worked the Reno area for more than thirty-years. His brief was to visit Darren Mack in Washoe County Jail and get a list of people who might help his case.

"I gave Mr. Mack a printed copy of his Rolodex," Shiffer said, "and asked him to go through [it] and highlight for me all the people that he wished me to interview [who might] have witnessed either irrational or violent behavior by Charla. And that's where I began my investigation."

Over several meetings in a small office adjacent to his cell, Mack ticked off a list of prominent people for Shiffer to interview, including prominent Reno politicians, society people, and a string of former girlfriends.

But when Shiffer approached them for interviews, many refused, not wanting to have anything to do with the notorious murder case.

At one meeting, Shiffer asked about the gun Darren claimed Charla had pulled on him. Shiffer said that, as Mack's defense investigator, he wished he had left it in her hand, where it would have been found with her blood and fingerprints on it.

"I said, 'Well what did you do with it?'" Shiffer recalled. "And his answer to me was that he had disposed of it. There were no specifics about where or how."

The experienced investigator was also puzzled as to why Darren would have taken the gun out of the garage to dispose of it.

"His answer to me never really made a lot of sense," Shiffer said. "And his explanation to me was it was a family item: it had belonged to his father. It was in a matched set and . . . he didn't want to leave it in the garage in his wife's hand. It was the heat of the moment of the thing."

When the investigator told Darren that the case would be far stronger if only he had left the gun in Charla's hand, Mack expressed surprise, asking how Shiffer thought that could change things.

"I said, 'I think if you had left it there, we'd have a very, very good chance; but without it being there, who knows what a jury's going to do?' "

About a week later, Shiffer told Scott Freeman about his troubling conversation with their client.

"Mr. Freeman said he really wanted me to keep it upbeat with Mr. Mack," the investigator said. " 'Keep him positive. Keep him focused . . . because he was going to have to give his story in court and testify.' And he really wanted him focused on that and not have any doubts."

On July 10, 2006, Darren Mack's defense team filed a motion to dismiss the case, citing District Attorney Richard Gammick's "flagrant disregard of the Defendant's right to a fair trial." In the scathing motion, Scott Freeman and David Chesnoff also accused Judge Herndon of "suppressing evidence."

The thirty-five-page motion described Gammick's press conference as a "legal tantrum" that had poisoned the jury pool. It said the district attorney had demonstrated "prosecutorial misconduct" with his "outrageous" and "unethical" statement while violating their client's constitutional rights.

The "appropriate remedy" for all the harm done to Darren Mack, the motion stated, would be to drop all charges. But in the event that the court declined, it continued, the trial should be moved to Clark County because of the "irreparable prejudice" to the Reno jury pool.

The motion also called for Gammick to be officially investigated for possible obstruction of justice and contempt charges arising from his press conference.

"Mr. Mack prays that this Honorable Court," read the motion, "dismiss the instant case for outrageous government and prosecutorial misconduct or, in the alternative, to sanction the prosecution for District Attorney Gammick's conduct."

When he read the motion, the district attorney labeled it "bogus," saying everything he'd discussed at the press conference had already been reported in the media.

"It's easy to throw this garbage around," he declared, "when you don't have a case."

At a special hearing on Friday, July 27, Judge Doug Herndon refused to dismiss the case or move the trial to Las Vegas. But he conceded that it might have to be moved later as a result of Gammick discussing Darren Mack's alleged confession in the media.

"Do I think the press conference was a bad idea?" asked the judge. "Absolutely. Was it an emotional and personal reaction to what happened in the case? Absolutely."

Judge Herndon pulled no punches, questioning the district attorney's professional behavior.

"I do expect more, as a former prosecutor, in terms of the conduct that took place," he told the court. "I don't think it's necessary to go out and refer to the defense as 'liars.'"

At the hearing, David Chesnoff accused Gammick of having "deliberately infected" the potential Reno jury pool and demanded the October 1 trial be moved to Clark County.

"I think it's an infection that can't be cured," he argued. "Mr. Gammick, like a petulant child, decides to hold a press conference to impugn the reputation of the lawyers, to call Mr. Mack a murderer—a confessed murderer—and to impugn the decisions of this honorable court."

Special prosecutor Chris Lalli called it all a "distraction," with little to do with the case.

"It's a shame when cases turn personal like this," he told the judge. "This is kind of a distraction and we really want to get to the business of trying our case."

Judge Herndon ruled a change of venue was premature, until potential jurors could be questioned.

* * *

In mid-August, the Washoe County District Court clerk's office sent out questionnaires to four hundred prospective jurors, asking what they knew of the Darren Mack case and if they had formed any opinions. The list of forty-seven questions, which had been agreed on by both sides, would also be used during the jury selection process.

"This case has received a great deal of publicity," stated the questionnaire, "and it would not be surprising or improper if you have heard, read, seen, or discussed this case."

Potential jurors were then asked to list their main source of news and approximately how many times they had been exposed to the Darren Mack murder case. Other questions included whether they had ever met Darren Mack or done business with him or his family; whether they had ever been involved in a divorce or child custody matter; and whether they had ever witnessed or experienced violence of any kind, and if they believed a person should be able to act in self-defense.

In the weeks leading up to trial, David Chesnoff urged Darren Mack to use an insanity plea on both counts. Chesnoff was concerned that if his client took the stand, as he wanted to do, the prosecutors would attack his claims that Charla had pulled a gun on him that had misfired.

"I told him not to testify," Chesnoff later explained, "that we would use insanity on both counts. If he didn't testify, he wouldn't be talking about the gun."

And on one occasion, Chesnoff told his client that he was skeptical of his story.

"I remember having a conversation with him where I said, 'Are you sure that the gun misfired? Because to me that's unbelievable," said Chesnoff. "And I think he said it was fired on two occasions. So I was saying to him as a lawyer, knowing the jury was going to evaluate what he said, that in fact I didn't believe that."

The experienced Las Vegas defense attorney is also a professional poker player, and he was keeping his cards very close to his chest. In fact, right up to the start of the trial, prosecutors had absolutely no clue that Darren Mack was anchoring his defense on his claim of Charla pulling a gun on him.

Chesnoff's favored defense strategy was to call psychiatrist Dr. Norton Roitman to testify. That way the jury would hear Darren Mack's version of events in the garage through his defense expert.

"And he wouldn't have to testify at all," explained Chesnoff. "Dr. Roitman interviewed him [and] would testify to the jury what Mr. Mack told him. He would tell the jury the story and it would became part of his basis for his hypothesis and his theory as to why he was insane. You avoid the defendant having to testify and be cross-examined and you present his explanation through."

But after Darren Mack insisted that he testify at trial, the defense was forced to change their strategy. Scott Freeman then started preparing Darren to take the stand, giving him an American Bar Association guide on how witnesses should testify.

"I told him, 'We're going to focus on [your] testimony, and we're going to work with [you],'" said Freeman. "I also told Mr. Mack that I would videotape him if need be, because he had a habit when he got mad and stuck: his jaw came out. And it was, quite frankly, scary."

In late August, Darren Mack finally told defense investigator Kemp Shiffer that he had disposed of the .22-caliber pistol and knife in a Dumpster. Mack also informed him that he had collected the gun from his mother's house the morning of Charla's killing. He said it was one of an antique matched set of revolvers that had belonged to his father, and there was an identical one still in its case at Joan Mack's house.

When the investigator told Scott Freeman that Mack had thrown the gun and knife into a Dumpster, the attorney said he had already tried unsuccessfully to find it more than a year earlier.

With a weak case, the defense now concentrated on trying to dig up dirt on Charla Mack. In mid-September, they hired forensic psychologist Dr. Edward Hyman to interview witnesses and prepare a report on Charla's propensity for violence.

Just one week before the trial was scheduled to begin, Dr. Hyman interviewed a string of witnesses, writing what they said verbatim on his laptop computer. Combining these interviews with what Darren Mack had told him, Scott Freeman stitched together a damning indictment of Charla Mack that he would incorporate into his opening statement at trial.

On Friday, September 21, Judge Doug Herndon met with both sides in his chambers to iron out any last-minute difficulties before jury selection. Special prosecutor Robert Daskas had previously announced his run for a Clark County congressional seat as a Democrat in the 2008 elections. But the forty-year-old chief deputy district attorney agreed not to campaign until after finishing prosecuting the Mack case.

After the half-hour meeting, Judge Herndon and the attorneys returned to open court, where the public gallery was packed with the press.

"Everybody's ready for trial on October 1?" Judge Herndon asked the attorneys, who all answered, "Yes."

Outside the court, Freeman told a TV reporter it would be hard to find an impartial jury in Washoe County.

"Not surprisingly," he said, "there's not many people that haven't heard of the case. Equally not surprisingly, there's not a lot of people that haven't already made an opinion about the case."

CHAPTER FORTY-ONE

Coming to Las Vegas

Over the weekend, the national media had descended on Reno for the long-anticipated Darren Mack trial. And a row of TV satellite trucks was parked in front of the Washoe County Court House on Virginia Street, just a block away from the Mills B. Lane Justice Center, where Judge Chuck Weller had almost been killed.

By 8:00 a.m. Monday morning, there was a line of reporters and members of the public outside Room 220, waiting for passes to attend the trial. Previously, Judge Herndon had agreed to allow fourteen members of the media to attend jury selection, as well as eight members of the public. Once the trial got under way, more would be admitted.

At 10:00 a.m., Judge Herndon entered the courtroom to begin the daunting task of picking a jury. He had flown in from Las Vegas the night before, and the airline had lost his luggage. So the balding, bespectacled judge began the proceedings with an apology for wearing blue jeans, quipping that he wasn't trying to set a new casual western fashion for judges.

The results of August's jury questionnaire had come in and were not too encouraging. For out of the 400 potential jurors questioned, 250 already believed Darren Mack was guilty. But the judge optimistically noted that "a surprising number" claimed to be open-minded.

"There's more people here," he observed, "who said they don't have an opinion than I would have expected."

Earlier that morning, David Chesnoff had filed another motion for the trial to be moved out of Reno, attaching a fat appendix of news articles.

At the start of the day's court proceedings, he handed Judge Herndon that morning's *Reno Gazette-Journal*, which had a huge photograph of Darren Mack being led into court at a previous hearing.

"There's a compelling need to give the defendant a fair trial," argued Chesnoff. "I ask you to consider, as a matter of due process, transferring this to another part of the state to avoid even the possibility of having to do this again."

Special prosecutor Robert Daskas then urged the judge to wait.

"If we can't get Mr. Mack a fair trial," Judge Herndon responded, "we'll pack up and move."

He then ordered jury selection to commence, saying that although there had been a great deal of publicity, he still wanted to give the legal process a chance.

"There's a lot of people who don't watch that much news," he noted. "I have to agree with the state."

The first panel of fifty-one potential jurors filed into the courtroom. For the rest of the day, the judge questioned them. His goal was to select thirty-five people before the defense and prosecution each used their nine peremptory challenges, whittling the group down to the final twelve jurors and three alternates. The defense had hired jury consultants to help cherry-pick the most advantageous jurors for their client.

One by one, the prospective jurors were questioned by Judge Herndon, with many being dismissed for strong opinions about Darren Mack's guilt. The atmosphere was tense as the proceedings moved along at a snail's pace.

When the judge recessed for the first day, only three men and three women had been approved.

Things went just as slowly the second day, with another

six potential jurors selected. And by the end of the third day—with only thirteen chosen of the thirty-five needed to move on to the next stage—Judge Herndon was running out of patience. Once again David Chesnoff called for a change of venue, expressing concern that some potential jurors had been "less then candid" in order to get on the jury.

Special prosecutor Chris Lalli said he sympathized with the difficulties of selecting a "solid panel" in Washoe County, but urged the judge not to give up yet.

"It's very disappointing how we proceeded today," said Lalli. "But I do request that we proceed with the process. Let's give it more time."

Judge Herndon then admitted his "optimism" had decreased, asking, "When does enough become enough?"

He said he needed the evening to think things out and would return in the morning with a decision.

"Wild developments at the end of today's hearing," wrote reporter Martha Bellisle in her daily trial blog. "Not only was one potential juror dismissed for being less than truthful, another is being looked at after some information was sent to the court. Add to that the slow painful redundant snail's pace of a process, and the judge sounded like he was leaning toward giving up. So we'll find out at 8:30 Thursday morning if he'll call more possible jurors in, or pack his bags for the next flight south."

At 8:30 a.m. on Thursday morning, Judge Herndon announced that he was moving the Darren Mack case to Las Vegas because of "a unique set of circumstances." It was the first time a murder trial had been moved out of Washoe County in almost a century.

But first he questioned the defendant about the change of venue and his feelings about it.

"Do you agree with the change?" asked the judge.

"Very much so, sir," replied Mack, who said he had discussed the move with his attorneys.

Then for the next hour the judge explained the reasons behind his decision, saying the Reno community deserved to know why.

"This case has caused me to lose a lot of sleep over the past few nights," said Judge Herndon. "I think it's apparent there's a reasonable likelihood that an impartial jury cannot be found here. There's been a pervasive amount of publicity that would compromise the case. For those reasons, a change of venue is warranted."

The judge announced the trial would resume in Las Vegas on Monday, October 15, when he would begin picking a Clark County jury.

The costs of packing up and moving the Darren Mack murder trial five hundred miles south would not be cheap. More than two hundred witnesses and others involved in the trial would now have to be flown to and from Las Vegas, and be put up in hotels. And from the outset, Clark County district attorney David Roger made it clear that Washoe County would be picking up the tab.

It was estimated that it would cost Reno taxpayers a minimum of $100,000 to give Darren Mack a fair trial.

CHAPTER FORTY-TWO

The Trial

At 8:25 a.m. on Tuesday, October 9, Darren Mack arrived at the Clark County Detention Center in Las Vegas, where he was officially handed over to the Las Vegas Metropolitan Police Department. In his processing papers, he gave his address as 5350 Franktown Road, Carson City, his former marital home, listing his attorney, David Chesnoff, as his nearest relative.

After being photographed and fingerprinted, the new inmate underwent a full medical examination and mental health assessment.

"He appears to be in good control of thoughts and emotions," his interviewer reported. "PT [patient] appears appropriate for GP [general population] or any other housing deemed suitable by classification."

After the examination, Darren Mack was housed in Module 2J, sharing a wing with thirty-three other inmates in the general population. It was from this cell that he started to prepare for his upcoming trial.

A few days earlier, special prosecutor Christopher Lalli had requested Detective Ron Chalmers come to Las Vegas for the duration of the trial.

"Chris called me and said I needed to be here," the detective remembered. " 'I need you to be available, Johnny-on-the-spot.' "

So Detectives Chalmers and David Jenkins loaded all the boxes of trial discovery and evidence in a police cruiser, preparing to drive it to Las Vegas. But before leaving, Chalmers received a call from Scott Freeman, asking him to collect some new defense evidence from his office.

When Detective Chalmers arrived, he was given a small presentation case with a North American Arms .22 Magnum mini revolver gun inside and some bullets. There was also an identical presentation case with the gun missing.

"So I asked Scott, 'Do you want to tell me where you got this?' " said Chalmers. "He said, " 'No, I just want you to book it into evidence.' "

When the detective asked exactly how these items related to the Darren Mack case, Freeman refused to answer.

The two detectives drove everything down to Las Vegas, dropping it off at the Clark County Regional Justice Center. When Detective Chalmers showed the two special prosecutors this new defense evidence, no one was under any illusions about what it meant.

"You know we played a game, for lack of a better term," Detective Chalmers explained. "Christopher [Lalli], Robert [Daskas], and I were trying to figure out what was the significance of this. I thought it was fairly obvious. He's obviously given me an empty box to show that it existed, to give proffer that the gun really did exist. Here's the box for it. And he's given us this gun to show the size and the conceivability. I expected ultimately they were going to put the missing gun in Charla's hand."

At 9:00 a.m. on Friday, October 12—three days before jury selection was scheduled to begin—Scott Freeman arrived at the Clark County Detention Center. That day he had received a $200,000 check from Landon Mack.

Darren complained to his attorney that his new cell was

not as comfortable as the one in Reno had been, although he did like the food.

"He said the . . . mattress was thin," recalled Freeman, "but the food was better than Washoe County. It's the only discussion he had. And I responded that I did not have the same relationship with the Clark County Jail, and I would pass it on to Mr. Chesnoff."

At 7:38 a.m. on Sunday night, Scott Freeman returned to the jail with David Chesnoff with a new designer wardrobe of clothes for Darren Mack to wear at his trial. These included several tan sports coats, a blue jacket, pants, shirts, ties, and two pairs of black shoes.

The two attorneys were upbeat, giving their client last-minute instructions before the all-important jury selection the next morning.

At 10:00 a.m. on Monday, October 15, Darren Mack was led into courtroom 10D, on the tenth floor of the Regional Justice Center in downtown Las Vegas. He was wearing a smart navy sports coat and sat with his attorneys, David Chesnoff and Scott Freeman, at the defense table. Directly behind them were Joan and Landon Mack and Alecia Biddison.

Court TV would be covering the trial, gavel to gavel, once it got under way, and the station's distinctive white satellite communications truck was parked outside.

There was an air of excitement in the courtroom, and over the weekend a dozen Reno reporters and television crews had relocated to Las Vegas for the duration of the trial, which was expected to last at least a month.

The national media was also there, with producers and reporters from *Dateline NBC* and the CBS show *48 Hours*, joining the other reporters on the two rows of benches reserved for the press.

But before the first panel of potential Clark County jurors was allowed into the courtroom, Chesnoff again asked Judge Doug Herndon to divide the murder and attempted murder charges into two separate trials.

Chesnoff argued that just having one trial put his client "between a rock and a hard place," for if he called Mack to the stand to testify about killing his wife in self-defense, he would then be exposed to prosecution questions regarding his defense of not guilty by insanity in the attempted murder charge.

Once again the judge refused, saying he would listen to arguments later and decide whether to restrict the scope of prosecution, questioning if the defendant decided to testify.

Finally, at 2:00 p.m., the first batch of thirty-six prospective jurors was seated in the courtroom, and Darren Mack's trial got started. Just as in Reno, things were painfully slow.

By 5:00 p.m., just six prospective jurors had been questioned, with all being excused for a variety of reasons. Finally, when Judge Herndon recessed for the day, two jurors had been selected to go into the eventual pool of thirty-five, to be cut down to the final twelve and three alternates.

On Tuesday, things moved a little faster. By the end of the day, a further eight prospective jurors, including a NASA scientist and a Christian pastor, had been selected to move forward to the next stage. By noon the following day, only four more prospective jurors had been picked, and Judge Herndon was becoming visibly frustrated.

"We have two hundred and we've gone through fifty and we only have twelve," he told Chesnoff and Freeman. "If [you] challenge every person and drill them for an hour, it will take forever."

But things hardly improved, with only three more jurors being selected that afternoon.

On Thursday morning—the day the opening statements had been scheduled to start—the next panel of potential jurors entered the courtroom for the fourth day of jury selection. That day, attorneys from both sides questioned fourteen people, selecting another five and bringing the total to twenty— still fifteen short of the number needed.

On Friday, another four prospective jurors were selected, meaning jury selection would go into a second week, delaying the start of the trial proper ever further. But when Judge Herndon recessed Monday night, after questioning three-quarters of the entire two-hundred strong pool of prospective jurors, the judge was still five short of the thirty-five needed.

Then on Tuesday morning—day seven of jury selection—five more prospective jurors were accepted, achieving the magic number of thirty-five.

"I have the theme music for *Rocky* going through my head," announced Judge Herndon triumphantly.

Then he ordered the selected jurors to return at 8:30 a.m. the next morning for the final stage of selection, in which each side would be able to dismiss ten prospectives without giving a reason, leaving the final twelve jurors and three alternates.

At 7:44 p.m. on Tuesday night, Scott Freeman and David Chesnoff visited Darren Mack to read him their opening statements. With them were key defense team members, trial strategist Dayvid Figler and psychiatrist Dr. Norton Roitman.

As Judge Herndon had refused to sever the murder from the attempted murder charge—and their client was insisting on a rare split defense, against their advice to pursue insanity pleas on both counts—Freeman and Chesnoff had decided to divide the opening statements between them. Freeman would address the questions of self-defense in the murder charge, while Chesnoff would use the killing as a triggering event, leading to Judge Weller's shooting.

On Tuesday night, Scott Freeman recited his dramatic opening to Darren Mack in front of Figler, Chesnoff, and Dr. Roitman. The experienced attorney had decided to use a rubber band as a demonstrative tool, showing the jury how Charla had finally caused him to snap. It would also provide the perfect segue for Chesnoff to take over the story.

"[Darren] was very pleased with it," Freeman recalled. "I asked him specifically if I had it. He said, 'You have it a hundred percent.' He was misty-eyed. I was gratified by that."

Freeman returned to his hotel to rehearse further, leaving Chesnoff to go over his opening with their client.

Chesnoff claims that after hearing his opening vividly depict how he had become delusional after Charla's attack, Darren Mack had given it his blessing, saying that was exactly how it had happened.

CHAPTER FORTY-THREE

"Her Death Was Personal"

At 10:15 a.m. on Wednesday October 24, 2007, after the final twelve jurors and three alternates were seated, Clark County special prosecutor Robert Daskas stood up to deliver his opening statement. There was an air of relief and excitement in Courtroom 10D as the trial of Darren Mack finally got under way—almost a month after the ill-fated first attempt to seat a jury in Reno, and sixteen months months after Charla's death and Judge Weller's shooting.

At the defense table, Darren Mack sat between his two attorneys, Scott Freeman and David Chesnoff. Wearing a somber black suit, white shirt, and tie, he looked uncomfortable, frequently scratching his head and nervously sipping water.

Directly behind the two special prosecutors sat Soorya Townley and Christopher Broughton as well as Charla Mack's friends Laura Cunningham and Jacqueline Ross, who had come to give support. Across the courtroom were Darren Mack's mother, Joan, and his brother, Landon.

Court TV and the KLAS-TV Web site broadcasted the trial live, and the two rows of press benches were packed with reporters.

"As far as Dan Osborne was concerned," began Daskas, "he thought he was doing a friend a favor."

The lean prosecutor, sporting a crew cut and a white fly-collar shirt and matching tie, told the jury how Darren Mack's friend had become an "unwitting participant" in the well-planned-out murder of his wife.

"It was a plan that was formulated and memorialized by the defendant in his own writing," said Daskas as the to-do list suddenly appeared on a large screen in front of the jury box. "Let me say that again: it was a plan that the defendant memorialized in his own writing. In fact, Dan Osborne's name appeared as the first entry on that list."

Daskas then outlined the tragic events of Monday, June 12, 2006, explaining how Dan Osborne had found himself in the middle of Charla Mack's horrific murder, and his escape from the defendant's Fleur de Lis condo with little Erika Mack, after the strange events of that morning.

He then backed up and told the jury that Darren and Charla Mack had had an "unorthodox marriage." He said the defendant had "persuaded" his wife to "engage in mutual, consensual sex with other people, and she had reluctantly agreed."

Then, after ten years of marriage, Darren and Charla had decided to divorce.

"Like most divorces," said the special prosecutor, "[the issue] involved money. What made the Mack divorce different . . . was the amount of money involved. Darren Mack and his family owned a company called Palace Jewelry and Loan in the Reno area, and it was a very successful business. In fact, in 2004, the defendant's estimated worth was around $10 million. His average annual income exceeded $500,000. Charla, on the other hand, had no income."

Daskas said things had become "very contentious" in the divorce proceedings after Judge Chuck Weller had ordered Mack to pay $849 a month in child support and $10,000 a month in spousal support.

He told the jury that Judge Weller had placed a financial restraining order against both parties, so neither one could "play games with the court," by disposing of or hiding any assets.

"Well, shortly after that order was entered," said Daskas, "the judge became concerned because the defendant transferred his interest in Palace Jewelry—at least his voting interest—to his mother, Mrs. Joan Mack. Then he filed for bankruptcy."

Daskas told the jury how Shawn Meador had then asked Judge Weller to hold Darren Mack in contempt for violating his court order. A subsequent hearing had been held to see if the defendant should be thrown in jail.

"As you can imagine," said Daskas, "the defendant was frustrated with the family court system. He was angry with Charla, his soon-to-be ex-wife, and he was furious with Judge Charles Weller."

Then, just before a hearing in early January 2006, Darren Mack's attorneys offered Charla a financial settlement worth almost $1 million, which she accepted. But soon afterward Darren changed his mind and wanted to back out.

"He had seller's remorse," said Daskas. "He filed pleadings with the family court, asking for permission to back out of the deal that he proposed.

"The defendant met up with a number of men from fathers' rights groups, advocates who thought the family court system was biased against fathers. Their mission, their goal, was to change family court for fathers. They thought it unconstitutional and there should be a revolt to fix the problem."

Then, as Darren Mack glared from the defense table, Daskas played a short excerpt from Mack's *On Second Thought* TV interview for the jury, saying it captured his "anger and frustration" just prior to the murder.

Jurors heard Darren rant about the family court system, declaring that it was time to make a stand against injustice.

As Darren Mack blanched, special prosecutor Daskas explained how Judge Weller had held a hearing on May 24, 2006, refusing to allow Darren to back out of his agreement with Charla.

"The defendant's frustration and anger grew," said Daskas. "The agreement he had proposed months earlier—the one he had tried so hard to back out of—was indeed en-forceable. Darren Mack had a problem. Eighteen days later, he found a solution."

Focusing on Charla's murder, the special prosecutor then showed the jury a series of horrific color photographs of the bloody murder scene and Charla's Mack's dead body on the floor of the garage.

"Darren Mack ambushed his soon-to-be ex-wife with a knife," Daskas told the jury. "Her death was neither sudden nor painless: it was personal. She was stabbed between six and seven times, and even though the defendant was much bigger, Charla Mack didn't go without a fight."

Daskas told the jury that Charla had "classic defensive wounds to her arms, wrists and legs, sustained as she desperately fought for her life.

"At some point she was on her back," he said, "trying to kick her husband, who was armed with a knife. But she was overpowered by somebody much bigger, much stronger, who was armed with a deadly weapon. Charla Mack didn't stand a chance."

As Darren Mack stared impassively ahead, Daskas showed the jury one particularly gruesome photograph of Charla lying on the cement floor, a deep, gaping gash at the base of her neck.

"The fatal wound was to her neck area," the special prosecutor said, approaching the jury box. "You can see it was delivered with such force, with such power, it left a gaping hole in her neck. In fact it severed her carotid artery. Charla Mack died on the garage floor of her soon-to-be ex-husband's town house while her daughter waited upstairs, watching television."

Special prosecutor Daskas told the jury that after murdering Charla, the defendant had followed his to-do list to conceal the crime, before proceeding to the next stage of it.

"Darren Mack left the condominum complex about 10:03 that morning," said Daskas. "The question was: Where was Darren Mack going? Well, he wasn't finished."

The prosecutor said that question was answered about an hour later, when a .243-caliber bullet shattered Judge Weller's double-paned office window, striking him and his administrative assistant. A color photograph then appeared on the screen, showing Judge Weller's chest with large cuts, one over his heart, sewed together with large stitches.

"It was fortuitous," Daskas explained, "that Judge Weller was facing the window sideways and the bullet fragment skipped off his chest. In fact, that probably saved his life."

He said that it didn't take investigators long to determine that the bullet had been fired from a parking garage across the Truckee River, offering a clear, unobstructed view of the judge's chambers.

"Finally," said Daskas, "the defendant's own words in his own writing will prove that he shot Judge Weller: the list—PARKING GARAGE . . . IF YES.' The defendant was finished for the day. In his mind he had ended the problem. He believed he had killed, and did kill, Charla Mack and he believed he had killed Judge Charles Weller. There was nothing left to do except run. And run he did."

Daskas said the evidence against Darren Mack was "overwhelming," proving conclusively that he committed both these crimes.

"You will learn that the defendant had a motive to kill both Charla Mack and Judge Charles Weller," he said. "In fact, you will see the defendant's plan in his own writing, outlining what he intended to do on June twelfth. And you will hear, in the defendant's own words, how he drew the line."

CHAPTER FORTY-FOUR

The Rubber Band Snaps

At 11:35 a.m., Scott Freeman walked up to the podium to deliver the first part of the defense's opening statements.

"Ladies and gentlemen, you've heard from the state," he began. "They've told you their version of the events and now it's time for the defense to tell you their story."

Reading from notes, the immaculately groomed gray-haired defender began by giving the jury a brief résumé of his client leading up to his meeting Charla Sampsell in May 1994.

"He thought he'd hit the lottery with this woman," said Freeman. "Funny, smart, beautiful, physically fit. She gravitated to his children . . . Jory and Elise."

But Charla was a violent person, said Freeman, and she had first attacked Darren on their honeymoon.

"She attempted to hit Darren in the groin in anger," he told the jurors. "They had a discussion thereafter as to why she would just strike at him like that. She claimed she didn't mean it. However, that experience was foretelling of things to come."

Darren Mack's defender told the jury that throughout their marriage his client had been a victim of Charla's violence.

"There were numerous examples," he declared. "Beating Darren in Elise's room eight to ten times, body-slamming Darren in their bedroom eight to ten times. Slapping him in the face at the airport in front of Jory and Elise. Two broken fingers, one when Darren and Charla were attending their tae kwon do class together. Charla was small but physically fit and very accomplished as a tae kwon do student."

Freeman said that at one tae kwon do class, Charla told Darren that she would kick at him and miss.

"She didn't miss," he said. "Broke his finger. Laughed when it happened. Another time Charla broke Darren's finger when he attempted to block a toilet brush that she had broken over his neck."

Then, as Charla's family and friends sat aghast in the public gallery, Freeman savagely attacked her character and morals.

"Charla had an unusual sexual appetite," he told the jury, rubbing his hands together. "She liked women. She liked to swing with men and women."

According to Freeman, it was three years before Charla even allowed her husband to participate in these sex games.

"She was the one in control, not Darren," he said. "Darren was open to allowing Charla to explore her fantasies, because his love was unconditional."

The defender maintained his client had initially been "hesitant" to accept this lifestyle.

"He wanted a monogamous marriage," Freeman explained, "like his mother and father. However, he wanted her to he happy so he agreed she could explore her sexuality."

Then Scott Freeman turned to Charla's "dark side," saying Darren had not been aware of its existence before they married.

"Charla had bragged to people that she had scored her big fish," he told the jury. "A handsome, successful businessman who could provide for her, so she wouldn't have to work. She told people she had married Darren for his money."

Charla's "dysfunctional childhood," said Freeman, had left her suffering from a borderline personality disorder.

"She could be sweet and affectionate one moment," he told jurors, "and abusive the next. Her mood swings were completely unpredictable. This abuse was fueled by alcohol abuse and self-medication. She liked to use the club drug Ecstasy . . . to enhance her sexual experiences."

Freeman said that as well as the physical abuse, there was verbal abuse.

"The verbal abuse was significant," explained Freeman. " 'I will destroy your reputation by filing false police reports. Who will they believe, me or you?' 'I will take your daughter and move to California, like your ex-wife did with your children.' 'I will cut your penis off and put it in a freezer.' 'I will kill you—I watch Court TV every day and I know how to do it.' "

Freeman told the jury that Charla had threatened to destroy his client's reputation unless she got what she wanted in the divorce.

"He was a third-generation Nevadan," Freeman said as Darren Mack sat taking notes at the defense table, "successful and credible in the community. This reputation was in the process of destruction if Charla did not get what she thought she was owed in a divorce."

He then turned to the events of June 12, 2006, saying Darren Mack always carried a concealed gun because of the "cash-and-carry nature" of the pawn business. Usually he carried a .40-caliber pistol in an ankle holster, but with summer approaching he had changed to a .22-caliber Derringer-type pistol so he could wear shorts.

"The gun was part of a matching set," explained Freeman. "His grandfather had the twin to that set, and it was located in his mother's home in Reno. The family has a gun collection room in his mother's house, and that's where the collector .22 was located."

The attorney explained that his client had wanted to renew his concealed-weapon permit but couldn't get the .22 pistol he needed to qualify for it until that Monday morning, June 12.

Suddenly, Freeman segued to Charla's step-grandmother Santea, whom he described as a psychic and clairvoyant.

"It should be noted that Charla had an unusual family," he told the jury. "Her mother had numerous relationships after divorcing Charla's father."

At one point Santea warned Darren that someone he trusted in his business wanted to steal from him. At first Darren did not take it seriously, said Freeman, but after a Palace employee had been caught embezzling $250,000, he began giving it credence.

Then, several months after the separation, Darren met Santea at his father-in-law's house, deciding to consult her about the divorce.

"Darren asked her if the divorce would go through," said Freeman. "[Santea] asked questions about Charla and their relationship and she went, as Darren describes it, in kind of a trance. She said, 'There's blood everywhere. You can't turn your back on Charla. She will stab you with a knife.'"

The defense attorney said his client had heeded this warning, in light of all the previous threats Charla had made as well as the accuracy of Santea's first premonition. So he had started wearing a knife, to defend himself against a possible attack from Charla.

Returning to Monday, June 12, Freeman said his client had gone to his mother's house early, collecting the .22 pistol from its collector's set in the gun room.

"All the guns in the Macks' collection room," said Freeman, "are always loaded. Darren put the gun in his change pocket, at the front of his denim jeans."

Then, after confirming with his mother that she would look after Erika later on, as he had errands, he left, returning home via Starbucks.

Back at his condo, Darren called Charla to confirm she was bringing Erika over to exchange custody.

"Charla also wanted to discuss settling the divorce," Freeman told the jury. "She had heard that Darren was going to appeal Judge Weller's most recent order to settle, and [she] wanted to discuss a potential settlement . . . without the lawyers, in light of the potential for this appeal."

Freeman said Charla had arrived at about 9:15, parking her Lexus on the street. Then she asked Darren for the Tupperware container used for Erika's lunches, so he went into the condo through the garage to get the brown paper bag that it is kept in.

After retrieving the paper bag, he brought it downstairs, putting it on the passenger's side of Charla's Lexus. He then went over to Dan Osborne's car, while Charla remained by hers.

"Charla begins to threaten," Freeman tells the jury, "and the rubber band starts to pull.

"'Darren, drop the appeal,' says Charla. 'Make your mother pay me. You know you owe me what I deserve, Darren.'"

Freeman said his client had replied that his appeal would be successful, and Judge Weller would soon be off the case and the divorce would be over.

"Charla sees her previous empowerment slipping away in the garage," said Freeman. "She threatens [that] Darren won't see Erika and that Charla's going to LA and Darren won't have a relationship with her. The rubber band is pulling."

At this point Scott Freeman dramatized what had happened next for the jury.

"Darren: 'Charla, you called my ex-wife Debbie the C word for doing that to me, taking my children to California so they wouldn't be with me. What does that make you, Charla?'

"That enraged Charla. The name-calling from Charla began. The terrorist split personality reared its evil head. She transferred into pure hatred. Darren couldn't communicate with her. It was obvious she had not come there to settle the divorce. She came to threaten Darren into submission.

"With that, Darren turned and said, 'We'll just see how the appeal goes. We're not making any progress this morning.' Darren turned his back to Charla as he walked from Dan Osborne's car location to the condo entrance through the garage leading to upstairs.

"Unbeknownst to Darren," Freeman continued, "Charla follows and bashes him in the right side of his face from behind. She knocked him over onto his left knee. He never saw it coming. She was calling him 'a fucking piece of shit.'

"She was going to punch him on the left side of his face but Darren gets up and pushes her back. With that, she stumbles towards the back of the garage. She steps on the. 22 gun that fell out of Darren's pocket when she knocked him to his knees. She picks up the gun.

" 'Charla, give me the gun,' " Darren says. " 'It's loaded.' " Charla looks at the gun, pulls the hammer back, smiles, and fires."

Then, in a moment of high drama, Scott Freeman suddenly produced a rubber band, snapping it apart in front of the jury box.

"Just like that, the rubber band breaks," he said gravely. "Darren believes he's been shot. He doesn't feel any pain. She aimed right at him. She pulled the trigger. The gun had misfired.

"Darren's worst fears were realized at that moment. Charla was really going to kill him. Darren thinks he's been shot; he's not.

"Charla starts to cock the hammer again. Darren lunges at her. All he gets was a handful of hair. Darren knew he was going to die. Charla rolled to her left. They both fell to the ground. Charla still has the gun. She is still trying to cock it.

"Charla: 'Let go of my fucking hair; I'm going to kill you.' The terror for Darren is overwhelming. Dan Osborne's pitbull dog jumps out of the car, barking wildly. Darren believes the dog is also running to attack. The knife Darren had been carrying is on his side on his belt. Darren reaches to pull it out. Darren believes he is going to die by Charla or the dog attack.

"Charla attempts to kick at the knife. It's caught in his shirttail. Darren can't get it out. Charla is bicycle kicking him. Darren can't get the knife out from under his shirt. Charla is kicking and he is trying to pull the knife out. She clamps on his arm with her legs. Charla is now putting the now-cocked gun back in Darren's face.

"Darren is able to free the knife, as Charla is now in front of him. They are both struggling on the ground. Darren plunges the knife into her neck once. Osborne's pitbull runs up to attack. Darren is bracing for that attack. The dog stops short and sniffs the blood that is now pooling. Charla's violence has stopped.

"Darren wanders around the garage aimlessly. It is all surreal, strange, not real. The rubber band has snapped."

Freeman told the jury that Darren Mack then went upstairs, walking past Dan Osborne and into his bedroom, where he showered and changed clothes.

"He's out of his mind," explained Freeman as Mack stared wide-eyed at the jury. "He is just dealing with things as they come to him. He sees a cup. He puts it in the dishwasher. He's thirsty. He gets a drink. He sees an inventory, some guns on a piece of paper on the right-hand side. He says to himself, 'I've got to get this organized.' He's an organized person. He makes lists. 'I've got to think this through. I need some time. What's happening here?' Defending himself from yet another attack from Charla."

Freeman told the jury that Mack then went into survivalist mode, deciding to go up in the Reno Mountains to clear his thoughts.

"He knows how to be a survivalist," said Freeman. "He's hunted before and he makes that as his plan."

Mack then began gathering the stuff he was going to need in the mountains, taking the guns he had used in target practice the day before and loading them into the back of the Ford Explorer.

"What happens next is he goes back into the house, looks for his hunting gear," Freeman continued. "It's in storage. He's not thinking. He didn't have it. He thinks . . . *I'll go to the airport. Regroup.*"

At that point, Freeman said, Darren packed a suitcase and

went into the kitchen to get a glass of water, where he saw the gun inventory that his mother had asked him to compile for the pawnshop. So he decided to make a list to help him organize his thoughts.

"*Then* he makes the list," Freeman told the jury. "Not before. Then. Trying to organize. Trying to think: What should he do? He's not himself. He'd snapped."

Then he'd gone downstairs back into the garage, and seen the gun and the bloody knife.

"It is very surreal," explained the defender. "He sees the gun and what he's thinking is: *That's my dad's gun. That's a family heirloom.*"

The bloody gun was caught in Charla's hair, Freeman said, but it was still cocked. So Darren removed it, leaving some of Charla's hair on the counter in the process. Then he tried to wipe off the gun and picked up the knife, but it was covered in blood. So he wrapped it in a towel, placing it in the front seat of the Explorer.

"The next thing he thinks he needs to do is leave," Freeman continued. "So he wants to put things away. Not covering up for a crime. This is what his orientation is: *I need to put things away.*"

So Mack drives the Ford Explorer out of the garage, bringing in Charla's Lexus and his Jeep Cherokee. Then he closes the garage door and drives off.

As he drove out of Wilbur May Parkway, he saw his cell phone and decided to call Dan Osborne and ask him to bring Erika to meet him at a nearby Starbucks.

"Dan Osborne says okay," said Freeman. "Darren drives from the condominium complex to meet Erika . . . and says to her, 'I love you very much. Remember your experience of me.'"

He then got back into the Ford Explorer and started driving to Reno Airport, to return the hired vehicle to the parking garage. But on the way he got sidetracked upon seeing the Sierra Pacific Power building, where Charla's divorce attorney Shawn Meador has his law offices.

"Instead of dropping the vehicle off, he turns to his left," said Freeman, "physically drives from the airport towards the Washoe County Court House. And with that, I turn you over to my cocounsel, Dave Chesnoff."

"At the time of the shooting of Judge Weller," David Chesnoff told the jury, "you will find that Darren Mack was suffering from what Dr. Norton Roitman, a brilliant and talented forensic psychiatrist, will describe to you as delusional disorder."

Then the bulky defender held up a copy of the American Psychiatric Association's *Diagnostic and Statistical Manual of Mental Disorders* (*DSM*).

"This book is kind of the bible of doctors and lawyers and courts on what mental illnesses exist in our world," he told the jury.

He then compared mental illness to cancer or diabetes, saying it was a disease that sufferers had no control over. He said a combination of factors had affected his client's sanity: his "tumultuous" relationship with Charla, their heavy use of Ecstasy during sex, and the stresses of the divorce.

"The lawyers were fighting," he told the jury. "The judge was fighting. The couple was fighting. They forced Darren's mom to participate. There was all sorts of emotion rushing through people's bodies and into their brains. And coupling that with the far too much drug usage by not just Darren but Charla as well."

He said the extracts from Darren Mack's television interview played by the defense proved his client was delusional.

"Mr. Mack equated his fight in the divorce court to the Revolutionary War," said Chesnoff. "If that's not delusional, I don't know what is. He was comparing himself to Ben Franklin. Darren acted upon his delusions in shooting Judge Weller, and the disease he suffers from causes the delusions to control his actions."

After "this terrible event with Charla," Darren went upstairs and took a shower.

"You will hear how Darren actually sees the individual

drops of water coming out of the shower magnified, like in *Fantasia*," he told the jury. "He's in what he describes as 'a superconscious state' where his brain is not even talking to him. There is no sound. Things happen. He hears the panting of the dog and nothing else. He sees the drops coming out of the shower but doesn't know he's in the shower.

"Everything is happening basically on automatic pilot, which is consistent with somebody suffering from the delusions that Darren Mack was suffering from at the time he went and shot Judge Weller. Darren Mack was suffering from a recognized mental disorder."

Chesnoff blamed Judge Weller for fueling Mack's delusions by threatening to put him in jail if he didn't pay up. He said his client was suffering from delusional grandiosity, believing he had some great insight into the family court system.

"Now, here's the dilemma that the state has," he said. "If everything was hunky-dory in the family court, and the judge was making rational decisions, everything was consistent with the way family court should operate. And Darren Mack thought that it was *the* worst corrupt system he ever saw: How is that not delusional?"

The attorney said Darren Mack believed the Second Amendment gave him the right to shoot a judge if he was breaking the rules.

"If the judge, in Darren's mind, is extorting him," said Chesnoff, "he's allowed to shoot him. That's what Darren believes. He's a soldier for a just cause. That's how he sees it."

Another symptom of Mack's fragile mental health, said the attorney, was his persecution complex that there was a conspiracy against him. He believed that Shawn Meador was in cahoots with Judge Weller to beat him.

"Darren thought that Charla had slept with Judge Weller," Chesnoff announced. "Delusion, I hope. We'll ask Judge Weller when he comes here. I guess the only way it won't be delusional is if he says he did."

Then Chesnoff turned to Darren Mack's heavy use of Ecstasy and other substances with Charla, calling it an agreed marriage therapy to fix their "disintegrating" relationship. He claimed they had both decided to use these drugs to "enhance" their sexual pleasure, creating an "unbelievably tight bond" between them.

"And you couple that with the psychology of this wife-swapping stuff," the attorney continued, "where you're supposed to have ultimate trust for your spouse, that they were both engaged in. Now, according to the literature, that makes them really in love."

Chesnoff said that Darren was heartbroken when Charla said she didn't want to be with him anymore, and the chemical intensity of their relationship only compounded this.

"The extended use of these drugs," said Chesnoff, "led to actually a firestorm in Darren's brain, and probably Charla's as well, that created the inability for Darren not to become a victim of the delusions created by his mental illness. Remember that commercial with the frying pan: First they showed this is your brain. Then they said, 'This is your brain on drugs,' and they showed the sunnyed-up egg crackling. That's what happened here."

Then picking up Scott Freeman's narrative, Chesnoff said that Darren Mack made a decision after seeing Shawn Meador's office on his way to the airport.

"It's a trigger," he explained. "He can either take off, or go on autopilot. He really doesn't make the decision volitionally. He's not thinking. His body and his mentally ill mind makes a decision to turn right.

"And as he's going there, he stops at a convenience store. Gets some water. Uses the restroom. And then he sees this gun that had been his father's—this heirloom. He tries to clean it, not because he's trying to clean up the evidence, but because it's his dad's gun. And that's in this delusional state. That's what he's focused on: the fact that it's his dad's gun. He can't get it cleaned; he throws it in a Dumpster. He heads to the parking garage.

"Now, one of the things that Dr. [Norton] Roitman will tell

you about this delusional disease is that the people who are suffering from it . . . there are kind of random events that [have] special meaning to them. Like, in this case, he gets to the parking garage and he doesn't know if Judge Weller's going to be in court, in the window, at home. But sure enough he pulls in: there he is. And he says to himself, *My, this must mean that I should do this.*

"So he's an expert shot. He shoots regularly. He's been around weapons his whole life. If fact, his friends call him "the Doctor" because he was surgically precise with his shooting. And he sets up and he says to himself, *I'm not going to kill him, because if I kill him it'll be about his death and not about the message.*

"And he shoots him here," said Chesnoff, pointing to his left shoulder. "The rest of the things you saw in the picture are from shrapnel. But the actual entry is here.

"And he consciously decides to wait till until the judge's assistant had left the area, because he's there about the message, not about the violence. That's the delusion. God's telling him, 'Now is the time to exercise your Second Amendment right and take down this tyrant. But not to hurt him, not to kill him, but to let everybody know that what's happened to me has got to stop.' And that's what he does.

"But then more things happen that make Darren think that this was divinely inspired. When he's taking off in his vehicle, he stops at another convenience store and there are two policemen there. And instead of the policemen walking up and arresting him, they turn around and walk the other way. And in his mind he thinks that was divine intervention.

"He gets to the border to go into Mexico, where they check everybody, and there's an accident and he gets waved through. This is while there's a manhunt going on. He thinks that's divine intervention, because he's delusional. It's not divine intervention. There was an accident; they waved him through. But in his mind it's these special things that are occurring that validate his illness."

Chesnoff told the jury that it was "very strange" for a defense attorney to be standing before them, saying, "My client did it."

Then, holding up the heavy *Diagnostic and Statistical Manual of Mental Diseases*, he said it described the delusional disorder Darren Mack suffered from.

"Please keep an open mind," he told the jurors. "Listen to the doctors. They have had years of training."

At 12:35 p.m., Judge Herndon recessed for lunch, saying the state would call its first witness when they returned.

CHAPTER FORTY-FIVE

A Faint Yelp

The state's first witness was Washoe County assistant medical examiner Dr. Katherine P. Raven. Under Chris Lalli's direct questioning, the forensic pathologist described Charla Mack's extensive stab injuries, using a series of twenty color photographs taken at the autopsy that Raven had performed.

She testified that Carla had desperately tried to fight off her killer and been stabbed six or seven times. The fatal wound had been one to the left side of her neck.

"And the weapon went in," Dr. Raven told the jury, "and the [blade] cut the carotid artery—which is the main artery that goes from the heart up to the brain on the left side—in half. It also cut the esophagus, where we swallow food. And it almost cut completely in half the trachea, or windpipe."

The pathologist also found evidence of blunt-force injuries on Charla's neck, arms and legs, which could have been caused by a punch or a kick.

Dr. Raven testified that Charla had actually choked to death on her own blood, and it could have taken up to five minutes for her to die.

"Did you come to an opinion as to the manner of death?" asked special prosecutor Lalli.

"Yes," replied Dr. Raven. "The manner of death is homicide.

"Death at the hands of another individual?" asked Lalli.
"Correct."

Then Scott Freeman stepped to the podium for his cross-examination.

"I'm not being facetious," he began, "but you were not present at the murder scene. Correct?"

After she agreed that she had not been, Freeman said Raven could not be sure if one person had started the fight, or had been reacting in self-defense.

"So it doesn't necessarily mean she was a victim," said Freeman. "She could have been an aggressor as well. You can't render that opinion, correct?"

"Initially, no," said the doctor.

Then the defender pointed out that the defensive wounds on Charla's body were consistent with a struggle.

"I'm not going to say it's a struggle," replied the doctor. "I mean, again, defensive wounds consist of someone trying to protect themselves or cover themselves."

"Or perhaps someone who began a fight," asked Freeman, "and then the tables were turned, so to speak?"

"I don't think I can answer that one way or the other," Raven said. "It's irrelevant to the injuries."

The state then called Corey Schmidt to the stand, and special prosecutor Lalli began by asking him about the luxurious Fleur de Lis complex, where he and his cousin Darren Mack had both lived.

"Is it in the ghetto?" asked the prosecutor sarcastically.

"I don't know what you'd define as [a] ghetto," replied Schmidt.

"Is it in a rather nice area in Reno?" asked Lalli, noting that it was a gated community with ponds and a clubhouse for residents.

Under Lalli's questioning, Schmidt said he had been backing his convertible BMW out of the driveway at about 8:45 a.m. on June 12 when he saw his cousin Darren and Dan Osborne standing there.

On cross-examination, Scott Freeman asked about a particular incident in October 2003 on board a Carnival Cruise ship.

"Was there an evening," asked the defender, "when Charla Mack attacked Darren Mack?"

"Yes, there was," said Schmidt, after acknowledging he had not actually seen any physical altercation.

"Tell the jury what you experienced," said Freeman.

"There was an incident that happened in the disco," said Schmidt. "Charla punched Darren in the stomach."

"Did Darren fall over a table?" asked Freeman.

"I was told that, yes."

Schmidt testified that his cousin had then left the disco "very disgruntled" and he had followed Darren back to his cabin.

"Charla came in the room verbally abusing my cousin, saying that he ruins everything and this always happens," he told the jury. "I was trying to get us back out to have a good time as a family."

In redirect, Lalli asked if Darren Mack was a competitive bodybuilder.

"To my understanding, yes," Schmidt replied. "I've never seen him do it."

"Nothing else," said Lalli, dismissing his witness.

At 8:30 a.m. the next morning the state called Dan Osborne to the stand. Under special prosecutor Dascas's direct examination, Darren Mack's old high school classmate described how he had been staying at the Fleur de Lis condo for a few weeks until he could find his own place.

Osborne told the jury that Mack was obsessed with his divorce, frequently complaining about being victimized by Judge Weller and the injustices of the family court system.

"Had the defendant ever said anything to you about the judge and Charla that caused you any concern?" asked Daskas.

"These things came up all the time," Osborne replied. "He talked about the judge and this divorce and [how] it's heavy on his mind."

Osborne said his friend was obviously "tormented," believing he was being unjustly persecuted.

"It's, like, essentially, 'I just wish I could get rid of all this stuff behind me and maybe start over, or maybe get a new attorney. Just get rid of them all, and just to try and get a fair shake," Osborne told the jury.

"You used the words 'get rid of,'" observed Daskas. "Did he ever use those words when he described his soon-to-be ex-wife and Judge Weller?"

"Well, he had said at one point, 'I'd just like to get rid of them all,'" said Osborne. "And I think he might have been referring to trying to get rid of the judge. Like, he was trying to get an appellant attorney. Someone that was going to listen to him."

Then Daskas asked about Monday, June 12, 2006, the morning Osborne was moving into his own place. Osborne said Charla had arrived to drop Erika off and Darren had asked him to keep her company while he went downstairs to talk to her mother.

"Did he pick up anything before he walked downstairs?" asked Daskas.

"Yeah, he did," Osborne replied. "There was a paper bag right by the stairway that he picked up. A Trader Joe's bag with paper handles."

Osborne said he and Erika were snacking and watching television, when she heard his dog.

"We're watching this show on Animal Planet on these dogs being rescued," he told the jury. "They're barking and one of them's dragging its back leg. And Erika said to me she thought she heard my dog barking. I thought that was kind of strange. I go, 'Oh, Rusty's out in the car outside.' And then I heard a faint yelping sound that was coming . . . maybe down from the garage."

Osborne had stood up and gone over to the stairwell so he could hear better. Then he heard a door shut and Rusty ran up the stairs, looking terrified.

"Then Darren came by," said Osborne, "right behind him. I looked up and here goes Darren past Erika and myself . . . he had a [bath] towel wrapped around his hand. He had kind of a weird look on his face."

"Did the defendant say anything to you?" asked the prosecutor.

"No."

"Did he say anything to Erika?"

"No."

"Did he say, 'My wife just attacked me?' "

"No."

"Did he say, 'My wife just tried to shoot me?' "

"No. He said nothing. He went into his room," explained Osborne.

"You said he had a weird look?" observed the prosecutor.

"Weird, scared kind of look," said Osborne.

Osborne estimated that Darren Mack had only been about five feet away from him and Erika, and there was bright sunlight flooding in.

"Anything to suggest or anything to cause you concern that he had just been in a physical fight?" asked Daskas.

"No."

"Just the weird look on his face?"

"Right."

"What did you do?"

"He went in his room," said Osborne. "Erika at that time said, 'Your dog has blood on him.' She was kind of kneeling down, and I went, 'What!' "

He had then grabbed his dog's head, taking a closer look and saw his fur was covered in blood. Then he "freaked out," telling Erika that they were going to her grandmother's house.

A few minutes later, after cleaning his dog in a nearby pond, his cell phone rang. Darren Mack was on the line.

"Darren called me and asked to see his daughter," said Osborne. "Meet him at Starbucks."

When they arrived in the Starbucks parking lot, Mack waved him down.

"It looked like he had changed his shirt," said Osborne. "He looks at me and says he wants to talk to Erika, and I said, 'Okay.' And he asked me if I wanted anything from Starbucks. I said, 'No.' He asked Erika. She said, 'Yes, I'll have a lemon bar.' And he said, 'Can you get me an iced tea.' "

Then Mack handed him some money and Osborne went into Starbucks, leaving Darren alone with his daughter.

About ten minutes later, Osborne came out with a lemon bar and an iced tea, handing Mack the change.

"He hugged Erika," recalled Osborne, "gave her a kiss and said, 'Okay.' We put her in the car and I said, 'I'm going to your [mom's]. I'll see you later,' and drove off."

During Scott Freeman's cross-examination, Osborne admitted helping Darren Mack research Judge Weller.

"So in terms of one divorced father to another," asked Freeman, "you were there and you were empathetic with Darren?"

"That's correct."

"And sometimes what happens is people blow off stream when they're talking to one another?"

"That's correct."

"Wouldn't you categorize what Darren said in terms of getting rid of people as kind of blowing off steam to you?"

"I would."

Under Nevada law, both judge and jurors are allowed to question witnesses after both sides have completed questioning. Judge Doug Herndon asked Osborne why he had not asked Darren Mack what had happened in the garage when he met him at Starbucks.

"I knew he carried a gun," Osborne replied. "I wasn't going to say anything. I thought he would tell me something. He didn't say anything and I wasn't going to say anything for the safety of both myself and Erika."

For the rest of the day, the state honed in on the investigation, calling three Reno police homicide detectives. But lead detective Ron Chalmers, who was working behind the scenes with the special prosecutors, was being kept in reserve for later rebuttal testimony.

Detective Dave Jenkins explained how, several hours after the shooting, he had interviewed Dan Osborne at his friend Toni Lackey's house. After hearing Osborne's story, he drove them straight to Darren Mack's condo, fearing "a seriously injured person" might be inside.

On arrival he was met by Detective Chalmers, with several other officers arriving soon afterward. After knocking on the front door and getting no answer, they tried the garage doors, which were closed.

"In the driveway," Detective Jenkins told the jury, "I saw several stains that I believed to have been blood."

"How many stains?" asked Daskas as crime scene photographs came up on a screen in front of the jury.

"I believe there were three," said the detective.

He said seeing the blood outside the doors raised his "anxiety level," so he called headquarters for the telephone number of the residence. Then he made two calls from his cell, which went through to an answering machine, before deciding to enter the garage.

"What did you see?" asked Daskas.

"As the door began to open," said the detective, "I bent down and was very close to the ground. It was very dark inside. I saw what appeared to be the form of a very small person laying on the ground at the front of [a Lexus] vehicle."

"Did you then go further into the garage?" asked the prosecutor.

"I did," Jenkins replied. "As I began to get closer, I could see a large stain of smeared blood that went across the front of both vehicles. And blood pooled underneath the . . . body, [which] was laying facedown in the garage."

Then, as the jury were shown a photo of Charla Mack's body facedown on the concrete floor, Daskas asked Detective Jenkins to describe the scene.

"That's the small woman," he said, "in the condition that I originally saw her in. The striation or smears in the bloodstains extending away from her feet are the first blood that I saw. And the blood pooling and trailing away from her upper torso."

He said he then looked for any signs of life.

"I felt that the skin was noticeably cold to the touch," said Jenkins. "I tried to manipulate the ankle a little bit, to see if it moved freely. I was immediately aware that there was what I believed to have been rigor mortis present, which is an artifact [*sic*] of death."

Defender David Chesnoff had no questions for the witness.

Homicide detective John Ferguson then took the stand to be questioned by special prosecutor Daskas.

"On June twelfth, 2006, did you respond to what we're calling 'the Courthouse Shooting' in the downtown Reno area?" asked Daskas.

"Yes," replied Detective Ferguson. " 'Controlled chaos' is probably the best way to describe it. The SWAT teams and several tactical officers were covering the area in the downtown corridor, trying to determine where the shot came from."

Later, the detective said he had gone to a parking garage on First Street and Sierra, where the shot was believed to have been fired from. He went up to the fourth floor, which offered a clear view of Judge Weller's chambers.

Daskas then asked about searching Darren Mack's condo two days later.

"We were there to collect items in regard to Judge Weller, Charla Mack—the shooting itself," Ferguson explained.

Inside Darren Mack's master bedroom, the detective found a black corduroy bag and seized it as evidence.

"There were multiple papers in there dealing with Judge Weller," said Ferguson. "The research we believe Mr. Mack had done on him."

He told the court that he had also discovered two Map-Quest maps in an envelope by Mack's bed.

"Without telling specific addresses," asked Daskas, "who lived at each of these two residences?"

"One was Judge Weller's address," he replied, "and the other was Shawn Meador's address."

"You mean the judge's work address?" asked the prosecutor.

"No," said Ferguson, "his home address."

Once again the defense had no questions, except to confirm that all the items impounded had been taken to the Washoe County Crime Lab for processing.

The last witness of the day was Reno police detective Shanna Wallin-Reed of the robbery/homicide division. She told the court that after the shooting, she went to the Washoe County Medical Center to interview Judge Weller.

When she arrived in the trauma room, the judge was lying on a table with an oxygen mask on. He was being worked on by medical staff.

"Did you ask him if he knew who potentially had shot him?" asked Chris Lalli.

"Yes," replied the detective.

"Did he provide you with a name?"

"Yes."

Detective Wallin-Reed then called her boss, Sergeant Randy Saulnier, to report.

"Tell me what you told Sergeant Saulnier," asked the prosecutor.

"That Judge Weller had provided the name of 'Daryl Mack,' who was the owner of Palace Jewelry and Loan, [and] could have potentially have been responsible for the shooting."

Two days later, she was involved in the second search of the defendant's Fleur de Lis condo. In the breakfast room she had found numerous handwritten and computer-printed papers as well as e-mails and books scattered on a table.

She then packed everything into an evidence bag, bringing it back to police headquarters for further inspection. The following day she started examining the papers.

"There was a notepad that . . . had some information on it that I thought was relevant," she told the court. "It was a yellow legal pad. There was writing on several pages."

Then a photograph of Darren Mack's to-do list was displayed on the screen in front of the jury box.

"What is that?" asked Lalli.

"When I was at the Reno Police Department, looking through the notepad, this is the one that really stood out to me," she replied.

"Objection to 'really stood out,' " interrupted David Chesnoff. "He asked, 'What is that?' It's been admitted?"

"All right," said Judge Herndon, "describe what it is."

"Do you want me to read what it says?" asked the detective.

"First of all," said Lalli, "it is a page in the legal pad that has been admitted."

"Your Honor," said Chesnoff, "I'm not trying to be obstructive. We know that it's an exhibit. It's been admitted."

"I understand," said the judge. "You may continue."

"Now, if you would read the entries for us . . . ," said the prosecutor.

"Objection, Your Honor," said Chesnoff. "The document speaks for itself."

"Response," said Judge Herndon.

"Well, as she is doing it," said Lalli, "I'm going to ask her if she recognizes any of the items on the page as relating to this case, such as Erika. Does she know a witness by the name of Erika, for example?"

"You can ask specific questions in that manner," ruled the judge.

"The first word on the pad is the name 'Dan.' Do you know an individual witness in this case named Dan?"

"Yes, I do." replied Wallin-Reed.

"Who is that?" asked Lalli.

"Dan Osborne."

"Just a little further down the page," said Lalli, "there's the name 'Erika.' Do you know a witness in this case by the name of Erika?"

"Your Honor," said Chesnoff, "we could start reading the witness list . . . and ask her if she knows the names. The document is in evidence. The jury is the trier of fact."

"Fair enough," said Lalli.

"Thank you," Chesnoff replied.

"Your Honor," said the special prosecutor, "that completes direct examination.

In his cross, David Chesnoff asked the detective if she had searched his client's condo looking for any materials relating to the family court system.

"Corruption in the court system," she corrected.

"Corruption," said Chesnoff. "And that's because you understood that there were issues surrounding whether or not the family court system in Reno was corrupt?"

"That's because that's what was listed on the search warrant," said the detective.

Then, at 2:30 p.m., Judge Herndon recessed for the day, telling jurors that the court would be closed Friday, as it was Nevada Day, and to be back in their seats on Monday morning.

With a three-day holiday weekend ahead of them, all the major players in the Darren Mack case headed straight for Las Vegas Airport to fly back to Reno. Taking the same afternoon flight on Southwest Airlines were Charla Mack's mother, Soorya Townley, Scott Freeman, and Reno detectives Ron Chalmers and David Jenkins.

CHAPTER FORTY-SIX

Forensics

At 8:52 a.m. on Monday, October 29, everybody was back in Courtroom 10D for the third day of the Darren Mack trial. The state had lined up seven witnesses to give forensic testimony, and shore up their case. Over the course of the day, the jurors would see dozens of photographs taken from both crime scenes, demonstrating how methodically and scrupulously Washoe County forensic investigators had collected numerous bloodstained items from Darren Mack's garage and Judge Weller's chambers.

The first witness was Lisa Harris, a forensics investigator at the Washoe County crime lab. Under special prosecutor Chris Lalli's direct, she described responding to Room 196 at Washoe Medical Center's intensive care unit after the June 12 shooting. Her brief was to photograph and document Judge Weller's and Annie Allison's injuries.

"Judge Weller was in the supine position," she testified. "He was on his back with injuries exposed."

The forensic investigator said she observed numerous injuries to Judge Weller's body, including his upper chest area, left arm, left knee, abdomen, and right hand.

Then the jury viewed the gruesome photographs she had taken of the judge, lying on his back with his eyes closed.

There was blood smeared across his chest and several holes along his left side from bullet fragments.

Later that day she went to the Fleur de Lis complex with other investigators, to document the murder scene and take swabs of suspected blood.

"It was photographed with the vehicles and victim Charla Mack in the garage in place," she said, "and with the vehicles removed and following the removal of the victim."

One of the photographs, taken after the garage was cleared, revealed an L-shaped blood trail from the door along the floor to the back where the body had been dragged. Investigator Harris told the jury she had found blood splatter on the wall by the turn in the long drag mark. She also discovered Dan Osborne's dog Rusty's bloody paw prints, as well as a hand print on the wall.

On cross-examination, Scott Freeman asked Investigator Harris about an unidentified bloodstain found in the garage on a workbench cabinet. It had been photographed and measured but never tested.

She said another investigator had collected that stain, and Freeman asked if it would have been processed back at the crime lab before being tested.

"It could be collected," she replied, "and then whether it's submitted for analysis is up to the detective."

"Well, in this case," said Freeman, "it's a bloodstain, so it would be of evidentiary interest. Would it not?"

"Oh, possibly, yes," she agreed.

"I mean, I'm not fencing with you," pressed the defender. "That's a bloodstain in the garage."

"I understand," said Harris.

"Where somebody died, right?"

"Correct."

"So do you think that would be of evidentiary interest to somebody. Right?"

"Right," she answered.

"I'm going to object," said Chris Lalli. "That's argumentative."

Judge Herndon overruled the objection, saying Harris could answer, but Scott Freeman deftly moved on to another subject, leaving the bloodstain question up in the air.

After a ten-minute recess, the state called Washoe County investigator Victor Ruvalcaba to the stand. He told the jury that he had been sent to Darren Mack's garage to assist Lisa Harris in processing the scene.

Investigator Ruvalcaba said there had been a number of bloodstains all over the garage, which he had swabbed with Q-tips for later analysis. He testified there had also been red stains on a light switch and a handle of a door leading from the garage into the residence.

He then swabbed more red stains on the banister going upstairs. Inside the kitchen area he swabbed a dead-bolt lock and the handles on a balcony door, both stained red.

In cross-examination, Scott Freeman immediately asked about the mysterious bloodstain in the photograph of the garage workbench drawer.

"Were you present when she took the picture?" asked the defender.

"I was at the scene during that time," said Ruvalcaba. "I don't recall if I was within the garage at the time she took the photo or not."

The investigator acknowledged that he had processed and collected the stain, and the defender asked how he had described it in his subsequent report.

"This location is described," said the investigator, "as a red stain located in the lower left cabinet door of the work-bench and it's outlined as 'red stain no. 4.'"

Ruvalcaba said that after swabbing the stain, he placed it in an evidence bag, which was driven to the crime lab for further processing and bar coding. But there his responsibilities ended.

The next witness was Investigator Dean Kaumans of the Washoe County Sheriff's Office, who had examined the two vehicles found in the garage at the crime lab.

"Now, did you examine the exterior of the Lexus SUV for the presence of blood?" asked special prosecutor Daskas.

"Yes," replied Kaumans. "There were areas on the driver's front quarter panel that had discoloration. Those were tested and produced a positive result for presumptive blood."

The investigator told the jury that there was also a key ring with a set of keys with red staining still in the Lexus ignition. And there was an obvious fingerprint in the blood on the ignition key.

"It's a visible print," said Kaumans. "Normal techniques that we used to lift it would probably destroy the print. So the technique that I used was photography to preserve this fingerprint."

In his cross, Scott Freeman asked the investigator about the copies of the checks found in the Lexus, attempting to show the jury that his client was regularly paying his wife child support and alimony.

The next witness, Ronald Young, a certified fingerprint expert, testified that the prints found on the Lexus ignition key, belonged to the defendant.

"They were made by one and the same individual," Young testified, "Darren Mack."

Scott Freeman had no questions for the latent print examiner.

After a brief recess, the state called senior criminologist Suzanne Harmon of the Washoe County Sheriff's Office. She told the jury that she oversaw all the initial testing of the samples in the crime lab, deciding if they required DNA testing.

"Quality assurance," she explained. "I'm the one that goes around with the clipboard and makes sure everyone is following the rules."

"Did you analyze any swabs collected from a Lexus?" said Lalli.

"I did," Harmon replied. "I had several swabs that were

described as 'red stain' and my results were positive presumptive for blood."

The senior criminologist testified that the presumptive presence of blood had been found on the steering wheel, the ignition keys, and Charla Mack's sweatpants.

"They were heavily stained with apparent blood," said Harmon, "and additionally there were numerous animal hairs . . . possibly that of a dog."

She said she also found blood flakes and numerous animal hairs in evidence bags attached to Charla's hands at the crime scene.

The presumptive presence of blood was also found outside the garage in the driveway as well as on a towel wrapped around Charla Mack's arm, a light switch, a banister, and the dead bolt on the door connecting the garage to the residence.

"In the upstairs bathroom, next to the mirror, there's a little spot of blood. Did you test that?" asked Lalli.

"Yes, I obtained positive results for the presence of blood," she testified.

Once again in cross-examination Scott Freeman focused on the unidentified bloodstain found on a drawer of a workbench in the garage. Harmon said that the two swabs taken from the stain had been logged into the crime lab case submission evidence summary as bar code number Q663660.

"Noticeably absent is the review of Q663660," noted Freeman. "Is that correct?"

"That's correct," she agreed.

"And that's because you were not given Q663660 to analyze, were you?" asked the defender.

"It would not have been requested on this work request," said Harmon.

Next up was the Washoe County forensic science division's DNA expert, Jeffrey Riolo. He said he had used a sample of Charla Mack's blood as a reference standard in his testing. His reference standard for Darren Mack came from a buccal swab (i.e., from the inside of the mouth), taken by

Detective Ron Chalmers when Mack arrived back from Mexico. The third reference standard had come from Dan Osborne, who had also supplied a buccal swab.

The DNA expert testified that he had examined four blood stains taken from Dan Osborne's work pants, finding a mixed DNA profile belonging to Charla Mack as well as Osborne.

"So what we're finding on Dan Osborne's pants is Charla's blood?" asked Lalli.

"Yes," he replied.

The prosecutor then moved on to Charla Mack's Lexus, asking if he had obtained any positive DNA results from the samples collected.

Riolo said he had found that the dominant DNA profile on the steering wheel belonged to Darren Mack, with a frequency number of 1 in 500 billion. He had also found a minor DNA profile of Charla's.

He said he had examined the Lexus ignition keys, obtaining a mixed DNA profile. This time Charla was the dominant profile, the minor one being too low a level to identify.

But Riolo did discover Charla's DNA in blood samples taken from inside and outside the garage as well as upstairs in the kitchen and a chair in the living room.

"Did you analyze a swab of that area of the chair?" asked Lalli.

"Yes, I did," said Riolo, "and Charla is the source, unless she has an identical twin."

After Chris Lalli passed the witness, Scott Freeman immediately asked him about the two swabs taken from the garage workbench.

"May I approach?" said the defender. "Take a look at this. Does this look like an evidence summary?"

When Riolo agreed that it was, Freeman continued.

"I've tabbed one particular item: Q663660," he declared. "I want you to take a minute and read that item to yourself. Take a moment and review your report and tell us your analysis of that particular sample."

"We're referring to Q663660?" asked the DNA expert.

"Q663660 is the bar code number I want you to focus on," said Freeman.

"My reports do not show that I looked at that item," said Riolo. "I missed that."

"You didn't miss it," snapped Freeman. "You didn't test it."

The final witness of the day was forensic handwriting expert Jimmy Smith, who worked for the Las Vegas Metro Police Department. As the jury was again shown the defendant's notorious to-do list on the screen, Smith said he had compared it with a known sample of Darren Mack's handwriting.

"I found no differences in these writings," Smith testified, "and identified this writer as being Darren Mack."

"In other words," asked Robert Dascas, "Mr. Mack wrote what is displayed on the monitor today. Everything on that page?"

"That's correct," Smith replied, adding that another expert had confirmed his findings in a peer review.

After excusing Smith, Judge Herndon recessed for the day, telling the jury that they would not be needed on Thursday.

"I think we are ahead of where I thought we'd be in the presentation of witnesses," he said, "so we're moving along very well. That's the reason I think it's appropriate and go ahead and do that on Thursday, for a variety of reasons."

Every day after court recessed, the special prosecutors met with Detective Ron Chalmers, who had been given an office at the Clark County District Attorney's Office. As the lead detective was on the witness list and could not attend the trial, Chris Lalli and Robert Daskas had to be very careful about what testimony he was able to hear.

"I met with the lawyers everyday after court," Chalmers said. "If they had something new that the defense raised during cross-examination, we would discuss what needed to be addressed with further investigation without going into details of what the testimony was.

"They would give me a to-do list," he said, "and then I

would make phone calls—either that evening or the following day—to try and find either witnesses or information."

After Scott Freeman claimed in his opening that Charla Mack had deliberately broken Darren's finger during a tae kwon do class, Chalmers was tasked with investigating if it was true.

"So I spent a significant time trying to identify where it occurred," he recalled. "As nobody knew where it had occurred, I ended up going through the phone book, calling all the different tae kwon do places."

Finally he tracked it down and talked to the instructor who had witnessed the incident.

"He says, 'Oh, yeah, I was there when that happened,'" said Detective Chalmers, "'and it was a joke and they were laughing about it.' Darren said, 'I should have zigged when I zagged and then she kicked me and broke my finger.'"

So the state lined up the instructor to call later in the trial as a rebuttal witness.

CHAPTER FORTY-SEVEN

"I've Never Had My Reputation Attacked"

At the beginning of the fourth day of the trial, the state screened Darren Mack's entire twenty-six-minute interview for the TV show *On Second Thought* for the jury. Then Special Prosecutor Robert Daskas called Washoe County Court security adviser Kevin Costa to the stand.

Costa, who had recently retired, testified that he had monitored Web sites and e-mails for potential threats to courthouse personnel. On October 25, 2004, there was a protest outside the Reno Courthouse, and he went undercover to investigate. He started talking to one of the people handing out fliers, discovering he belonged to a Yahoo! group called Redress2@yahoogroups.com who were protesting family court judges all over the country.

The security chief then invented a Yahoo! screen name and joined the group, arranging for all future postings to be sent to his e-mail address.

At 7:00 a.m. on Monday, June 12, 2006, Costa testified that he had arrived at the courthouse, logging into the group's e-mail messages and finding one posted by Dmack467@aol .com a couple of days earlier.

"Read to us what appears on page two of that e-mail?" asked Daskas.

"'It is not only in Las Vegas that attorneys are playing

with a stacked judicial deck,'" Costa began, reading to the jury the entire two-page e-mail in which Mack bitterly complained about the family court system.

"Later that morning, were you present in the courthouse when a shooting occurred?" asked Daskas.

"Yes, I was," Costa replied.

Then the state called Alecia Biddison to the stand. As the attractive blonde walked in the courtroom, the defendant gave her a big smile.

Under Chris Lalli's direct, Biddison told the jury how she had first met the defendant through the Legal Reader Internet site around January 2006 after posting a complaint about Judge Chuck Weller. They spent a few weeks exchanging e-mails and talking on the phone before meeting in person.

"Did you talk about family court?" asked Lalli.

"Yes," she replied.

"Did you talk about Judge Weller at all?"

"Yes, we did."

"Did you find that you shared a lot of the same feelings about family court?"

"We shared a level of frustration," she agreed.

"At some point does the relationship . . . develop more into a friendship and then eventually into a dating relationship?"

"Yes," she replied.

"Tell us a bit about that."

"I'm not sure what you're asking me," Biddison said tersely.

"Do you go to dinner together?" he asked. "Do you go on dates together?"

"Yes, we had dinner together. Yes, we had gone on dates."

"I don't mean to pry into salacious details about your personal life," said the prosecutor. "Did you ever have intimate or sexual relations with the defendant?"

"Yes," replied Biddison.

Lalli then asked about the dinner she had prepared for Darren Mack at her house the Saturday night before Charla's killing. And how Mack had invited her to go shooting with him, and several others the following day.

"Did you target shoot that day?" asked Lalli.

"Yes," she replied.

"What sort of guns were being used?"

"I used my personal handgun, which is a Glock .3540-caliber," Biddison said. "And the other gentlemen were using handguns and some rifles."

Biddison said that Mack had fired an AR-15 semiautomatic rifle at a long-range exploding target.

"When you saw Mr. Mack shooting at a target, did he hit it upon the first try?" asked the special prosecutor.

"No, he did not," Biddison replied.

"OK," said Lalli, "how many tries did he take before he hit it?"

"He didn't."

"He never hit it at all?"

"No."

"How many times did Mr. Mack attempt to hit the target?"

"I don't recall."

In cross-examination, Scott Freeman asked about Biddison's frustration with Judge Weller. She said the judge had been in charge of her child custody case in August 2005 and she had been "shocked and horrified" by what had taken place in his courtroom.

Then Freeman asked if Darren Mack had been frightened of his wife, Charla.

"Yes," she replied.

"Do you in fact have an experience where you heard Charla Mack on the phone related to a snakebite incident to the dog?" Freeman asked.

"Yes," she said. "Darren, my son, and I were attending a friend's holiday barbecue . . . and Darren received a phone call. It was Charla calling him. And I could hear her screaming at him [on] the phone, and so he stepped away . . . to take the call. So then he returned to us and had indicated that—"

"Objection," interrupted Chris Lalli. "Hearsay."

Judge Herndon sustained the objection, allowing the witness to answer if she had heard what Charla had said but without revealing what it was.

"No, Your Honor," she replied. "I didn't hear the specifics. All I could hear was screaming."

"And as a consequence," Freeman continued, "did you, without saying what was said, hear any violence, any threats, by Mr. Mack in response?"

"No," Biddison replied. "He was very calm and asked if he could use the home phone to call his daughter and check on [her]."

Once again Lalli objected, telling the judge it was all hearsay.

"I'll sustain the objection," said Judge Herndon. "That'll be stricken."

Then he told the jury to disregard Biddison's last statement.

"You need to wait for the questions," he told the witness, "and when I'm talking you need to not talk. Okay?"

"Yeah, sure," she replied.

In redirect, Chris Lalli asked if Biddison had called the Reno Police Department on June 12, 2006, after learning about Judge Weller's shooting. She said yes, after being transferred there by Sheriff Bill Ames.

"I told Mr. Ames that I was concerned I would be a suspect . . . because of my military background and because I know how to shoot high-powered rifles."

"Did you ever indicate any concerns that you might have fears of the defendant?" asked Lalli.

"Never," she replied.

"I just want to understand your testimony," said the prosecutor.

"You never told a detective at the Reno PD that you were afraid that the defendant would be seeking refuge at your house, and you wanted it searched?"

"No, I don't believe so," she answered. "I was afraid for my own safety, if I was going to be a suspect."

"And so if a detective from the Reno PD testified to that," said Lalli, "that would be incorrect?"

"Absolutely," she replied.

After both sides had finished, Judge Herndon asked Biddison if she had ever seen the defendant carry a gun or a knife. After she answered yes, Chris Lalli asked if Mack had carried the gun around in an ankle holster.

"That is correct," she replied.

"Would he always have a gun with him?"

"Yes."

"What about a knife?" asked the prosecutor.

"I did not see a knife," she answered. "I didn't actually see a gun, either. I knew he wore an ankle holster, because having been in the military in the dark I know the sound of an ankle holster being taken off."

"And again I apologize for this area of questioning," said Chris Lalli, "but I want to ask, you were at dinner on Saturday night on the tenth [of June], correct?"

"Yes," she answered.

"I mean, after dinner, are you intimate together?"

"At some point in time much later in the evening, yes," said Biddison.

"During that process of Mr. Mack taking off his clothes, did you ever see a knife?"

"It was dark," she answered. "The only reason I heard the gun—the ankle holster—is it's . . . because it's a—"

"You heard the Velcro?" interjected the prosecutor.

"I heard the sound that a weapon makes when it hits the floor."

"You never saw a knife, or you never heard anything associated with a knife?" he asked.

"I did not see a knife," replied Biddison.

There was much anticipation in the courtroom as Judge Chuck Weller slowly walked up to the stand, avoiding Darren Mack's gaze at the defense table. He testified that he was standing between his bookcase and desk at around 11:00 a.m. on June 12, 2006, when he had heard a very loud noise.

"I had a burning sensation right here," he told the jury, touching the left side of his chest. "I realized I was shot. I thought maybe my cell phone had exploded in my shirt. Then I realized I didn't have a cell phone in my shirt pocket."

The judge told jurors that he had then seen the window shattered, realizing that he had been shot.

"So I threw myself down to the ground," he said. "I crawled out of the room."

He told the jury that he was bleeding heavily from his chest and other areas and didn't know if he was going to bleed to death.

"One of the lenses of my glasses was covered in blood," he said.

The judge testified that when he was in the trauma room at Washoe Medical Center, a detective had asked if he knew who could have shot him.

"And what was the name you told detectives?" asked special prosecutor Daskas.

"'Daryl Mack,'" he replied.

"When you were providing the name 'Daryl Mack,'" asked Daskas, "who were you thinking of?"

"That man right there," replied the judge, pointing straight at the defendant, who looked back impassively.

Under Daskas's questioning, the judge said he had become aware of several Web sites, including one called Nevadans for Equal Parenting, that had been calling him corrupt and comparing him to Hitler.

He said he happened to know the person in charge of the site and had asked who was behind these attacks. He was told it was Darren Mack.

Judge Weller said he had last seen Darren Mack at a May 24, 2006, hearing when he had ordered him to pay Charla $1 million, as he had previously agreed to in their financial agreement. At the end of the one-day hearing, Judge Weller recalled Mack giving him a "mean, hateful, ugly glare" that he later described to Annie Allison as "a look of death."

In cross-examination, David Chesnoff immediately went on the offensive, attacking the judge on a string of allegations of misconduct. The defender's confrontational tone was intended to push the judge's buttons and make him lose his temper in front of the jurors. It worked.

"Judge Weller," asked Chesnoff, "are there statistics kept by the Washoe County Bar on whether lawyers think a judge should be retained?"

"There's an annual bar survey," agreed the judge.

"Right," Chesnoff continued. "And would you agree with me that in the year 2006 you had the lowest rating of any judge with respect to attention, among the 278 attorneys, who practice in Washoe County. Would you agree with that?"

"No," answered Weller resolutely. "I wasn't rated against 270. I was rated against the twelve judges who sit in Washoe County, and some small number of attorneys commented on it. Not 270. Certainly, 270 lawyers don't practice in the family court. What I don't dispute that in the judge survey of the twelve judges surveyed, I was number twelve."

Chesnoff then suggested that Weller should have removed himself from the Mack divorce case, after being told that Darren Mack was behind the Internet attacks on him.

"That's absurd," replied Weller. "There are rules on when a judge is to remove himself from a case, and it is certainly not when you are insulted publicly. It's a matter of degree. When he shot me, I removed myself from the case. That was across the line."

The defender then asked if telling someone who is "emotional, upset, and angry" that he was going to jail, could have an adverse effect on him.

"Sir, I'll answer your question," said Weller, bristling at the attorney's tone. "I run a fair but tough court, and when I took the bench, I didn't have to leave my common sense behind. What Mr. Mack was attempting to do in that case was the most egregious case of a violation of a court order that I had ever seen.

"The transfer of $280,000 and the voting control of a corporation, within a few days after getting his own order that said that wasn't okay, was nonsense. And I called a spade a spade, and I think it was the appropriate thing to do. I don't think I'm required in being nice to people . . . and allow them to do nonsense and pretend that it's justifiable."

Finally, in the middle of a heated debate on whether or not he had favored Shawn Meador in his rulings, Judge Weller lost it.

"I've never had my reputation attacked the way that you're attacking it, sir," he said angrily. "It's unfair and it's unwarranted."

"I'm going to strike it," said Judge Herndon. "Ladies and gentlemen, you'll disregard that statement. Judge Weller, you know better than that. This isn't a forum for that."

"I'm sorry," said Weller.

Then Chesnoff asked if Weller had a "secret deal" with Shawn Meador to hurt the defendant.

"No, sir," replied the judge.

"That would be crazy, right?" asked Chesnoff.

"It would be illegal, sir," replied Weller. "I don't know if it would be crazy."

"But if somebody thought that, that would be crazy, wouldn't it?"

"I don't think I'm competent to opine on what's crazy," answered the judge. "It would be incorrect."

Then, after apologizing in advance but saying he had an obligation to his client, Chesnoff asked if Judge Weller had ever slept with Charla Mack.

"No, sir," said the judge.

"Okay, that would be crazy, right?" asked the defender, prompting prosecutor Daskas to object.

"Sir," said Weller before Judge Herndon could rule, "I find in most cases that the person who loses the case either blames their attorney or the judge and refuses to take responsibility. I don't know if it's crazy. It's certainly a lack of the willingness to take responsibility."

After Judge Weller was excused, David Chesnoff demanded a mistrial.

"[Judge Weller] impugned me," the attorney complained to Judge Herndon during a jury recess. "Your Honor, it's completely improper for a lawyer, a judicial officer, to make a comment like that in front of the jury. So I make a motion for a mistrial."

Judge Herndon denied his request, saying he could quite understand why Judge Weller had made his outburst.

"I'll be honest with you," said the judge, "I've got great sympathy for Judge Weller. The man was shot at. Now he's on the stand with his credibility being questioned, his character being questioned. And I understand that that's a very difficult proposition for anybody to be involved in, whether it's a judge or anybody else."

On Wednesday, October 31—the fifth day of the trial—the prosecutors began wrapping up their case against Darren Mack. With all the state's key witnesses having testified, the prosecution focused on the first responders to the shooting and Mack's time on the run in Mexico.

United Airlines pilot Chad Ruff told jurors of his alleged encounter with Mack during a layover at the luxurious Meliá Cabo Real beach and golf resort in Cabo San Lucas, Mexico.

"Would it surprise you to know he was never in Cabo San Lucas?" asked Scott Freeman in his cross-examination.

"That would surprise me," replied Ruff.

"Would it surprise you that the first night he was in Ensenada?"

"That would surprise me, yes," answered the pilot.

"So if he was in Ensenada, you were mistaken about your identification?" asked the defender. "He couldn't be in two places at once."

"That's impossible, yes.

* * *

Judge Herndon had given jurors Thursday off, so on Friday morning, November 2, the Darren Mack trial resumed, with the state calling its final six witnesses.

First up was Patricia Eddings, a gunshot residue expert from the Las Vegas Crime Lab, who had tested the Ford Explorer after its return from Mexico. She testified that she had found a high concentration of the three common components of gunshot residue in the rear cargo area of the Ford Explorer, concluding that a firearm had definitely been fired there.

Then Kevin Lattyak, a firearms expert from the Washoe County Sheriff's Office, testified of going to Judge Weller's chambers after the shooting, where he'd found bullet fragments still embedded in the wall, books, and window. He had then reconstructed the path of the bullet, deducing that it had been fired from a parking garage across the Truckee River.

He had also analyzed three sections of a bullet jacket recovered from the south wall of the judge's chambers, finding that it would have been fired from a gun barrel with six lands and six grooves.

"Did you have a gun or a rifle," asked prosecutor Daskas, "to compare it to the rifling characteristics of the bullet jacket?"

"No," replied the expert. "No firearm was ever submitted for my examination or comparison to this bullet."

Nevertheless, the expert was able to calculate that the bullet had been fired from a .24- to .25-caliber rifle firing bullets approximately .243 in diameter.

"What are these caliber bullets used to hunt?" asked the prosecutor.

"Basically it would be light game," he replied, "deer, antelope, that sort of thing."

The jurors then heard from FBI Special Agent Steven J. Kling, who had supervised Darren Mack's surrender in Puerto Vallarta. Under Robert Daskas's questioning, Special Agent Kling described going to the Marriott Hotel on June 22, 2006, for the midnight surrender.

"I observed Mr. Mack walking into the hotel," he testified. "He was wearing an Angels baseball cap, a blue and orange jersey-type long-sleeved shirt, and blue jeans. And he was pulling a two-wheeled suitcase."

Soon afterward, two Mexican immigration agents arrived to assist Kling in taking the fugitive.

"The three of you now approached the defendant as he was at the registration desk?" asked Daskas.

"That's correct," Kling replied.

"Without telling me anything that anyone else said," asked Daskas, "did you say anything to the defendant?"

"Yes. I said, 'I believe we're the people that you're looking for.'"

Darren Mack then gave himself up peacefully and was transported to the local municipal jail. At the gates the two immigration agents got out of the van, leaving special Agent Kling alone with Mack.

"Did Mr. Mack say anything to you?" asked Daskas.

"Yes, he did," Kling said. "He told me that he had $37,500 in cash inside his suitcase, and he asked me who was going to remain with that suitcase during the evening."

"Based on his comments, was it your impression that the defendant was concerned about that money?"

"Yes," said Kling. "I assured him that I would take custody of his suitcase and his belongings, including the money it contained inside."

After leaving Mack locked up in the jail, special Agent Kling said he had returned to his hotel room and counted the money inside the suitcase.

"You're in Mexico with $37,000 in cash," noted Daskas. "You were concerned about that?"

"Well, it wasn't $37,000," Kling corrected him. "It was $36,201. Every bill was a hundred-dollar bill, except for the one-dollar bill."

In cross-examination, Scott Freeman noted how his client had been "very cooperative" when giving himself up at the Marriott.

"No violence?" asked Freeman.

"Correct."

"No guns?"

"No."

"As to the way Mr. Mack's demeanor looked to you," said Freeman, "it looked as though he was ready to go home and face the charges. Is that correct?"

"That's cause for speculation, Judge," Daskas objected.

"I don't know how his demeanor could convey that he was ready to go home," Judge Herndon agreed.

The state's last three witnesses were forensic investigators, called to document further scientific evidence for the jury. Toni Leal-Olsen, a forensic investigator with the Washoe County Sheriff's Office, described how she photographed Darren Mack after he was flown back to Reno.

She first photographed him in the clothes he was wearing, and then in various states of undress. She also testified that she carefully removed and photographed the contents of Mack's suitcase. Inside she found some jeans and Rockport shoes with red stains on them, three condoms, a set of keys to a Ford Explorer, binoculars, and various credit cards.

In cross-examination, Scott Freeman asked the forensic investigator about her visit to Darren and Charla Mack's onetime residence on Franktown Road, Carson City.

The defense attorney displayed one particular photograph she had taken for the jury, of a mirror in one of the bathrooms.

"Tell us where was that located," Freeman asked.

"That was located in the master bathroom," Leal-Olsen replied.

"And that says, 'So Long. Good Riddence,'" Freeman observed.

"Yes," Leal-Olsen confirmed.

"And 'Riddence' is kind of misspelled?"

"Yes, it is," she agreed.

Then the attorney asked if any forensic handwriting analysis or any other tests had been carried out on the handwriting scrawled in blue paint across the mirror.

"To my knowledge," she replied, "no one has."

The final witness for the prosecution was DNA scientist Jeff Riolo, making his second appearance. Chris Lalli questioned him about the Rockport shoes found in Darren Mack's suitcase on his return to Reno. The DNA expert testified that he had examined swabs of red stains taken from the soles of the defendant's shoes and was able to identify the DNA.

"Charla is the source of the DNA," he testified.

He had also analyzed a pair of jeans found in the same suitcase, identifying the DNA taken from the red stains as belonging to Darren Mack.

Lalli then asked if Riolo had analyzed a blood sample found on the keys of the Ford Explorer the defendant had abandoned in Mexico.

"I was able to get a DNA profile from that," he answered. "Charla is consistent with being the source of that DNA profile. And the frequency numbers associated with that are: 1 in 255 million in the Caucasian population; 1 in 515,000,700 in the African-American population; and 1 in 1,320,000,000 in the Hispanic population."

At 12:43 p.m., Judge Herndon told the jury that the state would formally close its case on Monday morning, dismissing them for the weekend.

CHAPTER FORTY-EIGHT

The Plea Deal

At 6:56 p.m. on Friday night, Scott Freeman and David Chesnoff visited their client at the Clark County Detention Center. During their brief visit, Freeman and Chesnoff discussed a weekend agenda to prepare their client to take the stand in his own defense, which is always a risky move.

"We talked about coming Saturday to work on testimony," Chesnoff recalled. "We outlined the order we thought we would go in."

The attorneys did their best to raise Darren Mack's morale, forecasting that they would soon be sipping beers together in Mexico.

"I was constantly pumping him up," Freeman explained, "being optimistic, in my view, for many different reasons."

At 9:40 a.m. on Saturday morning, the two defense attorneys returned with Dayvid Figler, who would help prepare Darren Mack to testify. Also with them were the defense expert psychiatrist Dr. Norton Roitman and law intern Darren Levitt. It was the first of three visits the defense team would make to Darren Mack's cell that day.

"We took him through a direct," remembered Chesnoff, "and then we began peppering him with a potential cross-examination."

In his mock direct, Darren Mack described numerous

situations in which he claimed to have suffered Charla's violence.

But when they began working on the far more difficult cross-examination, Mack became unusually candid about what had happened inside the garage that morning. For the very first time he graphically described placing his knee on Charla's head, after he had finished stabbing her and she was gurgling and choking to death.

"I got physically ill," recalled Chesnoff, "because it was the first time he had told me that."

After hearing this gruesome description of just how Charla had died, his attorneys became truly concerned about how this would play to the jury.

"It was a very graphic presentation by Mr. Mack," said Chesnoff, "which I felt did not inure to his benefit in claiming self-defense, in light of never calling the police, running away, and throwing away the evidence."

When Darren Mack asked Dayvid Figler what he thought of his testimony, the trial expert warned it could be a problem.

"The particular cross-examination," said Figler, "involved a very detailed and graphic description of the stabbing of his ex-wife. What was particularly striking and graphic about it was the depiction of Mr. Mack's knee upon his dying wife's head while the blood was spurting out of her neck. [This] was something that didn't fit into self-defense as I understood it. I remember using the words 'not well received by a jury.'"

The day before, the defense attorneys had discussed a possible plea deal with the two special prosecutors. Chesnoff said he had been contacted by an attorney, claiming Soorya Townley and Judge Weller wanted the case resolved and would be open to a plea deal.

But Lalli refused to make the defense an offer, saying he did not want to put the victims through an inevitable "emotional roller coaster."

However, the special prosecutor told the defense team that

he would be prepared to consider a serious offer from the defendant, agreeing to plead guilty in return for a certain sentence in the forty-years-to-life range.

On Saturday there were ongoing plea negotiations between the defense and the state. David Chesnoff was handling the delicate negotiations, as he already had a close working relationship with the two Las Vegas special prosecutors.

According to Chesnoff, Chris Lalli wanted Mack to serve at least forty years in prison.

"I came back and asked him to drop the gun," he said, "maybe construct something where he could still ask for close to forty and we would be able to ask for twenty. That's how the negotiations went."

David Chesnoff then told his client that he recommended cutting a deal with the state, as it was going to be a difficult case to win. As the day progressed, Darren Mack warmed to the idea, asking Scott Freeman how much time he would have to serve.

"He was concerned that it was going to be a life sentence," said Freeman.

The attorneys told him that he was looking at the mandatory minimum of twenty years, with possible parole after that, if they could persuade prosecutors to drop the deadly-weapon enhancement, which carried forty years.

Then the defense discussed creating a strong sentencing presentation for the court.

"He wanted to be close to his family," Figler explained, "and there were some other things he was hoping for. There were a lot of questions that were asked, that [the defense team] would work very hard with him in exploring all options to make his life in custody as good as possible."

On Saturday evening Darren Mack agreed that his attorneys should open negotiations with the state. David Chesnoff called the prosecutors, saying his client had decided to plead guilty and wanted to negotiate a plea. He said that Mack was now prepared to admit the charge of first-degree murder but without the deadly enhancement. He was also prepared to admit the attempted murder charge with the use of a deadly weapon.

But Lalli and Daskas said they would first have to talk to the victims and the Reno police detectives.

"If the police and victims are on board," Lalli told them, "we will send you a guilty plea agreement."

At 10:00 a.m. on Sunday morning, Detective Ron Chalmers was eating breakfast with his family at a Reno IHOP, when his cell phone rang.

"It was Christopher Lalli," he recalled, "and he said, 'Hey Ron, we have an offer from the defense.'"

At first Detective Chalmers was skeptical.

"My initial reaction was 'No, it's not enough time,'" he said, "'No, that's not a fair deal.' Chris said, 'Okay.' And I said, 'That's my initial reaction, Chris.'"

But the detective thought about it further and changed his mind.

"I'm familiar enough with the laws and sentencing structures, that I know first-degree murder at that time was life with or without parole," he said.

The prosecutor told him that under the agreement the state would not be seeking life without parole.

"So in Darren's case," Chalmers explained, "you get life with the possibility of parole after twenty years. That meant he had to do every bit of twenty years before he's even eligible to see a parole board.

"So I knew that he was looking at twenty years minimum on that. I also knew that the attempted murder was another eight to twenty, and with the deadly weapon enhancement it would be another eight years, and they must run consecutive."

With all the variables, the detective calculated, Darren Mack would probably receive about thirty-six years in jail for his crimes, meaning he'd be almost eighty years old when he finally got out.

"It was a little bit of a gamble from the state's side of

things," Detective Chalmers said. "You're rolling the dice a little bit. So that man needs to spend the rest of his life in prison for what he did, and I think this sentence gives him that."

He also took into consideration how the defense planned to launch an all-out attack on Charla Mack's character, and a plea deal would avoid that unpleasantness.

"It was going to be very ugly, whether it was true or not true, the things that they were going to say about Charla," said the detective. "It would be ugly for Soorya and Charla's friends, who would be there. And I didn't figure it was in Charla's best interests."

Prosecutors also contacted Charla's mother Soorya and Judge Weller, who both initially had reservations about it before giving it their blessing.

"Charla's mother was overwhelmed," said Ann Mudd, "and I think that law enforcement convinced her, 'Work with us, this is the best thing.' And they spent a little time explaining what he would have to look forward to in prison. He's going to be away for a very long time."

Late Sunday morning, the two special prosecutors faxed David Chesnoff a proposed guilty plea agreement they had drafted. The defense had several problems with the plea conditions, wanting Darren Mack to be able to take an Alford plea on the attempted murder charge. This meant he could maintain his innocence, while admitting there was sufficient evidence to convince a jury of his guilt.

That afternoon, after discussing the proposed agreement with Scott Freeman over a football game on TV, Chesnoff called Chris Lalli during the interval. The special prosecutor was at home preparing a pasta vongole dinner when he got the call. After dragging his heels a little, he agreed to make the changes.

Several hours later, Lalli met Chesnoff at a Starbucks in downtown Las Vegas, giving him an amended version of the plea agreement that reflected the defense changes.

At 6:30 p.m., Freeman and Chesnoff arrived at the Clark County Detention Center with the updated plea agreement. The two attorneys then sat around a table with their client, going through it line by line.

"I read it to him," said Freeman. "We had a specific conversation about [how] he could not say it was in self-defense because it was [done with] premeditation and deliberation. That's the elements of first-degree murder. So, as a consequence, it was that something happened and that he killed her. That's what we talked about."

While they were going through the five-page plea agreement, Mack had several questions for his attorneys, and Chesnoff scribbled notes on the agreement.

"We both went over it with him," said Chesnoff. "We talked about a lot of things involving the case, and I thought he clearly understood the plea agreement."

The attorneys told him that they expected Judge Herndon would give him consecutive time.

"I circled the '30,'" said Chesnoff, "because I kind of thought that's where it would end up. I indicated to him that was a potential sentence. I did not want to mislead him as to where I really thought his parole eligibility would be."

His attorneys also told him that the maximum sentence Judge Herndon could give him under the agreement was a minimum of thirty-six years in the Nevada Department of Corrections. (Later, Mack would deny his attorney's version of events that night, claiming not to have understood the full consequences of the agreement.)

Finally, Mack said that he personally wanted to tell his family about the plea deal, and it would go no further until he had done so.

"He was going to go forward," said Freeman, "but he wanted as a condition of that [to] speak with his family."

David Chesnoff said he would talk to Judge Herndon about it.

After leaving the jail, the defense attorneys called the judge, who was coaching soccer at the time.

"[They] asked whether or not I could make the courtroom closed Monday morning for the family to be with Mr. Mack," he recalled. "Because if he was going to accept a deal, he was going to want to talk with his family."

The judge agreed to Darren Mack's request.

At around 6:00 p.m., Scott Freeman called Landon Mack, asking him to have the family in the Las Vegas courtroom early the next day without mentioning the plea deal.

"Darren specifically asked me not to tell them about his decision," said Chesnoff. "He wanted to be the one to tell his family about his decision and explain it to them."

So Freeman told Landon Mack that his brother would be the defense's first witness, and needed the family there for moral support. After the call, Landon contacted Mack's mother and Jory and Elise Mack, and Alecia Biddison, asking them all to fly to Las Vegas that night.

"I told them Darren would be testifying first on Monday morning," said Landon, "that we were going there for a contact visit to keep him calm so he would come over well."

CHAPTER FORTY-NINE

"I Hereby Agree to Plead Guilty"

At 7:45 a.m. on Monday, November 5, Darren Mack's family arrived at the Clark County Courthouse. They gathered in Courtroom 10D fully expecting the defense to begin its case with Darren as the first witness.

During the night, Soorya Townley had had second thoughts about the plea deal. When she arrived she told Chris Lalli that she didn't want to go through with it. The special prosecutor and Detective Ron Chalmers then spent more than an hour persuading her it was best.

At 8:30 a.m. the press was barred from entering the courtroom for the resumption of the trial, leading to much speculation about what was going on inside. At one point Jory Mack came out in tears, refusing to talk to reporters.

"I remember running into Martha Bellisle [of the *Reno Gazette-Journal*] in the hallway," said Chalmers, "and her saying, 'What's going on, Ron? Something's happening.'"

Inside the courtroom, emotions ran high. When bailiffs brought Darren Mack in, he hugged each member of his family one by one. Then he tearfully broke the news that he had decided to plead guilty to all charges.

Over the next ninety minutes Darren Mack remained on his feet, talking to them as they sat around the defense table, bewildered. Scott Freeman and David Chesnoff were there to explain various points to the stunned family members and to answer questions.

It was the first time that Darren told the family his version of what had happened to Charla in the garage on June 12, 2006.

"He cried throughout," said Alecia Biddison. "He was very nervous, very anxious to begin speaking with us. One of the first things that he said to us was, 'My defense team feels that there is no way that we can win, and they have advised me that the best thing that I can do at this point is to take a plea agreement.'"

Scott Freeman later said his client essentially took the lead at the emotional family meeting.

"He told them what was happening," Freeman recalled. "He indicated a number of factors to them. I had stepped back because it was between him and his family. And if they had a particular question, I answered it."

Freeman said one of the questions raised was what would happen if he changed his mind, deciding not to go forward with the plea deal. David Chesnoff replied that Judge Herndon would probably recess for the day, picking up with Darren Mack's testimony the next day.

"We probably had about five days left for trial," said Freeman. "If he didn't want to take the deal, he didn't have to, and I would have finished the trial. The witnesses were on their way to Las Vegas."

Just after 9:57 a.m., the press was summoned back into the courtroom to be addressed by Judge Herndon without the jury present. The emotional Mack family sat behind the defense table, with Joan Mack and Alecia Biddison openly weeping. Charla Mack's mother, Soorya, and half brother, Christopher, sat with Judge Chuck Weller and high-profile civil attorney Gloria Allred.

"It is my understanding, gentlemen," said the judge, "that this matter has been resolved."

"That's correct," said David Chesnoff. "Mr. Mack feels

it's in his best interest to enter negotiations, for several reasons. He did not want to spend a week having his wife dispar-
aged, even though there were issues between them and she
had problems. That was a major consideration, as well as,
obviously, his own acknowledgment of his responsibility."

Then Scott Freeman outlined the agreement, stating
that in consideration of his client pleading guilty to murder
in the first degree, he would receive a sentence of life in
prison, being eligible for parole after serving twenty years.
He had faced a potential sentence of life without parole if
found guilty.

As part of the plea, Mack also acknowledged guilt in the
attempted murder of Judge Weller, and the state reserved the
right to argue for the maximum sentence and that the two
counts run consecutively. Mack also waived his rights of
appeal.

After Chris Lalli officially confirmed the agreement,
Judge Herndon addressed Darren Mack, sitting composed at
the defense table, as his family members wiped away tears.

"All right, Mr. Mack," said the judge. "Is Darren Mack
your true name, sir?"

"Yes, sir," Darren replied resolutely. "That is my correct
name."

Then, as Judge Herndon asked if he'd received a copy of
the amended charges dismissing the deadly weapon enhancement, the defendant stopped him.

"One thing I'm confused about," he said. "Mr. Lalli said
I entered a plea of guilty to the second charge. I thought that
was Alford."

The special prosecutor said the Alford charge did relate
to the charge of attempted murder.

Then Judge Herndon proceeded, asking if Mack understood the nature of the two charges of first-degree murder and
attempted murder with a deadly weapon.

"I do," he replied in an unwavering voice.

"You've had a chance to discuss the second amended information charges with your attorneys?"

"I have," replied Mack.

"Okay. As to count one, murder in the first degree, how do you plead?"

"Well," asked Mack, "isn't that . . . I'm accepting the guilty plea?"

"So you plead guilty to count one?"

"Yes, sir," he replied.

"As to count two, attempted murder with use of a deadly weapon, my understanding is that you're going to enter an Alford plea, at least in regards to the specific intent to kill. Is that correct?"

"Correct," said Mack.

"All right," said the judge. "Before I accept your plea, I need to be satisfied it's freely and voluntarily made. Is it?"

"Yes," declared the defendant.

"Anyone force you or coerce you to get you to enter your pleas of guilty and Alford this morning?"

"No."

"Did anyone make any promises to you, other than those contained in the plea agreement, in order to get you to plead guilty this morning?"

"Other promises—no."

Then when the judge showed him the written plea agreement, asking if that was his signature on page five, Darren Mack stopped him, saying there was something else.

"One question, Your Honor," he said, "before I go any further with this. There was one extra promise. It was informed to me that . . . at my sentencing, that I'll have all the time I need, because there are some very important things I would like to share, because I have remained quiet through this whole things. I would like to come forward and speak, and it was represented that I would have that with Your Honor?"

"Absolutely," replied the judge. "I'll probably set two days aside to consider sentencing. You'll have the opportunity to speak on your own behalf and explain whatever it is you want to explain."

"So my family," asked Mack, "people of that nature, can come in and testify on my behalf?"

"Yes," said the judge.

Then Darren Mack confirmed that that was his signature on the plea agreement and he had read it before signing.

"Did you understand everything in the plea agreement?" asked the Judge.

"Yes, sir," he replied. "We went through it pretty thoroughly last night."

"Did your attorneys answer any questions you had before you signed it?" asked Judge Herndon.

"Yes."

Finally, the judge canvassed him further on possible consequences of his plea agreement, as Mack repeatedly asked him to clarify certain points.

"Do you have any questions you would like to ask me or your attorneys before I accept your plea?" asked Judge Herndon.

"Nothing right now," he answered. "Before we end I would like to say something."

Then the judge formally read out the charges for the defendant to answer.

"As to count one, murder in the first degree, it's my understanding, Mr. Mack, that on June 12, 2006, in Washoe County, state of Nevada, you willfully, feloniously, and without authority of law stabbed at and into the body of Charla Mack, causing her death. Is that correct?"

"That's correct," replied the defendant.

"And that was done with premeditation and deliberation?"

"Correct."

"As to count two, it's my understanding that on the twelfth day of June 2006, within the county of Washoe, state of Nevada, that you did willfully, unlawfully, and without authority of law, shoot at and into the body of Charles Weller with use of a deadly weapon, to wit, a firearm, correct?"

"Correct," the defendant agreed.

Then there was some discussion about how the state could

prove Darren Mack's intent to kill Judge Weller. After Chesnoff explained how the Alford plea was to Mack's benefit, relating to his mental state at the time of the shooting, he agreed to enter the guilty plea.

Once again the judge asked Mack if he had any further questions before he formally accepted his pleas.

"One thing I wanted to tell the court," he replied. "I do understand, right now, my state of mind, that shooting at the judiciary is not the proper form of political redress.

"Also, one other thing I would like to tell you. I would also like to let you know that through this process, it has been a privilege to watch due process in action. I really accept Your Honor's integrity in performing a very high-integrity judicial process. Even though I have much at stake, it's been a pleasure to have somebody who takes their job seriously."

After accepting Darren Mack's pleas, Judge Herndon ordered that he be returned to Reno for a two-day sentencing hearing on January 17 and 18, 2008.

The jury were then called back into court and informed that the trial was over and they were excused.

Outside the courthouse, reporters excitedly swarmed around, trying to get interviews with jurors and other key players. Judge Chuck Weller's new civil attorney, Gloria Allred, described him as "an American hero for his courage to serve the community."

"I'm proud to be a judge," declared Judge Weller, "and I'm proud to be part of a legal system that gives every accused the right to a fair trial. I'm very glad this dark night is over—or at least a portion of the dark night is over."

Soorya Townley said she was pleased with the outcome, although she was still trying to make sense of the plea agreement.

"It is like eating an elephant," she told reporters. "It's just a huge, huge situation. All I can see in my mind was my daughter, who was slaughtered like an animal. She was the mother of his child."

Then she described Charla's killer as a "true sociopath," who had "hypnotized himself" into feeling he was the victim and therefore justified in what he had done. She said she couldn't wait to return to Reno and Erika and "try and be the greatest grandmother I can be."

Joan and Landon Mack left the courthouse together and got into a waiting car, refusing to discuss the matter.

Special prosecutor Robert Daskas told the Associated Press that the state's goal had been to see Darren Mack convicted of premeditated murder and attempted murder.

"Whether it was by jury verdict or guilty pleas," he said, "was insignificant to us."

Scott Freeman said there were no winners in this case, saying it had been "a very, very long, difficult experience."

His colleague, David Chesnoff, said his client still wanted to tell his story to the public.

"I wish, in hindsight," said Chesnoff, "a lot more people would have listened to him, because I don't think he's the type of person who would have found himself in his circumstance. He's an honorable guy. He's a good father. He's been a good citizen. Events just overwhelmed him, and he wound up in what he calls a perfect storm."

Several of the jurors held an impromptu press conference, expressing a strong dislike for Judge Weller's demeanor on the stand.

One female juror described the judge as a "jerk" for his outburst during testimony, leading to the judge's admonishment.

"If Judge Weller got out of line and acted like that here," said a male juror, "imagine how he would act in his own courtroom where he [had] godlike powers."

Corey Schmidt watched a live video feed of the trial from his office computer at Palace Jewelry and Loan. He could not believe that his cousin had suddenly pleaded guilty.

"And I started bawling," he recalled. "I started crying. I personally felt betrayed. I thought, *What have I done for the last two years but defend you and the family, and now all of a sudden you're pleading guilty. What's going on?"*

Darren Mack's girlfriend, Alecia Biddison, was also flabbergasted by his decision to plead out. On Tuesday afternoon, she asked him why he had done it.

"And he stumbled around," she recalled. "And because I kept pushing and asking repeatedly, 'Why did you do this?' He finally said, 'Well, what else do you do when your attorneys throw up their arms and say, "We can't defend you."

Biddison then began researching the Nevada statutes for information on withdrawing guilty pleas prior to sentencing. She convened a Mack family meeting, which was attended by Joan, Landon, and Jory Mack, gaining their support for the idea.

She now went on a mission to get her boyfriend a brand-new trial and give him a second chance to take his case to a jury.

CHAPTER FIFTY

Buyer's Remorse

On Thursday, November 8, Darren Mack was flown back to Reno, and returned to Washoe County Detention Center. Soon after being processed, he was visited by Alecia Biddison, who told him that he might be able to withdraw his guilty plea.

"He was absolutely receptive to set[ting] the record straight," said Biddison.

Later that day, Mack's attorney friend Mike Laub also visited, wanting to know why he had pled out.

"Didn't make sense to me," said Laub. "I wanted to know what happened—the sudden change in position."

Laub says Mack was "really distraught" as they were placed in a cell together with a guard outside.

"I asked him what had happened," said Laub, "and he told me his lawyers had abandoned him."

Mack told him that Freeman and Chesnoff had promised to spend at least three weeks preparing him to testify, but had only given him thirty minutes' preparation time.

"I told him that if he felt strongly about it, he should seek separate counsel to review what had happened," said Laub.

Soon afterward, civil attorney Mark Wray visited his client to gauge how his decision would affect the outstanding lawsuits he was handling. It was a foregone conclusion that his admission of guilt would have a negative affect on all the civil suits, including the Charla Mack estate's wrongful-death suit and Annie Allison's personal injury suit.

"I wanted to understand the implications of what had happened," Wray explained. "Everyone wanted to understand that and nobody could."

Then Mack asked if Wray would withdraw his plea for him, but Wray explained he was not qualified, advising him to consult Scott Freeman instead.

Landon Mack also talked with Scott Freeman and David Chesnoff about his brother withdrawing his guilty plea.

"My brother was very uptight about what had happened," said Landon.

Over several telephone conversations, in a special pawnbroker's code they had developed at Palace, Landon kept his brother apprised of developments.

Soon afterward, Scott Freeman visited the Washoe County Detention Center, for a meeting with his client on his upcoming sentencing. And as soon as he entered his cell, Darren Mack turned on him.

"He expressed his displeasure with me," said Freeman. "He said, 'You guaranteed me that I would be acquitted.' I said, 'I never guaranteed you anything like that.' That absolutely blew me away."

After leaving the jail, Freeman called David Chesnoff, informing him that Mack had now changed his mind about pleading guilty and had "buyer's remorse."

A few days later, Chesnoff flew to Reno and went to the jail with Freeman, who had previously requested that Darren Mack be shackled for their protection.

"I was concerned for sure," said Chesnoff. "He'd shot a judge and stabbed his wife and apparently was angry with me."

Later, Chesnoff would say he felt "an obligation" to discuss Mack's concerns, especially because he was aware that he had discussed plea withdrawal with another attorney.

* * *

On November 16, David Chesnoff wrote a four-page letter to Darren Mack, arranging to have it hand delivered to the jail. He repeated his belief that the plea agreement had been in his best interest.

"I believed you acknowledged our hard work and challenges," he wrote. "I'm sure you even saw the strides we made during the trial, none as dramatic as the cross-examination of Judge Weller. There can be no better proof that Weller has been discredited and humiliated and his arrogance and impartiality exposed, than the fall out from this court exchange.

"Dismantling and exposing a judge in such a fashion is an area where I assure you few lawyers dare ever tread, and yet it was a mission for you on my part."

Chesnoff said that, going into the trial, they had no idea of how his claim of self-defense would play. But the prosecution case involving Charla's first-degree murder was "compelling and impenetrable."

He described the plea deal as "a gloss of hope," saying it allowed Mack to keep his dignity.

"And specifically at the sentencing hearing," wrote Chesnoff, "where you are guaranteed an unfettered right to say what you need to say, with the eyes and the ears of the world upon you and listening."

On November 27, Darren Mack fired Scott Freeman and David Chesnoff, hiring a new criminal lawyer named William Routsis. The pugnacious middle-aged attorney has a law office in South Lake Tahoe, Nevada, and also works out of the Laub & Laub law offices, owned by Darren Mack's close friends Mike and Mel Laub.

"Routsis has been retained," Landon Mack told the *Nevada Appeal*, "to correct a huge manifestation of injustice and to withdraw the pleas."

The Mack family also issued a press release, quoting Mahatma Gandhi and Mark Twain.

"The details surrounding the abrupt end to the trial," it

read, "and circumstances that culminated with Mr. Mack's guilty plea will be revealed in the appropriate time."

On December 5, Routsis filed a motion to withdraw Darren Mack's guilty pleas, claiming his client had been "confused" and had not realized what he was admitting.

It also stated that Mack had asserted his innocence of murdering his wife for fourteen months and had always wanted to testify in his own defense.

"This was of utmost importance to Mack," read the motion. "However, on the Sunday before the defense was to present its case, the defense team came to Mack and presented him with a very different picture, which included a plea agreement. The result was that Mack suddenly felt abandoned by his attorneys."

The motion also presented "further evidence" of Darren Mack's state of mind, claiming he had been "unreasonably hot" throughout the trial, resulting in his being seriously dehydrated. It also alleged that while being held at the Clark County Detention Center, he had been in "a tremendous amount of pain" from a bad back, and not sleeping or eating properly.

When Chris Lalli learned Darren Mack wanted to withdraw his plea, he was not surprised, given his previous track record.

"Whenever anybody signs up for a sentence of this magnitude," said the special prosecutor, "it's not uncommon to have buyer's remorse. Unless he can show that the [pleas] were not knowingly, voluntarily, and intelligently entered, it won't be accepted."

On Monday, December 10, 2007, Judge Doug Herndon held a status hearing back in Reno to decide how to proceed. Darren Mack was back in the Second District Court with his new defense attorney, William Routsis. And Chris Lalli had flown in from Las Vegas, telling the judge that it was still undecided who, if anybody, would replace Robert Daskas, who was now on the campaign trail.

The judge heard that Routsis had now received all nine thousand pages of discovery from Freeman and Chesnoff.

At the brief hearing, Routsis asked Judge Herndon to postpone the sentencing, giving him time to focus on withdrawing his client's guilty plea. But the judge refused, saying that there would be enough time: they had to focus only on the sentence for the charge of attempted murder with a deadly weapon and whether the two sentences would run concurrently or consecutively. For the first-degree murder charge was covered under the plea agreement, with a compulsory sentence of life with possible parole after twenty years.

Lalli then asked Judge Herndon to waive Darren Mack's attorney-client privileges in regard to Freeman and Chesnoff so they could be questioned about the plea agreement.

Judge Herndon asked the defendant if he agreed to do so; he did.

Then the judge ordered an evidentiary hearing into the plea deal to be held in Reno on January 15 and 16, with oral arguments on January 17.

Outside the court, Landon Mack conducted an impromptu press conference, vowing to right his brother's "betrayal" by the Nevada justice system.

"We've prepared a flow chart," he told reporters, "to show how many of the players are working together and have obvious conflicts in this judicial nightmare. They use their roles to further themselves and are intent on destroying Darren Mack, our mother, myself, and the Mack family financially and spiritually."

That same day, Soorya Townley issued a statement saying Darren Mack still refused to be accountable for his murderous actions.

"I have seen no remorse from Darren Mack for his barbaric actions or regret for the profound suffering he has caused," she said. "The greatest lesson the entire Mack family has to learn is accountability. I honestly don't think they will ever humble themselves enough to look within [and] be still for a while to recognize that their actions have led them to the place they are in now. Judge Weller didn't lead them there, nor did Charla."

Alecia Biddison had been busy behind the scenes helping William Routsis prepare for the January plea withdrawal hearing. She typed up declarations from herself and members of the Mack family on Laub & Laub letterhead that were duly included in a flood of new defense motions filed four days before Christmas.

On January 5, 2008, Routsis filed into court a seventy-three-point declaration from Darren Mack himself, claiming he had been "brainwashed" and "psychologically raped" by his two former defense attorneys. The rambling thirty-page statement claimed that Scott Freeman and David Chesnoff had assured him of acquittal on all charges, only changing course after receiving the final payment of their $1.25 million legal fee.

Mack also claimed that he had never signed the plea agreement and the signature was a forgery.

"I was so mentally and physically broken down," he wrote, "I couldn't resist the continual verbal assault on me from my defense team . . . that I couldn't win and they couldn't help me and I had to sacrifice myself and go to prison for the rest of my life."

He also claimed that Dayvid Figler, of the defense team, had promised him preferential treatment in prison if he took a plea.

In a state motion opposing plea withdrawal, special prosecutor Chris Lalli said prosecutors had presented "a compelling case" with "overwhelming evidence" of Darren Mack's guilt.

"Rather than present a case and be subjected to cross-examination by the State," read the motion, "the Defendant elected to enter a negotiated plea of guilty, accepting responsibility for Charla's murder and for the shooting of Judge Weller."

The motion also revealed that after leaving the courtroom

that day, Mack had personally thanked both special prosecutors in his holding cell for their "professionalism" in handling his case.

"Justice requires that those who brutally and senselessly
murder their estranged wives and attempt to assassinate a
member of the judicial branch of government be punished
severely," the motion stated. "The State respectfully requests
that the Defendant's Motion to Withdraw Pleas of Guilty be
denied."

CHAPTER FIFTY-ONE

The Circus Continues

On Monday, January 13, the day before the hearing to determine if Darren Mack could withdraw his plea agreement, the Mack family summoned the press to Palace Jewelry and Loan. There, Joan and Landon Mack addressed reporters, as Alecia Biddison and Jory Mack stood at their side.

"He's excited," Landon told reporters. "He has been muzzled. He's been trying for a very long time to tell his story."

The now scheduled four-day hearing was being viewed by the national media as part two of the Darren Mack trial, and teams from *48 Hours* and *Dateline* were back in Reno to cover the proceedings. Court TV also planned to carry the Mack hearing, and KOLO-TV was streaming it live.

At 1:00 p.m. on Tuesday, January 14, Judge Doug Herndon convened the hearing in the same courtroom where he had tried unsuccessfully to seat a jury ten weeks earlier.

Under William Routsis's sympathetic direct examination, Landon Mack claimed that he had paid Scott Freeman and David Chesnoff $1.25 million in a "packaged deal" on the understanding his brother would be acquitted of murder.

Landon Mack testified that the first he had known of the plea deal was when his brother walked into the courtroom on what should have been the start of the defense case.

"He looked right at us," said Landon, "and his exact quote

was: 'My defense team says I can't win,' that the defense team said it would not be good to drag the mother of his child through the mud for a week."

As soon as Chris Lalli started his cross-examination, Routsis objected to him referring to Charla's Mack's death as murder.

"I don't believe there was a murder," the defender argued. "And until a jury makes that finding, I don't think there has been a judgment."

Lalli told the judge that it was clearly murder and the defendant had even admitted it.

Judge Herndon overruled the objection, agreeing that the defendant had pled guilty and they were now deciding whether or not to allow him to withdraw the plea.

During his often aggressive questioning, Lalli asked whether Landon Mack wanted Chesnoff and Freeman to refund some of the money he had paid them.

"It has never been about the money," he replied.

"Have you ever talked about suing them to get some money back?" asked the prosecutor.

"I don't recall," he said. "I may have. They did not fulfill what they said they were going to do."

The next witness was Alecia Biddison, who testified her boyfriend had been in tears when he told the family that he would have to plead guilty to killing Charla, but would be able to say it was self-defense.

Routsis then asked her what Darren Mack had told the family had happened in the garage, the morning of Charla's death.

"He began by telling us that on the morning of June twelfth that Charla had come over," she said. "And that she had attacked him from behind in the garage. And that she had obtained a gun and turned—Darren had indicated that the gun was loaded—and that she then smiled and pulled the trigger, and he thought he was dead. But he wasn't. And they began to struggle over the gun, and she was trying to fire it another time."

She said Darren had described how Dan Osborne's dog had run into the garage during the struggle.

"He was afraid he didn't know what the dog was going to do," she said, "and at some point something else happened and Charla was killed."

The final witness that day was nineteen-year-old Jory Mack, who said he was being groomed to take over the family pawn business.

"What was your relationship with Charla?" asked Routsis.

"She was my stepmom," he replied. "I loved her very much. She was basically a mother figure to me for many years."

He testified that he had only attended the trial the day his father pled guilty.

"I went to Vegas," he said, "because I was told by my uncle that we were . . . going to calm down my dad. Or just talk to him and maybe hear what he was going to testify about."

Jory said his father had explained to the family about the plea his attorneys wanted him to take.

"He said that he would . . . just have to say that he got in a fight," said the teenager. "She pulled the trigger. Something happened and he defended himself. He said that he had to say that he decided to kill her."

"Did you feel something was unusual about your dad that day?" asked Routsis. "In his demeanor?"

"He seemed really rushed to talk to us," replied Jory.

Chris Lalli had no questions, so at 5:45 p.m. Judge Herndon recessed for the day.

The next morning William Routsis called David Chesnoff to the stand.

"Mr. Chesnoff," he began. "I know this isn't going to be pleasant."

Darren Mack's new defense attorney then began peppering his predecessor with critical questions about his and Scott Freeman's approach to the case. He asked if it had been wise to follow Freeman's self-defense opening statement claiming Darren Mack was delusional and insane.

"Were you proud of the fact," asked Routsis, "that you told the jury that, prior to the death of Charla, Darren Mack's brain was so fried on drugs . . . that he had lost reason and judgment? Are you proud of that statement?"

"Absolutely," declared Chesnoff.

The Las Vegas attorney testified that he had repeatedly told his client to plead insanity on both counts, but he had insisted on arguing self-defense for his estranged wife's murder.

"Then," said Chesnoff, "I repeatedly moved to sever the counts, because I believed there was an inherent potential for a conflict. But the judge did not allow that."

Routsis asked Chesnoff why he had told Darren Mack that the prosecution's cases was impenetrable.

"Because I knew, for example, on rebuttal, they were going to bring in a blood spatter expert that was going the describe the gurgling and the movement of the body," Chesnoff replied. "That was one. The other thing—"

"Did you think—" interrupted Routsis.

"May I finish my answer, sir?" said Chesnoff. "The other thing was Darren, in preparing for his testimony, had told us that after he stabbed [Charla] he put his knee on her head and she was gurgling. When he told that to us in preparing for his testimony, I got physically ill, because it was the first time that he had told me that."

"Really?" asked Routsis dismissively.

"Yes, really," said Chesnoff.

In cross-examination, Chris Lalli asked about the problems the defense had encountered after Darren Mack started rehearsing to take the stand. Chesnoff said the Saturday before the plea deal was the first time he had ever mentioned putting his knee over Charla's head, as she lay dying on the garage floor.

"And that was in some respects consistent with some of the scientific evidence that you guys had presented, which corroborated your presentation," said Chesnoff. "He also didn't respond well to the cross."

"You just made a fist and punched your hand," observed Lalli.

"Right," agreed Chesnoff. "This wasn't the first time."

Then Dayvid Figler took the stand, and Chris Lalli asked if he had ever told Darren Mack that he had enough "juice" with the Nevada Department of Corrections to get him housed in a particular prison. Figler testified that he had explained that most of his clients with murder convictions were sent to the maximum-security Ely State Prison but could be transferred to another, depending on a number of factors.

"He wanted to be close to his family," said Figler, "and there were some other things he was hoping for. As far as I could answer, field those questions, I certainly did—"

"Okay," the special prosecutor interrupted. "I just heard Mr. Mack tell his lawyer that what you are saying is all bullshit. Is what you're telling us today bullshit?"

"You know, Mr. Lalli may be taking it out of context," Routsis told the judge.

"That is what I heard, Your Honor," Lalli insisted.

"I suggest," Judge Herndon said sternly, "that Mr. Mack keeps his voice down. You can answer the question."

"To the regard that one can answer that question, Mr. Lalli," said Figler, "there were a lot of questions that were asked and certainly anything that the defense team could do . . . had been offered to Mr. Mack to assist him from the time of potential sentencing in creating a real sentencing presentation to the court that would be unrivaled."

On Thursday morning, Darren Mack finally got the chance to take the stand to testify. Although in shackles, he was dressed in a charcoal gray jacket, white shirt, and a polka-dot tie.

As he sat down and composed himself, he smiled at his mother, his brother, and Alecia Biddison, who were sitting behind William Routsis at the defense table.

"Darren, take a deep breath," said Routsis, "and we're going to go through this today, okay?"

For the next four hours, Darren Mack articulately explained the details of what had taken place on June 12, 2006, resulting in the death of his estranged wife and the shooting of a judge. Using his hands to make points and frequently sipping water, Mack had a fixed smile, even when describing the most horrendous things that had happened.

He testified that he had told Scott Freeman from the beginning that he would never cut a plea deal with the State. He said his defense team had assured him that they were going to trial and he would be acquitted.

Then, the day after the state rested its case, Mack's lawyers conducted a mock cross-examination, giving him a D+ and making him feel he had been abandoned. He claimed that Dayvid Figler had told him he was going to be "slaughtered" and Daskas and Lalli were "vipers."

He claimed they had persuaded him to take a plea due to his physically weak condition caused by insomnia, "paralyzing" back pain, dehydration, and not eating properly.

"It was like a psychological rape," he explained. "I mean, I have a whole new relationship to compassion for women who are raped. It's not just the sex that's taken from them. It's their will. And that is, like, one of the most horrifying things to have your will taken from you."

But this uncharacteristic glimpse of emotion was in stark contrast to his explanation of how his bloody thumbprint, with hair, had been found on some furniture in the garage.

"As I was trying to get myself together," he said matter-of-factly, "I looked down and the gun was laying in her hair when she was laying on the ground."

He then described untangling his dead wife's hair from the hammer of the gun as it lay in a bloody pool.

"I had the hair all stuck to my fingers," he said flatly, "and I walked over and went like that to get the hair off my thumb."

Under Routsis's gentle questioning, Mack claimed to have been pressured into an insanity defense by David Chesnoff.

"I'm not insane," he declared. "And I told him I did not want to lie for my defense."

Then, after a brief recess, Special Prosecutor Chris Lalli stood up to begin his long-anticipated cross-examination of Darren Mack. He immediately zeroed in on the gun, Mack claimed Charla had attempted to fire at him.

"Okay," began Lalli, "I want to talk to you a little bit about the gun and some of the things you say in your declaration about a gun."

Lalli asked why Darren had never mentioned the gun to Dan Osborne, his brother, Landon, or Garret Idle, all of whom he had spoken to after Charla's killing.

"You spoke to your own brother," noted the prosecutor, "and you never mentioned a gun to Landon Mack, did you?"

"That I don't recall," Mack replied, looking uncomfortable.

But he conceded that he had never mentioned the existence of the gun to Freeman and Chesnoff at their first meeting after his return from Mexico.

"Okay," said Lalli, "wouldn't you agree with me that the gun, or the idea of Charla having a gun on the day you killed her, is probably one of the most significant aspects of your defense?"

"Absolutely," replied Mack.

"And you didn't bother to mention it to your lawyers until after you had meditated on it; is that what you are telling us?"

Initially Mack admitted that he had not mentioned the gun at that first meeting, but then had a change of heart.

"I can't say I didn't mention it," he said. "We did not discuss it in any depth."

"Okay, so if Scott Freeman were to testify that you never used the word 'gun' in your first conversation with him, would he be lying about that? Yes or no?"

"I . . . I don't believe he would be. I can't . . . I can't . . ."

"There's no question, Mr. Mack," replied Lalli coldly.

The special prosecutor then observed that he had been in the courtroom to hear Chesnoff and Figler testify earlier.

"[Y]ou told them," said Lalli, "that you placed your knee on Charla's head as blood was coming out of her throat."

"I never said that second part," snapped Mack angrily. "I did not describe it that way."

"What exactly did you tell them about placing your knee on Mrs. Mack's head? Don't describe the whole scenario, just what about that."

"I put my knee on her head when the dog was attacking me," he replied.

"That's what you told them?"

"That what I told them."

"So they are wrong about blood coming out?"

"Well, there was blood coming out," he conceded, "but it wasn't described that way."

Then, under Lalli's scathing questions, Darren Mack admitted being "partially" responsible for Charla's death but fully responsible for Judge Weller's shooting.

"Isn't it true," asked the special prosecutor, "that if you had seen Shawn Meador that day, you would have killed him, too, or at lest attempted to. Isn't that true?"

"I don't know what I would have done that day. That day was . . . I was . . . my reality was pretty shattered that day."

"You told Scott Freeman," said Lalli, "that had you seen Shawn Meador, you would have killed him too."

"I said that went through my mind," he admitted. "I had a thought. I was angry. But I wouldn't do that. That's what I said."

Mack also accused his attorneys of telling him to lie about where he got the $36,000 in one-hundred-dollar bills found in his suitcase in Mexico.

"Scott Freeman told me the best way to handle that," he explained, "would be to say I withheld it from bankruptcy. I told him I wouldn't do that because that would be bankruptcy fraud and I'm not going to lie about these things."

Lalli then asked exactly where he had gotten the money. Mack replied he had gotten it from a Middle Eastern man named Ben in Los Angeles while on his way to Mexico. He said he had previously met Ben in the Palace store and just happened to have his card in his ankle wallet and called him.

"I don't know his last name," said Mack. "His first name is Ben."

"So, when you were a fugitive, you met with Ben?" asked Lalli.

"Yes."

"Does Ben, whose last name you don't know, just give you $36,000?"

"He did," said Mack. "That's why they wanted me to lie about it."

Later that day, Scott Freeman took the stand to defend his legal reputation and set the record straight. In his direct, Chris Lalli asked about Darren Mack's claim that he had no idea of the defense's opening statements before they delivered.

"I had wanted Darren Mack to hear it," said Freeman. "So I went to the jail and I did it with some emotion . . . and provided it to him."

"What was his . . . impression upon your opening statement?" asked Lalli.

"He was very pleased with it," answered Freeman. "I asked him specifically if I had it. He said, 'You have got it a hundred percent.' He was misty-eyed."

Then Lalli asked the attorney about Mack's claim that he had never signed the plea agreement and someone had forged his signature.

"Do you know that to be an absolutely false statement?" asked the special prosecutor.

"I do know that to be an absolutely false statement," replied Freeman. "He signed it in open court right next to me. That's the way it is."

"So the declaration that the defendant made in this case—that he signed pursuant to penalties of perjury—you know to be absolutely incorrect?"

"That is correct," said Freeman.

After taking a short recess, William Routsis began his cross-examination of Scott Freeman.

"Mr. Freeman," declared Routsis, "do you think Darren Mack is delusional or insane?"

"When?" replied Freeman.

"Right now," snapped Routsis.

"I have no way of knowing."

Then Routsis asked if he was aware that David Chesnoff's opening had said Darren Mack's brain was so fried by drugs, he had lost all reason and judgment.

"Quite frankly, Scott," said Routsis, lawyer to lawyer, "I read your opening . . . and I think you eloquently articulated self-defense."

"Thank you," replied Freeman.

"The concern I have, Scott, is, wasn't it your understanding that David Chesnoff was going to be giving an opening argument on temporary insanity at the time of the death of Judge Weller?"

"Shooting," noted Judge Herndon. "He is still with us."

"Yes, he is still with us," agreed Routsis. "Can I just ask you that question, Mr. Freeman?"

"Sure. The answer is that Mr. Chesnoff did his own opening statement, so I really didn't know what he was going to say before he said it."

Routsis then questioned how the defense team could tell a jury that Darren Mack was delusional because of heavy drug use and then ask them to acquit him of killing Charla Mack in self-defense by finding that he had "great reason and judgment" in doing so.

"You realize on its face that is a compellingly inconsistent defense?" asked Routsis.

"Let me explain how our defense worked, so you know," said Freeman. "What I did during my opening statement was indicate that the death of Charla Mack was the triggering event . . . that contributed to his delusional thought to shoot the judge. That's how it worked.

"If you saw my opening statement . . . I did a demonstrative thing—I snapped a rubber band—and then the way Mr. Mack was going to describe how he had some sort of out-of-body experience, that in my view . . . fit the best way we could do it without a severance [of the two charges]."

Routsis then questioned Freeman's judgment in not presenting more of a character case, by subpoenaing judges and other influential people to vouch for Darren Mack's good character.

"Okay, you made a tactical decision," observed Routsis.

"I did."

"I guess my question to you, Scott, is I don't understand it. You have a character case, and . . . I know you to be a great attorney. I just think, in this case, would you agree that when you have a murder case, that there are generally two very important premises when you go in: if you could get the jury to like the defendant, and if you can get the jury to understand that the victim may be a violent person, and that the premise I look at. You didn't see it that way in this case?"

"I did," replied Freeman. "I'm not going to insult you in any manner, William. I know you haven't tried a murder case in Nevada. I'm not insulting you."

"Scott," said Routsis, "you know my record on homicide cases, so let's not go there."

Toward the end of the cross-examination, Routsis asked Freeman if he had ever told Darren Mack he had been unable to locate the Dumpster where he claimed to have thrown the gun, knife, and towel. Freeman said he hadn't because at the time he reasoned that either his client was "being less than candid" or the Dumpster had been moved.

"Either way, it didn't matter to me," he explained, "because that was his story, and we were going to develop it in another way, and that was the sister gun issue."

Freeman said that, in his mind, throwing out the murder weapon, the gun, and the bloody clothes was inconsistent with self-defense.

"It is consistent with premeditation," he said, "because

you don't throw away guns, knives, and bloody clothes. So I didn't want to go there. My belief was I have got his story. I'm going to work with his story."

Freeman said Mack had mentioned that there was a sister gun to the one he claimed to have had at his mother's house.

"And I'm, like, 'Cool,'" said Freeman, "because I can use as demonstrative evidence the sister gun to assist me with his story. And, sure enough, I contact Landon Mack . . . who provides me with the gun, the gun case, and an empty gun case. I don't ask any questions. It was provided to me by Mr. Mack.

"Boom, I have got my gun. I don't have to worry about this dagger. I don't have to worry about bloody clothes infecting my defense, and I have a great way to show it. So I waited. And I didn't provide it to Mr. Lalli, through Detective Chalmers, until I absolutely had to, and that was when we won change of venue. That's when I had to reveal it to them, and they were all over it, just like I assumed they would be."

Then Routsis asked if he had believed his client was telling him the truth about what had happened inside the garage, leading to Charla's death.

"I don't know how to answer that," replied Freeman. "He was telling me what his version of the events are, and I, as a defense lawyer, ethically am following what my client is telling me.

"Do I have an opinion on his truthfulness? I don't think I have a place here to say whether he is truthful or not. I'm going with what he tells me. I mean, let me tell you, there's some parts of this case that cause me some concern."

"What's that?" asked Routsis.

"Well that's not the answer to your question," Freeman continued. "Did I believe in the truth? He tells me a story. I go with that version. That's what lawyers do."

Then at 6:40 p.m., after hearing a total of seventeen witnesses, Judge Herndon ordered both sides to be back in court the next morning and present their arguments before he made a ruling.

*　*　*

At 8:40 a.m. on Friday morning—the fourth day of the hearing—William Routsis presented his closing argument to Judge Herndon. In a long, rambling speech, full of emotion, the defense attorney urged the judge to give his client a new trial so he could take his story to a jury.

He told the court that Mack was willing to risk a double life sentence if a jury was to convict him, because he did not feel he had been properly represented by his former defense team.

"It just shocks the conscience of the court," he declared. "This is an obscenity, Judge. This case begs for a jury to hear this man testify."

Judge Herndon then asked the defender what had prevented his client from stopping the guilty plea canvass, saying he did not understand it.

"I mean," said the judge, "even the most uneducated, down-on-their-luck, not-a-dime-in-the-bucket guys stand before me on a daily basis and stop plea canvasses and tell me they don't understand something that's going on. I don't have ESP, or I'm not clairvoyant when I'm taking a plea canvas for somebody."

Then special prosecutor Chris Lalli stood up, telling the judge how criminal defense attorneys sometimes have to tell their clients things they do not want to hear.

"And many times those clients perceive those comments as coercive," said Lalli. "They don't like them; they don't believe their defense attorney is their friend anymore because they're giving them bad news. That's the reality of criminal practice."

He said that the prosecution's case against Darren Mack had been "overwhelming," and his chances of acquittal "bleak."

"I think," he said, "what is abundantly clear from the testimony of Mr. Chesnoff and Mr. Freeman, is that they cared about this defendant. They zealously represented him from the very, very beginning. They cared about him, and at every turn they did what they believed as good lawyers. And they are excellent lawyers. They did what they believed was in his best interest."

After hearing both sides' arguments, Judge Herndon said that the claim that Freeman and Chesnoff had not discussed the implications of the plea deal with their client "strains credibility," and Mack's claim that his signature had been forged on the plea agreement was "incredible."

The judge also noted how Mack had even shaken the hands of the two special prosecutors in his holding cell, thanking them for giving him the opportunity to resolve the case.

Then, turning to Routsis's plea to give Mack another trial, he said the law just did not work that way.

"There is a knee-jerk reaction," said the judge, "when something occurs like this to say, 'Fine, let Mr. Mack withdraw his plea, let him go to trial, no problem. Have the state put all the penalties back on the table.'"

But, Judge Herndon said, the rules of law were important, having evolved over time to give "guidance and structure" to society, and no one is above them.

"The defendant admitted he killed his wife," said the judge. "He admitted he shot the judge and, quite honestly, now wants a do-over. You know: 'I've seen my jury, I've heard all your evidence and your theories, and now I want to start over.' I don't think that's fair. I don't think that's just."

Then the judge ruled that Darren Mack's guilty plea agreement would stand, ordering him to be sentenced for his crimes on February 7 and 8. During the two-day hearing, Judge Herndon assured Darren Mack that he would have his opportunity to make a statement.

On Friday, February 1, William Routsis called an emergency hearing in a last-ditch attempt to postpone sentencing. Darren Mack and his mother Joan attended the hearing in Washoe County Court, while Judge Doug Herndon and special prosecutor Chris Lalli were on speakerphone in Las Vegas.

Routsis asked the judge to delay sentencing for three weeks to allow his client to be interviewed by Nevada Division of

Parole and Probation officers for a presentencing report. Ironically, Routsis had previously refused to allow Mack to be interviewed for this.

"I'm not going to use the name 'gamesmanship,'" the
judge said. "I think it's woefully late. I can't understand why
the request wasn't made ages ago."

"I've been in the middle of fighting for this man's life,"
replied Routsis. "It slipped my mind."

Then, as Judge Herndon announced that he would not
postpone sentencing, Routsis interrupted him.

"Mr. Routsis," said the judge sternly, "I'm making a ruling
now. I've heard your argument, thank you very much. I know
more about Mr. Mack than I know about anyone I have ever
dealt with as a judge. There comes a point in time when
things have to be taken care of, and a late and inadequate request to delay the proceedings aren't going to be accepted by
the court."

Just hours before sentencing, William Routsis petitioned the
Nevada Supreme Court to intervene. But the three supreme
court justices ordered sentencing to proceed, arguing that
Darren Mack could later appeal his conviction and sentence,
as well as Judge Herndon's ruling not to let him withdraw
his guilty pleas.

"[We] are not satisfied that this court's intervention by
way of extraordinary relief is warranted at this time," read
the justices' ruling.

CHAPTER FIFTY-TWO

"I Lost a Wife Too"

Darren Mack's day of reckoning finally came on Thursday, February 6, at the Washoe County District Court. Security was extra-high and nobody, including law enforcement, was allowed into the courtroom with a firearm.

Once again there was heavy media coverage, with Court TV broadcasting the sentencing live. TV crews from *48 Hours*, *Dateline NBC*, as well as three Reno network affiliates and a dozen print reporters also packed the courtroom.

Now a convicted man, Darren Mack's designer suits had been replaced by a regulation red jumpsuit. He sat dispassionately, his legs manacles and a heavy chain around his waist, at the defense table, his family occupying the rows behind him. Across the courtroom sat Charla Mack's family and friends, some of whom would deliver victim impact statements to the judge. Sitting with them were Judge Chuck Weller and his administrative assistant Annie Allison, who would also be addressing the court.

At 10:00 a.m., sentencing began with William Routsis announcing that the defense wished to call forensic psychologist Dr. Edward Hyman to testify about Charla Mack's "violent tendencies" as a mitigating factor

Chris Lalli objected, saying Darren Mack should not be

allowed to bring in an expert to "trash Charla Mack more than he already has."

Judge Herndon denied the prosecutor's request, saying Dr. Hyman's testimony about Charla's alleged violent tendencies was not a mitigating factor.

"That, to me," said the judge, "is trying to attack whether or not Mr. Mack was guilty of first-degree murder. He has pled guilty to first-degree murder. The issues for sentencing are what can mitigate his punishment in terms of his character."

Then Chris Lalli addressed the court, calling for the maximum possible sentence for Darren Mack's crimes. He told Judge Herndon that the state had received a report from the Department of Parole and Probation, which had considered the matter.

"They conclude that Darren Mack ought to receive the maximum sentence," said the special prosecutor, "forty years in the Nevada Department of Corrections with a minimum parole eligibility of sixteen years. And they conclude that that sentence ought to run consecutively. I share their opinion and urge the court to do just that."

Lalli told the judge that the Darren Mack case represented a "direct and violent attack" on the government of the state of Nevada.

"It is an attack on our judiciary," he said, "and it is an attack on the rules of law of this community. And the question is: What does justice require of a person who commits such an act? It is incumbent upon the court to send a message that this will not be tolerated."

Lalli told Judge Herndon that Charla's murder and Judge Weller's shooting were premeditated, as evidenced by the to-do list.

"The pistol," he said, "is a figment of his imagination."

Lalli said it would be appropriate to consider the brutal manner in which Charla Mack was murdered.

"And I'm not going to parade those photos around again,"

he said. "But consider the fact that her head was severed almost completely from her body; that he dragged her body around on the cold, hard floor of that garage."

"I'll object!" shouted Routsis angrily. "That's not the medical evidence, that the head was severed almost from her body. It was a stab wound that cut the artery. That's not a fair comment."

"It actually impacted her spinal cord," said Lalli.

Judge Herndon said he had seen the photographs and would allow the statement to stand.

The prosecutor observed how the court had also learned more about the murder, during the recent post-trial hearing.

"How the defendant placed his knee on her head as she was gasping for air," he said. "This was by all accounts a particularly brutal murder."

Lalli told the judge that Darren Mack had never expressed any remorse.

"I think it is incredibly telling when he describes how the murder happened," he said. "And we heard about that when he testified. There is no remorse. It was completely matter-of-fact. There is no emotion for killing the mother of his child. No remorse for attempting to murder a sitting judge. And I think that gives the court some insight into his soul, some insight into who he really is."

Lalli told Judge Herndon that another victim of Darren Mack had been the entire Reno community, which had been "impacted by the fear and horror" that this could happen again.

"Nothing less than the maximum punishment is appropriate," said Lalli.

After Lalli sat down, William Routsis asked the judge to swear in all the character witnesses, as he intended to cross-examine them. Chris Lalli said he had no intention of doing so unless they went "over the line."

"I agree with Mr. Lalli," said Judge Herndon. "I didn't expect you to cross-examine each other's witnesses."

But Routsis insisted that they take an oath, and Judge Herndon reluctantly agreed.

Corey Schmidt was then sworn in to testify about his cousin's character. He emotionally described growing up with Darren.

"I have gone through some of the deepest parts of my memory," he told the judge, "and I honestly can't remember anything bad, damning, hurting, or anything that Darren has done purposely bad to myself or any others."

He called his cousin "a mentor" and his "best friend," saying it had been a dream come true when he'd moved to Fleur de Lis and they'd become neighbors.

"I live it every day as I walk outside," he said, "and I look across the street and I think about all that has been lost."

Alecia Biddison then testified, saying that although she had only known Darren Mack for three months before the crimes, she knew him to be an "upstanding member of the community" and a good person and father.

"Those of you who followed this case closely," she said, "know I care deeply for Darren, his children, and his family. My life, too, is forever impacted by the heartbreaking events of June twelfth."

She then urged the judge not to send Mack to the "farthest reaches of Nevada," as it would make it hard for his children to visit.

Joan Mack then told Judge Herndon how she and her husband had first come to Reno and started Palace Jewelry and Loan. She described an idyllic family life that was shattered after her husband, Dennis, was tragically killed in a plane crash.

"When I lost my husband, the children's father, [Darren] took over the store," she said.

Then William Routsis asked her about a statement she had made to him that she had never seen her son lie until he took the guilty plea.

"Yes, I never caught my son in a lie in all the years," she

said. "I am not saying he never lied to me, but I never caught him. And I felt, when he was taking his plea, he was very confused and he was lying, if he was saying that he had premeditated murder, because that is not the son that I know."

Then Routsis asked if the way the state had portrayed her son's character had been "insulting to the truth."

"It isn't the son that I know," she said tearfully. "He has admitted to killing Charla. I know he has felt some deep remorse. Things happen. I don't excuse it. I don't try and explain it."

She then attacked the media for exploiting the high-profile case.

"I mean . . . everybody wanted to get on the bandwagon," she said, "and it became some notorious crime that just got out of hand."

Then her grandson, Jory, testified, talking about the father he knew and loved, and how the tragedy had changed his life.

"June twelfth was the absolute worst experience that anyone could go through," he told Judge Herndon. "I lost my stepmom and can't hang out with my father. Nobody here has any clue how it feels to know that your father is innocent and to have to look at him through glass and talk to him on the phone."

Wiping a tear from his eye, Jory said his father had been his life coach and had always been there for him.

"My dad was a victim of enormous corruption from Judge Weller," he said. "I saw the enormous amounts of stress that he was going through and I felt terrible for him."

Jory said he had loved Charla Mack deeply and still did today.

"I ask that my dad get the absolute minimum sentence or a new trial," he said, "so that he can present himself in the truth in front of a jury. And I cannot imagine going the rest of my life without my dad, my mentor, and my best buddy."

Landon Mack followed his nephew to the stand, complaining that the Nevada court system had failed his family.

"It is just a surreal thing," he said, "for me to really to go into the large words of expressing one's ideas and opinions of a gentleman who has qualities which nobody chooses to express back. It's been a very appalling venture."

After a short recess, Darren Mack finally had the chance to tell the world his side of the story. And for the next three hours, referring to copious notes, he held forth on his philosophy of life, his victimization by Charla, and how he had become a scapegoat for the corrupt family court system.

Under his defense attorney's sympathetic questioning, Darren Mack said he did not want to disparage Charla but wanted to discuss her two sides, one of which few people were even aware of.

"There is that wonderful, beautiful human being," he told Judge Herndon, "that I fell in love with and that I married. And then there is also the other part."

He claimed that Charla had often threatened his life. Twice he had gone to Reno police for help, and even sought refuge at a battered-women's clinic.

He said her borderline personality disorder was not readily apparent.

"It's not like somebody walking around dribbling on sidewalks," he explained. "It is somebody who is brilliant, somebody who is wonderful, giving. And I don't want to take away from that. That is part of Charla."

He said he fully understood how Charla's death had impacted everyone around her.

"But the thing a lot of people don't recognize," he said, tearing up, "[is that] I lost a wife too. And even though this happened, I still love Charla. I just couldn't live with her and I was afraid of her. I still cared for Charla."

After William Routsis had finally finished questioning his client, Chris Lalli cross-examined him. The prosecutor asked him about the manner of killing his estranged wife. He cited Scott Freeman's opening statement, claiming Charla had struck him with enough force to make him fall to the ground.

"Yeah, it was pretty shocking," the Darren agreed, "because it came from behind."

"And I think," continued Lalli, "if I understand what you are saying today, is you stabbed Charla and then somehow after that is when she pointed the gun at you?"

"No," replied Mack. "The gun was already in her hands."

"So you stabbed her in her neck. I mean, you heard the testimony of Dr. Raven regarding the depth of the injury, the fact that the knife actually struck her spinal cord."

"I do. But that was much different than almost cutting off her head, like you misrepresented."

Then, after the prosecutor asked why he had no injuries thirteen days later on his return to Reno, Darren said he had a question for Judge Herndon.

"I didn't know that I was subject to cross-examination," he complained.

The judge told him that he had been willing to allow him to take the witness stand without being sworn in, but his defense attorney had insisted on it.

"For whatever reason," said Herndon, "you all decided to testify and swear an oath to get up there. And so obviously I am going to allow him to cross-examine you."

"Okay, I was under a misunderstanding that I would not be subjected to cross," said Mack. "It was my choice."

Then the special prosecutor observed how much bigger Mack was than his five-foot-four-inch, 134-pound wife.

And you were stronger than she was," he asked, "or was she stronger than you?"

"That's a hard question," Mack replied. "When she got into her fighting mode, she exuded some amazing energy."

"So she was stronger than you?"

"I'm fairly strong," he said, "but I am not used to exuding energy on the person I love."

Then Lalli noted that Mack had used the word "liar" a lot.

"Back during the course of your divorce," said the prosecutor, "you accused Shawn Meador of being a liar, right?"

"He lied so many times, I thought it fit."

"Okay. You have accused me many times today of being a liar?"

"You are still doing it."

"Which is a first for me," quipped Lalli. "You have accused Mr. Daskas of being a liar?"

"Anybody who misrepresents fact—"

"Did you accuse Mr. Daskas of being a liar?"

"I did."

"You accuse Mr. Freeman of being a liar?"

"That is correct."

"You accuse Mr. Chesnoff of being a liar?"

"That's correct."

"But isn't it true that you testified . . . that you had been untruthful to Judge Herndon on five separate occasions?"

"Under extreme duress, I was," he conceded.

At about 5:00 p.m., Judge Herndon told Darren Mack he could step down, calling a recess and instructing everyone to be back in the courtroom the next morning for the state's presentation, followed by sentencing.

"And my intent is we'll go until we are done tomorrow," said the judge.

CHAPTER FIFTY-THREE

"No Remorse"

The second day of Darren Mack's sentencing began with William Routsis's summation. Once again the defender passionately appealed for leniency.

"Judge," he began, "this case has all the elements that challenges the ability of all of us involved to act beyond our fears, to look into our fears and try and do justice at all costs."

In his often emotional speech, Routsis maintained that Darren Mack had never confessed to first-degree murder and deserved to get a new trial, so he could put Washoe County district attorney Richard Gammick on the stand.

"I believe that the truth has been slain," Routsis declared, "and I want to go over how the truth has been slain throughout the course of this case, from the first meetings with David Chesnoff to the plea agreement."

He told the judge that anyone who had ever spoken to Darren Mack knew he was not insane. His state of mind that led to Judge Weller's shooting was the result of "a traumatic situation" and not premeditated.

He then asked Judge Herndon to reconsider his decision not to allow Darren Mack a new trial.

"So, in all due respect, Judge," he said, "I ask you to reflect a little bit. Because I feel . . . you are the only one that can do justice. And to stand up and do it might be difficult.

But I think you will be able to look in the mirror for the rest of your life, and that's more important than anything else I think we have. Because that's all we have as people. Thank you, Your Honor."

Then Judge Herndon asked Chris Lalli to call his first witness, Annie Allison.

Reading from a prepared statement, Allison said that she had been in the wrong place at the right time, becoming "an unwitting victim" of the defendant's "horrific crime spree."

She said the events of June 12, 2006, had changed her life forever, and she was constantly in fear of another sniper attack.

"I keep my office blinds closed," she told Judge Herndon, "and my windows at home closed day and night."

She said she couldn't even go to church without worrying she might be caught in the middle of "someone else's irrational rage."

"I know it's paranoia," she said. "It is time-consuming and it is burdensome. But it is my reality."

Finally, she appealed to the judge to "reward" Mr. Mack's crime with a punishment befitting his actions.

Chris Lalli then called to the stand Judge Chuck Weller, who first read out a short statement written by his wife, Rosa. She said she had initially been reluctant to discuss the events of June 12, 2006, but with all the resulting negative publicity she felt it was time to speak out.

"When Chuck and I discussed his running for family court judge," she said, "I had no idea this would be the path we would have to take. We still fear for our safety due to continuing threats of violence."

She said it was time for her family to move on and "begin the arduous journey of healing the emotional, physical, and psychological scarring we have endured."

Judge Weller went on to outline the Mack divorce case, ending with the final May 24, 2006, hearing at which Charla had expressed fears about her estranged husband knowing where she lived.

Then, as Lalli was about to replay Charla Mack's tearful appeal to Judge Weller, William Routsis angrily objected.

"Judge," said the defender, "how is this relevant to sentencing."

"I'll allow it," replied Judge Herndon.

It was an electrifying moment as the lights dimmed and Charla Mack appeared on a large screen in front of the court. Darren Mack looked away without a hint of emotion.

"And I have a commitment that he knows where [Erika] lives when the divorce is over," came Charla's tearful voice through the speakers around the court, "but he gets so angry and so worked up that I just don't feel comfortable right now knowing personally where I live."

Judge Weller continued his statement, saying he still keeps the curtains in his home, and his office blinds, tightly closed.

"My wife and I don't go out like we used to," he said, "because we live in fear that the violence is not over and someone with the same beliefs as Mr. Mack may seek to finish what he started."

The previous Christmas—eighteen months after the shooting—he had received a death threat, making the same false allegations as the defendant and vowing to finish the job.

Judge Weller told the court that Charla Mack had come into his courtroom seeking justice, and he had had done everything possible to be fair to all parties.

"Darren Mack wouldn't accept that," he said, looking straight at the defendant. "And instead he murdered his wife, the mother of his child, and shot me. He has demonstrated that he is too dangerous to live in a free society. Judge, I trust you chose the right thing to do."

After a brief recess, Charla's half brother, Christopher Broughton, took the stand.

"I thank the court for the opportunity to offer a statement as a victim of the murder of Charla Marie Sampsel," he began. "I use her birth name because she should no longer be associated with the name 'Mack.' "

Describing his sister's murder as "the most gut-wrenchingly painful experience" of his life, Broughton described the harrowing task of choosing a casket and tombstone.

"I have had to witness," he told Judge Herndon, his voice quivering with emotion, "the cold dead corpse of my sister, once vivacious, then shrunken, hard, cold, and cut up by a brutal butcher. I will be haunted by these memories until the day I die."

Looking straight at Darren Mack, he said he had been forced repeatedly to "face the murderer and his family," who had no remorse or regret and refused to accept guilt.

"The crocodile sheds tears," he said, "yet he remains still a crocodile."

Then Broughton appealed to Judge Herndon to sentence Darren Mack to the "harshest sentence" allowed.

"Assign Darren Mack to a prison in the furthest hinterlands in Nevada—in Ely," he said. "Let him never again breathe the air of a free man. Let him forever remain caged until the day he dies.

"This punishment will never bring my sister back, but it will assure that Darren Mack is never again a threat. May he die in prison."

Charla's father, Jan Sampsel, then addressed the court. He said he was not there to eulogize his daughter, but just hoped Darren and his family would finally let her rest.

"To me Darren is already dead," he declared. "He has taken away part of us in a brutal, senseless fashion. And even more pathetic, he wants everyone to believe that he was threatened by Charla with his own gun. He had no other choice but to stab her to death in self-defense."

Sampsel told the judge that although his ex-son-in-law had murdered his daughter and tried to assassinate a judge, he still refused to accept responsibility for his actions.

"Decisions aren't going his way," said Sampsel, "just fire the lawyers. He did it twice in the divorce case and now again in this trial. Decisions aren't going his way: Defy the court. Move assets. Declare bankruptcy.

"When this transparent action was not accepted, cry foul and claim persecution by the judge. And finally, when decisions aren't going his way, kill the antagonists.

"In the past, he has always had his father's name and his family's money to rely on when things were rough. Not this time. The crimes are so outrageous that he will be forced to accept the consequences on his own. This time he will be held accountable without regard to money or perceived social status."

He then asked Judge Herndon to send the defendant to prison for as long as the sentencing discretion allows.

The final state victim witness was Soorya Townley, who read out an emotional statement about her beloved daughter.

Taking a big breath, she described how they had overcome past mother-daughter conflicts to find a deep, meaningful relationship with each other.

"We were supposed to have a destiny together," she told Judge Herndon. "A sublime intelligence gave us life to be fully expressed as a mother and a daughter. Now an indulgent cowardly man has interrupted our path of growth.

"This man who thought he knew a better plan—who decided to play God—Darren has just hurt so many people on this earth."

After her daughter's murder, Soorya said, she had developed shingles as well as asthma-related problems.

"The doctor says it's common when great stress and grief overcome the body," she said. "In all these years I have rarely gone to a doctor, because I have never been ill. Instead of Charla, wheezing is now my constant companion. The doctor said that the muscles around my trachea have become hardened. Interesting to note that Charla's trachea was cut right where mine has suddenly hardened."

Soorya told the court how she would be haunted by mental images of her daughter's brutal killing until the day she died.

"I cannot stop thinking about Charla," she said, fighting to overcome emotion, "lying facedown on that cold, dirty cement floor of a garage with her shoe flung in front of her body, where she desperately fought for her life. Charla lying in her own river of blood. I keep seeing how her face looked as the [medical] examiner held her up to the camera. Charla had a face so beautiful that people would often gasp when they first met her. Now I am left with how beaten, bruised, bloodied, and dead her body looked."

She then speculated on her daughter's final minutes on earth.

"Darren slit her throat in such a way that Charla suffocated in her own blood," she told the judge, "and she didn't die immediately. We will never know for sure, but I'm certain knowing her child was only a few feet away was unbearable for her. The greatest agony was in the surrender of having to let go and leave the little girl behind with a madman. Judge Herndon, this is what I think about all the time."

She said she was now raising Erika, which was a full-time job. After the trauma the little girl had experienced, she had to be especially vigilant.

"On top of my personal grief," she told the judge, "and my parents' grief and the grief of all of Charla's friends, I must first manage the grief and feelings of a little girl whose trauma cannot be underestimated. There are no maps to guide on this one. This is uncharted territory."

She asked the judge to give Darren Mack the maximum sentence, and to run it consecutively.

"He is a dangerous, manipulative man," she told Judge Herndon, "and I believe he is a true danger to any community. Darren is a person who has zero capacity for personal insight; therefore he cannot be rehabilitated. He needs to be kept away to protect the rest of us. Thank you."

"Ms. Townley," asked Chris Lalli, "may I ask you a question?"

"Yes," she replied.

"You brought a CD too? To play for His Honor?"

"Yes. Charla was pursuing her musical career. And she was working out her angst about Darren . . . and there was a song that she wanted to sing to Darren, and I thought it would be really appropriate to end this with."

Then Charla's moving country-and-western-style song "Be True to Me (Be a Man)" was played, and many inside the courtroom openly wept.

> *So you think you got it figured out*
> *What a woman desires most . . .*
> *The house, the car, the ring, the bank account . . .*
> *Sense of security . . . you ain't even close.*
>
> *Your talking 'bout the icing on the cake you gotta live*
> *up to the love you made . . .*
> *If you want know what it really takes . . .*
>
> *You better be true to me . . . don't fool with me . . .*
> *Don't stray from me . . . Don't play with me . . . turn*
> *away when you are tempted too . . .*
> *Don't lie to me . . . do right by me . . . stand beside*
> *me when your feeling weak, think about your woman*
> *and think again. Oh be a man . . . on think about your*
> *woman and think again . . .*
> *Be a man!*

At 11:55 p.m., after taking a short recess, Judge Doug Herndon began his sentencing of Darren Mack for the first-degree murder of Charla and the attempted murder of Judge Weller.

Judge Herndon said that, since he had refused to allow Darren to withdraw his plea and get a new trial, the defendant and his family now viewed him as "a true suppressor and conspirator with many liars as part of a corrupt system that is trying to wrong him."

He said he had assessed carefully what message the sentence he was going to deliver would send to the defendant as well as other potential "Mr. Macks who may contemplate violence against elected officials as a means of solving problems."

He said a civilized society cannot condone shooting people just because one felt wronged about decisions they made in their job.

"This case, in my mind," said the judge, "obviously cries out for incarceration. And the defendant is going to be incarcerated for a very long time."

He commended the Mack family for standing by Darren, saying it would have easy to walk away and not suffer the embarrassment and humiliation of a "notorious" case like this.

Then turning to Charla's murder, Judge Herndon said he found some of Darren Mack's claims of how she died not "completely credible."

"And the nature of what a stabbing is cannot be overlooked either," he told him. "This is a very up-close-and-personal—I think Mr. Routsis referred to a hand-to-hand-combat—manner of inflicting death."

The judge said that all through Darren Mack's three-hour statement the day before, he had been waiting for some kind of apology.

"I let him go on in part," the judge explained, "[to see] if he would ever say what he never did. Despite that, he never said, 'I'm sorry.' Even in the context of maintaining innocence. There was never an 'I am sorry Charla Mack is dead. I'm sorry I killed Charla Mack. I'm sorry I had anything to do with her death. I'm sorry I shot the judge. Regardless of what my intent may have been, or my mental state was, I'm sorry for these acts.'"

The judge told the defendant that showing some remorse, apart from guilt or innocence, would have been appropriate.

"But there was nothing," he said. "Which leads me to the conclusion, Mr. Mack, that you are not sorry that Charla is dead, and you don't regret her death at your hands. Saying 'I wished that day had never happened' is not the same as expressing remorse for your culpability in someone's death, and for your culpability in shooting someone and the damage you have inflicted upon Judge Weller and his family, in the physical and psychological ways that you did. And that type of attitude and conduct deserves severe punishment."

Judge Herndon told the defendant that his sentence needed to leave no questions in the community about how the judiciary will impose its checks and balances on this "type of senseless, brazen, and unremorseful violence."

He then sentenced Darren Mack to the maximum possible custodial sentence allowed by law.

"As to count one, Mr. Mack," he said, "I sentence you to life in the Nevada Department of Prisons, with the possibility of parole beginning after a minimum of twenty years has been served. As to count two, the attempted murder charge, you will receive a maximum twenty years, with a minimum eight years, for the attempted murder, and an equal and consecutive maximum twenty years, with a minimum of eight years, for the use of a deadly weapon."

The judge then ordered the murder and attempted-murder sentences to run consecutively, meaning Darren Mack would be eligible for parole in thirty-six years, when he is eighty-three years old.

After the sentencing, Judge Herndon appealed to both sides of the family to put little Erika Mack's welfare first and bury their animosity toward each other.

"You have a young child at a very impressionable age," said the judge, "that's going to move into her teen years and then into her young adult life. And you can either choose to raise her, disparaging her parents on each side, or you can try and get past the criminal case, whatever you think about that, and be the bigger person and rise above.

"And hopefully you don't want to raise an angry and spiteful child who doesn't know who in her family to trust. She needs to be raised with hugs and kisses and not talking bad about each of those people."

The judge said that anytime there is a domestic homicide involving children, it is "a bigger tragedy" than any loss of life.

"A child without a mother," he said, "and now without a

father for a great many years, is going to need a whole lot from both sides of the aisle."

After Judge Herndon's sentencing, Soorya Townley hugged Judge Weller.

"I'm so glad this is over," she told a reporter, "so we can move on."

But the Mack family vowed to keep fighting.

"The truth of this case is that it was not first-degree murder," Routsis said defiantly. "This case will define the community when the truth comes out."

Speaking for the family for the first time, Jory Mack told the *Reno Gazette-Journal* that they had been expecting the long sentence and were prepared.

"It was about the judge's shooting," he explained. "[Judge Herndon] was willing to put an innocent man in prison rather than risk another judge shooting."

Immediately after sentencing, Darren Mack was transported to the Northern Nevada Correctional Center in Carson City. There he would undergo a three-week review, before being assigned to the prison where he would probably spend the rest of his life.

EPILOGUE

Two weeks after sentencing, Judge Chuck Weller sued Darren Mack in Washoe County District Court for punitive damages totally more than $100,000. The lawsuit named Mack as well as unnamed "Doe" conspirators who had "aided, counseled, encouraged and assisted and participated" in the shooting attack on him.

Darren Mack's civil attorney, Mark Wray, told the *Reno Gazette-Journal* he was "mystified" by the lawsuit, as his client had no money left.

On February 27, William Routsis filed a motion requesting that Judge Herndon once again reconsider his refusal to allow Darren Mack to withdraw his plea as well as reconsider Mack's prison sentence.

In the motion, Routsis accused prosecutor Chris Lalli of being guilty of professional misconduct for claiming that his client had "almost sliced or slashed Charla's head off."

"Christopher Lalli knows how important words are," wrote Routsis, "and the prosecution knows that a stab wound to the neck is not even in the same ballpark as almost slashing one's head off. Why would he say such a thing? Why would this court not hold him in contempt for perpetuating a fraud on the court?"

A month later, Routsis tried unsuccessfully to have Judge

Herndon thrown off the Darren Mack case because of his acknowledged friendship with his client's former attorney David Chesnoff. But Nevada chief judge Kathy Hardcastle threw out the motion, saying a judge who did nothing wrong could not be disqualified for adverse rulings.

On Wednesday, March 19, in Reno a Washoe County District Court jury awarded more than $590 million in damages to Charla Mack's estate and her nine-year-old daughter, Erika. It was the largest noncommercial payout in Nevada State history.

After two days of testimony, during which Darren Mack and his attorneys were noticeably absent, the eight-strong jury panel took just over two hours to reach its decision.

"Let justice be heard throughout this community," said attorney Kent Robison, who represented Charla's estate. "Speak powerfully. Speak Loud. You have to determine the value of Charla's pain and suffering. Try to imagine what was in her mind when the assault was initiated. What fear, what terror, was there, knowing her daughter was upstairs while Darren was doing the very thing that, for weeks, she feared."

The jury awarded punitive damages of $375 million, plus other damages totally $215 million. Even though Robison acknowledged that it was unlikely the damages would ever he paid in their entirety. he said it was important that the Reno community understood how Darren Mack had ruined an entire family.

The jury's decision was later upheld by the Nevada Supreme Court.

On April 15, 2008, Judge Doug Herndon held yet another hearing in Washoe County Court, to rule on William Routsis's latest motion to withdraw his client's guilty plea. But Darren Mack, who had started serving his sentence in the general population of Ely State Prison, was denied permission to come to Reno for the hearing.

After a long, often combative hearing, Judge Herndon denied the defense motion before launching an astonishing attack on William Routsis for unprofessional behavior.

"If you want to act like a petulant child," he told the defense attorney, "and complain about things with rhetorical questions and personal attacks against people, do it on your own time, not on the court's time."

He accused Routsis of taking "an immature approach" to law, saying it was an honorable profession.

"We didn't go to law school and take the bar exam to get out and do it in this fashion," he said.

The following day, the Mack family issued a press release condemning Judge Herndon's decision.

"There was new case law presented," it read, "and new arguments raised . . . that went unaddressed by both the state prosecutor Christopher Lalli and Judge Herndon.

On Tuesday, November 4, 2008, Darren Mack's new civil attorney, Julia Vohl, was in the Nevada Supreme Court, arguing that her client should not have to pay the Charla Mack estate the $1 million divorce settlement as ordered by Judge Weller. Vohl argued that it had not been a binding contract and could not be enforced, as Charla Mack was dead.

"If, under the unique facts of this case, you kill your wife during your divorce, it means the decree was never entered," said the estate lawyer, Egan Walker. "Now, in his strange universe, he kills her and says there is no agreement. 'I killed her, so all of the promises I made on record don't mean anything.'"

On March 26, 2009, the Nevada Supreme Court upheld the divorce settlement, ordering Mack to pay Charla's estate more than a million dollars.

Citing Nevada's "slayer statute," the supreme court ruled that the convicted killer "may not benefit from his wrongful act of killing Charla."

In June 2010, the Nevada Supreme Court denied an appeal by Darren Mack against Judge Herndon's refusal to let him withdraw his plea. The state's highest court ruled that Mack had understood the plea and been given adequate information to make his decision.

Darren Mack's new criminal attorney, Marcus Topel, said he would advise his client to file a petition.

"I believe the facts and the law we presented to the court," he said, "merited a reversal of the guilty plea and an opportunity for a new trial."

A month later, the Ninth U.S. Circuit Court of Appeals ordered Joan Mack to give Charla Mack's estate her son's $500,000 Palace Jewelry and Loan pension fund.

In February, 2012, Darren Mack's newly hired criminal attorney Richard Cornell appealed to a federal court for a new trial, on the grounds that all his previous lawyers were incompetent. The petition also claimed that Mack's constitutional rights were violated when he was denied the chance to withdraw "an involuntary guilty plea" to Charla's murder and the shooting of Judge Weller.

Cornell's motion, filed into the U.S. District Court in Reno, also accused his former attorneys Scott Freeman and David Chesnoff of suggesting that if he pled guilty the governor might eventually commute his sentence.

"Those representations were so unrealistic as to fall below the standard of reasonably effective counsel," Cornell's motion stated.

Made in the USA
Las Vegas, NV
28 March 2023

69777392R00239